Young Learners Diverse Children

Celebrating Diversity in Early Childhood

Virginia Gonzalez

Foreword by **Eugene E. García**

CORWIN
A SAGE Company

For information:

Corwin
A SAGE Company
2455 Teller Road
Thousand Oaks, California 91320
(800) 233-9936
Fax: (800) 417-2466
www.corwinpress.com

SAGE India Pvt. Ltd.
B 1/I 1 Mohan Cooperative
   Industrial Area
Mathura Road, New Delhi 110 044
India

SAGE Ltd.
1 Oliver's Yard
55 City Road
London EC1Y 1SP
United Kingdom

SAGE Asia-Pacific Pte. Ltd.
33 Pekin Street #02-01
Far East Square
Singapore 048763

Printed in the United States of America.

Library of Congress Cataloging-in-Publication Data

Gonzalez, Virginia.
Young learners, diverse children: celebrating diversity in early childhood/Virginia Gonzalez; foreword by Eugene E. Garcia.
     p. cm.
Includes bibliographical references and index.
ISBN 978-1-4129-6813-3 (cloth)
ISBN 978-1-4129-6814-0 (pbk.)

   1. Early childhood education—United States. 2. Multicultural education—United States. 3. Education, Bilingual—United States. 4. Children with social disabilities—Education—United States. 5. Educational tests and measurements—United States. I. Title.

LB1139.25.G657 2009
372.21—dc22   2009017324

This book is printed on acid-free paper.

09   10   11   12   13   10 9 8 7 6 5 4 3 2 1

Acquisitions Editor:	Jessica Allan
Editorial Assistant:	Joanna Coelho
Production Editor:	Libby Larson
Copy Editor:	Codi Bowman
Typesetter:	C&M Digitals (P) Ltd.
Proofreader:	Caryne Brown
Indexer:	Jean Caselegno
Cover and Graphic Designer:	Michael Dubowe

Contents

Lists of Figures and Tables

FIGURES

TABLES

Foreword

Presently, one in three children eight years old or younger living in the United States is of linguistically and culturally diverse origins. Current estimates suggest that these children are raised in home environments where variable amounts of English and a second language are spoken. However, educational skills and achievement lag significantly for this population, creating an unacceptable achievement gap at the beginning of kindergarten, which grows even further by the end of third grade. Considering the growing size of this young-child population and the large number of them being raised in multilingual environments, it is critical that practitioners address basic questions related to language, culture, cognition, and educational opportunity. This book provides a synthesis of empirical work, which spans several decades, and conceptual frameworks associated with the linguistic development and the early education of young children. Linguistic, psycholinguistic, anthropological, psychological, sociological, and educational contributions that underscore research and practice are reviewed. Emphasis is placed on the practices associated with educational concerns—including teacher competencies, instructional strategies, curricular content, programs, parent involvement, and related policy. In accordance with the literature reviewed, the author offers specific educational-practice alternatives that have demonstrated achievement enhancements for these children.

Young linguistically and culturally diverse children age zero to eight years old are currently the largest and fastest growing population in the United States (Hernandez, 2006; Hernandez, Denton, & Macartney, 2007). As educational programs, policies, and practices move forward—especially those targeting the youngest groups of children—it is important that *relevance* and *appropriateness* continue to be resonating themes. But what can be concluded about a large population of children with diverse language and educational experiences at home and in school? What can be ascertained from the empirical literature, theory, extant programs, and policies associated with language and early learning for young Hispanic children? And what home and school factors are important to the differences in early cognitive development and educational well-being? This book explores these questions in a systematic fashion, relying on current theory and evidence with a focus on educational practice.

Because language is a central feature to the cognitive development and early learning for this population (García, Jensen, & Cuéllar, 2006), topics explored in this book are linked to questions of language use and practice. Bilingualism, second-language learning, and related issues, therefore, appear and reappear throughout this synthesis. The author recognizes that not all these children are English-language learners. Many are raised in English-only homes. Moreover, these children represent various racial groups, national origins, social classes, geographic locations, and immigrant generations. Although the author makes the incredible diversity found within this group very clear, there are general trends, patterns, and themes significant to the students as a whole. These are important to understand, as efforts are made to improve educational opportunities for this young, diverse set of children. To avoid gross generalizations, the book addresses key characteristics of this group of children in terms of proportional representation and provides, where possible, descriptions of samples of children in the studies reviewed. As in most reviews, the evidence must be weighed, critiqued, and understood in its proper context where applications are made to individuals or small groups.

A review of this sort is likely to be of most use to practitioners and those that "professionally develop" them. In some cases, policymakers and researchers can profit from it. Our hope is that discussing research findings and relevant theories while focusing on educational practices will allow appropriate examination of what we know and that if implemented that knowledge base can make a difference in student achievement and overall well-being. Language and its many parts—phonology, morphology, syntax, pragmatics, vocabulary, word literacy, text literacy, and reading comprehension—must be analyzed and understood not only in terms of mechanics (e.g., word attack, reading fluency) but also in terms of context (e.g., person-to-person interactions, relationships, activity settings). This necessitates an analysis of culture, which is inherent in language. Although several studies have described the cultural context in which young children from linguistically and culturally diverse backgrounds use and develop language, few have made the conceptual and methodological links necessary to understand how home and school contexts (including differences between contexts) influence early literacy and learning outcomes (Rueda, August, & Goldenberg, 2006).

In addition to research on language and literacy development, the book reviews the literature on school program effectiveness, including dual-language programs, research on assessment, English acquisition, cross-linguistic transfer, and directions that can lead to better educational practice.

This book both "complexifies" and simplifies our evolving educational knowledge base. For example, as the study of early language has morphed from a consideration of habits and innate structures to an interlocking study of linguistic, psychological, and social domains, educational researchers must continue to expand the integration of diverse theories and empirical research associated with language, cognition, and socialization to understand early development and educational appropriateness for young children, particularly those children who come to school from highly diverse settings. Theory and qualitative and quantitative research incorporating multiple academic disciplines—linguistics, education, anthropology, psychology, and sociology—underscore historic and concurrent work reviewed here. The author's work is organized thematically and explores, with a particular focus on the educational practice, the specific findings our national examination of these issues.

This book should help educational practitioners who serve as architects of educational environments and instructional experience for young students and those who implement the educational interventions. It is directly focused on programs, practices, and policies that demonstrate a positive relationship in reducing the achievement gap for young, diverse learners. Although research and theory are addressed as important grounding, the author informs the reader about key educational circumstances that exist for this population and addresses specific program, instructional, and related educational interventions that have been developed to serve these students, and finally, describes, in detail, the educational interventions that have actual evidence for enhancing the teaching of young, diverse learners.

Eugene E. García
Arizona State University

Preface

A Letter to the Reader

Dear Reader:

The real-life story told by this book is dedicated to all early childhood teachers of diverse learners. I hope you enjoy reading this story and find the philosophical and pedagogical principles and multiple teaching strategies described and exemplified in this book useful. To tell my story, I have used many real-life classroom teaching and learning experiences of young, diverse children, their teachers, and their families.

THE CONTEXT FOR THE STORY TOLD BY THIS BOOK

Before telling my story, I have to give you some contextual information. About nine years ago, I moved from Texas to Ohio to work as a professor at the Teaching English as a Second Language (TESL) program at the College of Education, a department of the University of Cincinnati. At the time, I was the first (and only) Hispanic faculty member in this particular, almost 100-year-old, college of education.

My move to Ohio followed some demographic changes in minority representation in this Midwest medium-size city. Historically, Ohio had experienced diversity only as a racial issue represented by African American minorities or by low-socioeconomic-status (SES) Appalachian white populations. The exception was Cleveland, with a constant influx of immigrant, diverse groups (pretty much like any other large city). Until the early 1990s, cities like Cincinnati typically showed overrepresentation of African American children in low-SES, inner-city public schools and low-SES, Appalachian white children in suburban public schools. In the last decades, Cincinnati has experienced periods with some presence of middle- to upper-class international families (mostly from Asian and Latin American countries) brought by transnational corporations.

In the mid-1990s, a new immigration wave started in the medium-size cities of the Midwest, comprising Hispanic, eastern European, African, and Asian families. Some of these diverse families were new immigrants to this country, but most families were migrant groups moving to unsaturated smaller cities in search of better jobs and salaries. During the mid- to late 1990s, culturally and linguistically diverse immigrant families started to settle in low-SES neighborhoods and attend public schools in Cincinnati. This new wave of diverse immigrants challenged public schools because of their English-as-a-second-language (ESL) educational needs. In addition, the new immigrant groups created racial and ethnic tension with the African American community because together with Hispanics and Asians they were categorized as historically underrepresented groups and competed for the same federal and state resources for housing, education, health care, and other services.

These immigrant families were attracted to Cincinnati because of the traditional presence of industry and service jobs, lower cost of living, stronger unions pushing for higher salaries in blue-collar jobs, and less saturation of social institutions and services, such as public schools and health care. However, at the same time, minority immigrants had less support from an established ethnic community and minority leaders that advocated for their social needs. The situation for ESL educators was privileged because of the *fresh* attitudes and less *saturation* of social services for immigrant, diverse families, but at the same time, it was challenging because of the need to establish new partnerships and institutionalized services in social institutions, such as the school system. The advantage of a community such as Cincinnati was the tradition of ESL German immigrant settlers that entered America through Ellis Island during the mid-1800s to early 1900s. These German settlers succeeded in maintaining their German language and culture, together with English bilingualism, until the Anti-German sentiments brought German media and schools to an end around the start of World War I. Between the early to mid-1990s, many generations of monolingual English descendants had forgotten about their ESL and German roots established by earlier German settlers.

THE STORY TOLD BY THIS BOOK

Now, we go back to our story. Consider the real-life story that depicts my experience as a cultural bridge and mediator between the mainstream school system and Hispanic families and their young children. During a typical morning in my new office, my phone rang. It was an administrator from a suburban mix-income public school district (including schools located in low-SES to middle-class neighborhoods). She wanted to meet with me to discuss ways we could collaborate to serve the new Hispanic, Asian, eastern-European, and African immigrant low-SES children and their families at the preschool level. She explained that some educational services were in place, as mandated by the federal government, to serve the elementary and secondary ESL students (including Hispanic, eastern-European, and Asian groups), but there was no ESL program for the three- to five-year-old children who had started to show up in the last few years. However, she had some funding from Head Start to serve the low-SES mainstream and diverse preschool children within a mainstream setting. She asked me if I would like to visit and discuss ways we could reach out and adapt the educational services to the ESL, low-SES immigrant children and their families.

Soon after, I paid her a visit and observed some Head Start classrooms located in a primary school full of eager, young, diverse learners. I was encouraged by the experience of meeting some open-minded school administrators and teachers! who had a genuine interest in better serving ESL youngsters. I was happy to see that Cincinnati's administrators had a fresh attitude, much more positive and open-minded than other states, where ESL students have a historical presence and are perceived by many educators with a *saturated* attitude. When I moved to the Cincinnati community, ESL minorities were portrayed as the "news" in the local newspapers and television programs. This visit also made me realize that school administrators in the Cincinnati community were charging me with an important social responsibility: to act as a liaison, cultural bridge, or mediator between the school system and the newly immigrated diverse ESL families and their children.

Soon after my visit, my phone rang again; it was a director of a nonprofit community-based speech pathology organization, who was offering me a former preschool classroom to start a preschool program for ESL youngsters in collaboration with his organization. Again, I went on a field trip. It was a-dream-come-true situation! There, I found a beautiful facility. The large classroom was complete with furniture, educational materials, its own restroom, kitchenette, and adjacent computer room. Best of all, the director and her colleagues had very positive, fresh attitudes toward language-minority groups and were eager to put their facilities to use. They explained to me that recently they had lost their mainstream preschool clientele because of competition with public schools expanding early childhood special education services for youngsters with speech and hearing handicaps and language disorders. The director asked me, "Would you be interested in leading the effort of recruiting and implementing an ESL preschool program in collaboration with us?" Again, I was perceived as a liaison between diverse children and their families and a mainstream organization.

Soon after, my phone rang yet again. By now, I was getting used to meeting educational administrators and being perceived by them as an advocate for diverse children and their families. It was the director of a regional Head Start program, who was offering me financial support to serve ESL preschool children and their families. His regional Head Start program had started to collaborate with some inner-city public schools to diversify their service to minority families and children, from the historical African American groups to the new immigrant ESL families. They had recently approved the implementation of some Head Start classrooms in an inner-city school, but they had been unsuccessful reaching and recruiting ESL families. Though they tried hard, he explained that they sent many fliers, translated to their native languages, to potential ESL parents and posted some ads in community papers, but so far, they had received little to no response. He asked me if I would help them recruit diverse ESL families and their children for these inner-city Head Start programs, and if I would be interested in starting some Head Start classrooms to serve ESL children and their families. I paid him a visit; his large office was located in a suburban public school, and I was happy to meet more administrators with fresh attitudes who were interested in funding preschool services for ESL children and their families.

Back in my office, I reflected about my visits with educational administrators, and I felt overwhelmed by the social and moral responsibility of establishing so many partnerships between schools, organizations, and diverse families. But I also felt overjoyed by the fresh attitudes toward diverse immigrant families and their children. After some thought, I decided to put together this enthusiastic group of individuals and form a collaborative consortium, in which we would collaborate to serve ESL children and their families. This is how the Bilingual Preschool Development Center (BPDC) was established, as a partnership among inner-city and suburban public schools, a regional Head Start center, a nonprofit community organization, and faculty and students at the University of Cincinnati. I was to serve as a cultural bridge or liaison between diverse ESL children and their families, a leader in ESL preschool curriculum development, a recruiter and trainer of ESL student teachers from our graduate ESL program at the university, and a recruiter and advocate of diverse ESL families and their children. Funding was committed in different forms by the participating organizations. These funds were used to pay for student teachers, children's school transportation, consumable educational materials, and snacks.

Finally, after about nine months of hard work and many meetings, we were ready to open our doors for the upcoming school year. All that we needed now were children. But we hit a wall; we advertised; we waited, and nobody came, exactly as the Head Start programs in inner-city schools had experienced. We met, we worried, and we wondered why diverse ESL parents were not coming. I felt committed to continuing with this initiative, but I was puzzled. How could I serve as a liaison for recruiting diverse children? I wondered about possible strategies for solving this puzzle. By analyzing the situation in light of research literature, I realized that formal channels of communication were not working because many diverse immigrant groups rely on traditional oral communication styles, and therefore, church was a trustworthy community organization they attended. This eye-opening experience made me a true advocate and led me to announce to my colleagues with renewed confidence, "I will bring you diverse families from their church communities; please plan open houses at our preschool classroom and provide transportation on Sundays."

Then, I embarked in a series of Sunday visits to churches serving the new immigrant, diverse families in town. I started with a Catholic community center that offered masses in Spanish to hundreds of new Hispanic families. I asked for the support of the priest and nuns, and with their permission and endorsement, at the end of several Sunday masses, I announced, in Spanish, our open house in the preschool classroom. After each mass, I talked in Spanish with mothers and fathers and won their trust and friendship, and I established rapport and empathy by using language and culturally appropriate behaviors as a member of their Hispanic community. Through establishing rapport, I persuaded them to board our bus and visit our preschool classroom on Sunday afternoons. I realized the power of face-to-face interaction for establishing trust and respect with diverse families following an oral tradition of social relationships.

I also realized the differences between the cultural values of diverse families and the mainstream school culture, such as minority parents being unaware of the need for preschool education. Low-SES minority parents parents from a traditional cultural background, such as Hispanics, consider that their three- to five-year-olds are still babies and do not need to go to school yet. I explained to them that these young children need extra time to learn English, to continue to develop their Spanish, and to develop school readiness to start kindergarten in the mainstream school system. In the open-house meetings, we arranged for parents to meet teachers and fill out registration paperwork in their native languages, and soon, we realized that many were not literate or could hardly read or write in their first and only language. We had to arrange for volunteer university students to serve as mediators for diverse parents so the parents could fill out paperwork in their native language.

We also realized that many parents came with their extended family to the open house, and soon, we received some referrals for children of relatives and neighbors. I repeated the mass visits every weekend for the rest of that summer, in different parishes and communities. By the end of summer, we were ready to start with our first group of young, diverse children, and we were featured in the local newspapers and TV programs as the first bilingual English/Spanish preschool classroom opening in Cincinnati's history. With this advertisement, we also added some middle-class children from diverse immigrant and international families and other minority children (African American, Asian), whose parents were interested in an ESL preschool program. As time went by, other diverse preschool classrooms opened in the Head Start locations on the west side of town, which had a large proportion of low-SES Appalachian children. So rather than isolating the diverse children, we adopted an integrated model. In each preschool classroom, we balanced the number of monolingual English Appalachian children with the number of diverse ESL children. This integrated instructional model worked beautifully, as the diverse children started learning English much faster from their mainstream peers rather than from their teachers only.

As the BPDC story depicts, the effort to serve newly immigrated, diverse families resulted from the fresh and caring attitudes of a group of local educators who took social and moral responsibility and an advocacy position toward young, diverse children and their families. This book will use this real-life story for illustrating the ethnic-educator philosophy, assumed by the BPDC educators, and the pedagogical and assessment model and strategies that emerged from the implementation of pilot preschool classrooms serving young, diverse children throughout a four-year period.

THE STORY TOLD BY THIS BOOK ENDORSES AN ETHNIC-EDUCATOR PHILOSOPHY FOR EARLY CHILDHOOD DIVERSE EDUCATION

This book endorses an ethnic-educator philosophy and a *pluralistic* view of education and schooling, which includes different languages and cultural backgrounds as part of America's educational values and beliefs, processes, and products. This book's philosophy endorses integration and *transculturation* (leading to multiple languages and cultural identities) and opposes *assimilation* (leading to enforcing the mainstream culture and language only), both educational processes for immigrant students. The ethnic-educator philosophy endorsed in this book strongly stands behind an *integrated* approach to the linguistic and cultural adaptation of young, diverse students and their families, in which they can maintain their diversity while becoming American. In this book, I invite readers to become aware of the fact that the value of schooling lies in teachers serving as *liaisons* to facilitate young, diverse children's cultural adaptation, access, and integration, to middle-class America. I am hoping to inspire early childhood teachers and *awaken* their ability to *make a personal connection to young, diverse children and their families*, and by doing so, develop rapport, commitment, and advocacy to nurture, mentor, and mediate the cultural and linguistic adaptation processes among the increasing numbers of young, diverse children who populate preschool classrooms in the United States today. The four main philosophical principles of the ethnic-educator approach, with its embedded pedagogical principles, form the core of the BPDC curriculum presented throughout chapters in this book. The Appendix presents the summary of the ethnic-educator philosophical principles aligned with its pedagogical principles that the reader can use as an advance organizer or map for this book.

The most forceful message throughout the chapters of this book is that early childhood teachers need to rethink and rediscover the *learning potential* of young, diverse children and endorse and demonstrate through their classroom practice that *high-quality teaching can make a difference*. The diverse theoretical and philosophical approaches, pedagogy, and instructional and assessment strategies proposed in this book represent best educational practices that committed early childhood teachers can use to develop academic skills in young, diverse children. Best educational practices need to include and value the cultural, linguistic, and socioeconomic backgrounds of young, diverse students, in relation to content areas and methodologies used. The recommended educational practices have a core message to stimulate early childhood teachers to become *committed advocates* for helping young, diverse students in their *cultural adaptation process* to achieve at higher developmental levels.

I hope that this book will inspire early childhood teachers to develop *social and moral responsibility* and to become *committed advocates* for young, diverse students. I hope that this book will inspire readers to engage in personal reflections about the philosophical orientation that they use the most in their practice (based on an Erikson's concept of searching for a professional identity). In the *pluralistic school environment* that I have envisioned in this book, early childhood teachers and parents collaborate as partners to increase young, diverse students' achievement and developmental levels though high-quality education and parental involvement, which transforms research-based knowledge into educational practice in the classrooms.

I hope that the story I tell in this book becomes engaging, inspirational, and useful as a handbook for solving real-life challenges when teaching and facilitating learning for young, diverse children and building a partnership with their families and communities.

THEME AND OVERVIEW OF THE BOOK

The central theme of the book is the ethnic-educator philosophy and its derived pedagogical models and strategies, which link assessment to instruction, actual lesson plans, and alternative assessment tools. The book presents an insider's perspective on diverse early childhood education by unveiling a real-life story of a successful school laboratory for diverse preschoolers that the author established: the BPDC.

The book is divided into three parts. Part I includes the first two chapters and establishes the ethnic-educator philosophical and theoretical framework. Part I provides a context for understanding the pedagogical models introduced in this book and its unique features that interface cognition, language, and culture to meet the educational needs of low-SES young, diverse children (preK through Grade 3). These *young, diverse* children may come from *language-minority groups*, who have English as a second language (ESL), such as Hispanics, Asians, Native Americans, and Pacific Islanders, or from *sociohistorical minority groups*, such as African Americans, or who may be *mainstream* in terms of ethnicity but share the *low-SES* background with such minority groups as Appalachian and other white children.

Chapter 1 introduces the ethnic-educator philosophy. This educational approach and its pedagogical principles endorse advocacy and moral responsibility in teachers acting as liaisons and cultural bridges between the mainstream school culture and young, diverse children and their families. The central idea in the ethnic-educator philosophy is that the teacher's personality is the most important tool for the assessment and instruction of young, diverse low-SES children. Based on the ethnic-educator philosophy and some evidence from research (see Gonzalez, 2006; Gonzalez, Brusca-Vega, & Yawkey, 1997; Gonzalez & Yawkey, 1993; Gonzalez, Yawkey, & Minaya-Rowe, 2006), there are multiple factors embedded in teachers' personalities (i.e., attitudes, expectations, cultural beliefs and values, knowledge level, and level of familiarity with diverse languages and cultures) that affect their instruction.

Chapter 2 presents a pedagogical model that follows the ethnic-educator approach, which is based on research evidence (Carnegie Task Force on Learning in the Primary Grades, 1996; National Research Council, 1999a, 1999b). This ethnic-educator pedagogical model has been pilot-tested with young, diverse children in the BPDC. This pedagogical model is *holistic* because it integrates developmental areas (i.e., cognition, language, social, and emotional) with content areas (i.e., language arts, math, science, and social studies) across concepts represented by themes and topics in the curriculum.

The conceptual framework presented in the Part I will support the actual educational applications of the ethnic-educator approach presented in Part II, which includes Chapters 3 through 8. These five chapters will present (a) how to implement the pedagogical models through the derived instructional strategies, (b) how to develop lesson plans that integrate standards across developmental and content areas, (c) how to implement the classroom-based assessment tools for linking assessment with instruction and meet pedagogical and accountability purposes, and (d) case studies and lesson plans illustrating the recommended praxis.

Chapter 3 presents four main clusters of pedagogical strategies that follow the ethnic-educator pedagogical model presented in Chapter 2, which are research-based and meet the educational needs of young, diverse children. Then, Chapter 3 translates the ethnic-educator approach, with its philosophical principles, into an actual praxis or clusters of pedagogical strategies that build a curriculum. Examples of teachers using the ethnic-educator pedagogical strategies at the BPDC are provided to portray the unique educational needs of young, diverse children.

Chapter 4 integrates the pedagogical strategies of the ethnic-educator approach with academic content standards for young, diverse children. The first section of this chapter explains how pedagogical strategies link assessment to instruction through *classroom-based assessments* (observations and evaluation tasks) that represent academic content standards endorsed by Head Start and Teaching English to Speakers of Other Languages (TESOL, 2005). The second section of this chapter discusses the instructional purposes of assessment and presents the rationale explaining why classroom-based assessments are alternative measures that are more valid and reliable when assessing young, diverse children. The third section presents an integration of the ethnic-educator approach with TESOL academic content standards in the BPDC curriculum. Finally, sample lessons of the curriculum used in the BPDC are presented as examples of integration of the ethnic-educator curriculum with TESOL academic content standards and links to classroom-based observations.

Chapter 5 presents developmental tasks as alternative strategies of the ethnic-educator approach for assessing academic content in young, diverse children. Developmental tasks link assessment and instruction and provide teachers with classroom-based assessments that tap verbal and nonverbal mental processes and behaviors in young children. A case study is used for illustrating the implementation of this alternative assessment for young, diverse children.

Chapter 6 presents storytelling developmental tasks as an alternative tool for assessing semantic development (i.e., the intersection of cognition, culture, and language) in young, diverse children. Storytelling developmental tasks are classroom-based assessments that represent the philosophical and pedagogical principles of the ethnic-educator approach. As a developmental method of assessment, storytelling tasks link assessment to instruction and provide early childhood teachers with measurement tools that tap verbal and nonverbal mental processes and behaviors (i.e., semantic development) in young, diverse children. The storytelling developmental tasks presented in this chapter complement the classroom-based observations presented in Chapter 4 and the developmental tasks of academic content presented in Chapter 5. All the alternative methods of assessment presented in Chapters 4, 5, and 6 are classroom-based assessments that can be used by early childhood teachers for instructional purposes with young, diverse children.

Chapter 7 presents an ethnic-educator approach to alternative reading instruction for young, diverse children. These pedagogical reading strategies represent academic content standards endorsed by TESOL, which (1) support reading instruction through reading fluency interventions and the guided-reading approach; (2) are based on a socioconstructivistic, theoretical framework, centered on schema theory and proficient-reader research; and (3) support family involvement for increasing reading skills in young, diverse children. Some examples of the application of the guided-reading strategies are provided for the language arts content area as well as concluding remarks about best reading instruction practices for meeting the educational needs of young, diverse children.

Chapter 8 presents excerpts of interviews with teachers who were participants in the BPDC project and in ESL graduate-level courses and with parents of BPDC children. These interviews illustrate patterns and transparent conclusions for the book. The teachers' and parents' interview excerpts represent the topics covered throughout the chapters of the book. The main objective in Chapter 8 is to represent the teachers' and parents' end-of-the-school-year reflections on their teaching and parenting experiences and their feedback about some lessons learned from praxis.

Acknowledgments

I am grateful for all early childhood teachers who participated in the bilingual preschool classrooms, who inspired the story of this book. These early childhood teachers were master's students at the Teaching-English-as-a-Second-Language (TESL) Program, Division of Teacher Education, College of Education at the University of Cincinnati. Students who participated in this project during the 2001 through 2005 period included in this book were Carla Amaro, Griselle Zeno, Samantha Pittinger, Mendy DiMatteo, Jennifer Taylor, and Rachel Burns. I would also like to express my appreciation to Lorraine Schnier for her assistance in evaluating the children for the project discussed in Chapter 6. At the time of the project, Ms. Schnier was also a master's student at the College of Education at the University of Cincinnati.

I also appreciate the parents for providing their consent for their children's participation in this book project. Their teachers and I learned a lot from making *personal connections* with these young, diverse children and their families. I am sure that these children's unique educational experiences have become engraved in our minds and souls as personal and professional lessons to share with future generations of educators through the story told in this book. The most forceful message throughout chapters of this book is that early childhood teachers need to rethink and rediscover the *learning potential* of young, diverse learners and endorse and demonstrate through their classroom practice that *high-quality teaching can make a difference.*

I also want to express my deepest appreciation to my colleague Dr. Eugene García for graciously agreeing to write the foreword for this book. His scholarly work and leadership contributions to the education of diverse students have been an inspiration for my work. He has been a mentor, role model, and dedicated advocate for many scholars and diverse children and their families.

Last, but not least, I am very grateful to Ms. Jessica G. Allan, the acquisitions editor from Corwin, for her interest in supporting a book about the education of young, diverse children and her constructive feedback on improving the plan for this book. I also deeply appreciate the six external reviewers selected by Corwin for providing expert and helpful recommendations that definitely improved the content and format of this book:

Yolanda Abel, EdD
Instructor
Johns Hopkins University
Baltimore, MD

Amie Beckett, PhD
PhD Specialization Coordinator
Early Childhood and Primary Education
Richard W. Riley College of Education and Leadership
Walden University
Austin, TX

Katina Keener
Second-Grade Teacher
T. C. Walker Elementary
Gloucester, VA

Michele Pecina
Executive Instructional Manager
LitConn (ELL Materials, publisher of lessons)
Fresno, CA

Danielle Waldrep Rich, PhD
Assistant Professor and Clinical Supervisor
University of Montevallo
Montevallo, AL

Diane Senk
ELL Teacher
Sheboygan Area School District
Sheboygan, WI

Happy reading,
Virginia Gonzalez
Cincinnati, OH

About the Author

 **Dr. Virginia Gonzalez** has an interdisciplinary professional and academic background (BA in psychology from the Catholic University of Lima-Perú; MA in bilingual special education and PhD in educational psychology from The University of Texas at Austin). One of Dr. Gonzalez's major areas of expertise is the development of multidisciplinary models explaining sociocultural and linguistic factors influencing alternative assessment, learning and developmental processes, and instructional programs in bilingual/English-as-a-second-language (ESL), low-socioeconomic-status, Hispanic children. Dr. Gonzalez has conducted multiple research studies that have been published in the form of books and journal articles, have been disseminated at national and international conferences, and have been applied to the assessment and instruction of diverse learners in the public school setting and of international ESL students in higher education. These studies have generated alternative models and research methodologies, with important educational applications for the assessment and instruction of ethnic minorities. In light of this scholarly work, Dr. Gonzalez has been recognized as an outstanding and prolific scholar by major professional organizations in the interdisciplinary fields of second-language learning, bilingual education, and cognitive and language development. Among the many recent recognitions that Dr. Gonzalez has received for her scholarly and service work are (1) being elected to serve as a member of the Executive Special Interest Group (SIG) committee and the program committee for the American Educational Research Association (AERA) for a three-year term (2007–2010); (2) being presented with a service award by the AERA Bilingual Education Research SIG in April 2007; (3) serving as a chair and discussant for an invited presidential symposium, titled "Sociohistorical Factors Affecting ESL U.S. Immigrant Public Schools Students' Academic Achievement," presented at AERA 2008 annual meeting in New York City; and (4) being selected by the Council for International Exchange of Scholars (CIES) as a recipient of a Fulbright Senior Specialist grant with the University of Costa Rica in December 2008.

The real-life story told by this book is dedicated to all early childhood teachers, and the children and their families who participated in the bilingual preschool project. I hope that the story that they inspired me to tell in this book becomes inspirational and useful in solving real-life challenges when teaching young, diverse children and building a partnership with their families.

PART I

Ethnic–Educator Philosophical and Theoretical Framework

1

The Ethnic-Educator Philosophy

Chapter 1 introduces the ethnic-educator philosophy and pedagogical principles endorsing advocacy and moral responsibility in teachers acting as liaisons and cultural bridges between the mainstream school culture and young, diverse children and their families. The central idea in the ethnic-educator philosophy is that the teacher's personality is the most important tool for the assessment and instruction of low-socioeconomic-status (SES), young, diverse children. Based on the ethnic-educator philosophy and some research evidence (see Gonzalez, 2006; Gonzalez, Brusca-Vega, & Yawkey, 1997; Gonzalez & Yawkey, 1993; Gonzalez, Yawkey, & Minaya-Rowe, 2006), I believe there are multiple factors embedded in teachers' personalities (i.e., attitudes, expectations, cultural beliefs and values, knowledge level, and level of familiarity of diverse languages and cultures) that affect their teaching. It is important to note that *all* teachers can assume an ethnic-educator philosophy, regardless of their personal ethnic, racial, cultural, and language backgrounds. That is, mainstream and minority teachers can assume a commitment for respecting and celebrating diversity among their students. This chapter engages *all* teachers in reflecting about how much high-quality education for low-SES, young, diverse children depends on teachers acting as committed mentors who value and celebrate cultural and linguistic diversity as an asset and who nurture and believe in young, diverse children's learning potential. Endorsing an ethnic-educator philosophy, this book proposes that once teachers become committed mentors and advocates, they need to become knowledgeable about pedagogical models and strategies that meet the diverse educational needs of young children.

The Bilingual Preschool Development Center (BPDC), which I organized in collaboration with public schools, a regional Head Start center, a community organization, and my university, is used as a real-life laboratory where the ethnic-educator approach was tested and implemented for serving young, diverse children and their families. Throughout this book, excerpts from reflections of student teachers acting as BPDC lead teachers will be used as illustrations of the ethnic-educator philosophy and principles in action. The creation of the BPDC consortium and the real-life story behind this book is told in the Preface, as a letter to the reader.

The ethnic-educator philosophy and principles discussed in this chapter are also embedded throughout the book because *diversity* is approached as a broad term encompassing ethnicity, minority cultures and languages, and low-SES backgrounds. The young, diverse children whom this book refers to may come from *language-minority groups* (English-as-a-second-language [ESL] groups, such as Hispanics, Asians, Native Americans, and Pacific Islanders), from *sociohistorical minority groups* (i.e., African Americans), or from *mainstream* groups in terms of ethnicity but *low-SES* backgrounds (i.e., Appalachian and other white children living in poverty). The term low-SES is preferred in this book, rather than poverty, because it encompasses many social factors associated with low income and economic disadvantages that negatively impact development and learning in young children. For instance, among the most important factors, SES encompasses (1) occupation of parents and the associated levels of education and literacy in parents and, especially, caregivers, such as mothers, grandparents, or siblings; (2) resources present at home—from books and computers to basic needs, such as food and clothing; (3) physical and mental health of parents—related to emotional availability of parents, resilience, resourcefulness to identify social services, and the quality of the parent-child relationship; (4) cultural adaptation of parents and siblings—related to level of English-language proficiency in minority and immigrant families; and (5) number of siblings and birth order—older siblings have a higher risk of underachievement.

Philosophical principles are defined in this book as theoretical frameworks and perspectives that the author endorses as a vision for educating young, diverse children. Pedagogical principles are defined as general instructional approaches supported by research-based studies and theoretical paradigms. Together the four central *philosophical principles* and the embedded *pedagogical principles,* as listed and fully described later in this chapter, form the ethnic-educator philosophy presented in this book. Table 1.1 lists the ethnic-educator philosophical and pedagogical principles with a brief description.

- *Philosophical Principle 1: Developmental and Humanistic View of Learning*

Philosophical Principle 1 describes a *developmental* and *humanistic* view of learning and academic achievement in low-SES, young, diverse students. Teaching as a social and affective experience is emphasized throughout the chapters of this book, stimulating teachers to develop advocacy, commitment, empathy, and rapport for assuming social and moral responsibility when serving young, diverse children.

- *Pedagogical Principle 1: Socioemotional Nature*
  of Learning and Teaching Processes

Pedagogical Principle 1 represents the *socioemotional nature of learning and teaching processes* in nurturing classroom or home environments in which educators and parents are able to establish a trusting friendship with mutual respect for individual, cultural, and linguistic differences and a personal connection with the child (i.e., bonding or *rapport*). This rapport stimulates children's learning potential, the

Table 1.1 The Ethnic-Educator Philosophical and Pedagogical Principles

Philosophical Principles	*Pedagogical Principles*
Principle 1 *Developmental and Humanistic View of* *Socioemotional Nature of Teaching and Learning*	*Learning Processes*
• A *holistic* **developmental perspective** for learning across cognitive, linguistic, and socioemotional developmental and academic areas (language arts, mathematics, science, and social studies)	• **Developmental and humanistic** view of learning processes and academic achievement • The *socioemotional nature of learning and teaching processes* in nurturing classroom or home environments, in which educators and parents are able to establish a trusting friendship with mutual respect of individual, cultural, and linguistic differences, and a personal connection with the child (bonding or *rapport*)
Principle 2 *Holistic View of Learning and the* *Curriculum*	*Internal and External Factors Affect Resilience and At-Risk Conditions*
• **Socioconstructivistic** theoretical perspective with the interaction of internal and external factors in developmental and learning processes	• Learning and developmental processes are affected by the **interaction of internal factors** (maturational, psychological, and biological) and **external factors** (cultural, social, schooling, and family settings) • Internal and external factors affecting low-socioeconomic-status (SES), diverse, young children can support or hinder their *academic achievement* (becoming resilient or at risk of underachievement)
Principle 3 *Pluralistic and Transcultural Perspectives*	*Culture and Language Represented in Assessment and Instruction*
• **Pluralistic pedagogical approach** because it celebrates cultural and linguistic diversity as an asset, enriching the development and learning potential of young, diverse children into multicultural and multilingual minds and spirits	• Language is a conceptual tool for learning and representing sociocultural, affective, and emotional processes (i.e., cultural and bicultural identity)

Principle 4 Teachers as Advocates and Cultural Mediators	Teachers as Advocates and Cultural Mediators
• **Advocacy position** that calls teachers to raise their cultural awareness and develop *personal connections* between their family history and their students' sociohistorical backgrounds	• Teachers need to develop *nurturing learning communities* in which diverse, young children can collaborate, participate actively, and have a sense of belonging and intrinsic motivation • Teachers act as *cultural bridges/mediators* between the mainstream school culture and minority families • Teachers need to act as *mentors* for developing *rapport* with diverse children and *partnerships* with parents to establish mutual trust, respect for cultural, linguistic diversity, and idiosyncratic differences

negotiation of cultural and linguistic meanings with teachers and parents (or peers and siblings), and socioemotional learning processes (i.e., related to their individual differences and personality characteristics, such as temperament, motivation, interests, attitudes, cultural identity, cultural adaptation processes, cultural values and beliefs, identification and internalization of role models, imitation, self-concept, and self-esteem). Thus, stimulating learning in young, diverse students goes beyond the creation of an academic context, but requires a caring and committed teacher who can offer praise, encouragement, celebration, and reassurance of the value of minority linguistic and cultural identities.

- *Philosophical Principle 2: Holistic View of Learning and the Curriculum*

Philosophical Principle 2 describes a *socioconstructivistic* theoretical perspective with a *holistic* view of development (i.e., with interaction across cognition, language, and socioemotional areas) and the curriculum (with interaction across content areas—language arts, mathematics, science, and social studies). This holistic view of education acknowledges the interaction of internal and external factors in development and learning in young, diverse children. Assessment also has a holistic approach in which alternative or qualitative measures need to be used with process and problem-solving tasks. The ethnic-educator philosophy endorses the development of verbal and nonverbal concepts as mental tools for thinking and learning and high-level critical-thinking skills and problem-solving strategies that can actualize young children's potential for learning into academic excellence. It is considered that children's learning potential continues to develop across their life span, from lower- to higher-developmental levels.

- *Pedagogical Principle 2: Internal and External Factors Affect Resilience and At-Risk Conditions*

Pedagogical Principle 2 states that *internal* (i.e., developmental and psychological characteristics) *and external factors* (i.e., school and family environments) *interact*, resulting in resilience or at-risk conditions for underachievement in young, diverse children. A developmental perspective considers that young, diverse children are unique individuals with idiosyncratic differences that are the product of the interaction between internal and external factors. That is, development is dynamically influenced by individuals' unlimited potential for learning that is actualized and expressed differently across cultural and linguistic environments. Young, diverse students need to be respected and valued by teachers as individuals with rich heritages and cultural and linguistic backgrounds.

- *Philosophical Principle 3: Pluralistic and Transcultural Perspectives*

Philosophical Principle 3 describes a *pluralistic* pedagogical approach because teachers must celebrate cultural and linguistic diversity as an asset that can enrich the developmental and learning potential of young, diverse children into multicultural and multilingual minds and spirits. A pluralistic approach endorses *transculturation,* not assimilation, to use education as an enrichment tool that nurtures, maintains, and develops young children's culturally and linguistically diverse identities. Transculturation allows diverse children to move freely between their minority and mainstream personalities, enjoying the freedom provided by a truly democratic classroom and schooling process. In this way, the American Dream pursued by diverse families will become a reality for their children.

- *Pedagogical Principle 3: Culture and Language Represented in Assessment and Instruction*

Pedagogical Principle 3 states that teachers need to understand how to represent cultural and linguistic backgrounds of diverse children in assessment and instruction, through classroom-based assessments with instructional purposes. A battery of alternative assessments across developmental and content areas needs to be used to evaluate the individual child (i.e., readiness to learn across first and second languages [L1, L2] and nonverbal developmentally appropriate abilities), the social learning contexts in the school (school readiness), and family diverse settings. Assessment as an inseparable element for high-quality teaching requires the use of instruments that have demonstrated validity or accuracy for a particular use and population, as well as highly trained educators who can evaluate young, diverse students' learning and development through classroom-based assessments.

- *Philosophical Principle 4: Teachers as Advocates and Cultural Mediators*

Philosophical Principle 4 states that teachers need to take an *advocacy* position to raise their *cultural awareness* and develop *personal connections* between their family history and their students' sociohistorical backgrounds. Many teachers may have diverse ancestors, because about one-third of U.S. citizens today come from diverse ethnic, cultural, and/or linguistic backgrounds. By finding a personal connection

through family history, educators can build rapport that fosters high-quality pedagogy and success for young students' learning and academic achievement.

- *Pedagogical Principle 4: Teachers as Advocates and Cultural Mediators*

Pedagogical Principle 4 states that teachers need to reach out to diverse
parents to become collaborative partners, mentors, cultural mediators (or liaisons),
and committed advocates in the successful schooling process of young, diverse
students. Moreover, educators need to generate emotional or social bridges between
home and school by creating an integrated curriculum and a school environment
that authentically resembles students' real-life experiences of language and culture in their natural home environment.

Thus, the ethnic-educator philosophy stimulates teachers to engage in a
reflection about central philosophical and pedagogical principles affecting low-
SES, young, diverse students' learning, development, and academic achievement.
Research evidence and educational implications of how these central philosophical and pedagogical principles lead to high-quality teaching for young, diverse
learners are presented throughout the book. Case studies of classroom imple-
mentations as well as teachers' personal reflections are used to illustrate the
implementation of these central philosophical and pedagogical principles in
classroom practice through the BPDC project.

Now that all four central philosophical and pedagogical principles have been
summarized, I will discuss each one in light of some examples from the BPDC
experience.

EXAMPLES OF PRINCIPLE 1
The Developmental and Humanistic
Views of the Socioemotional Nature of Learning

Consider the following examples regarding the first philosophical principle of a
developmental and humanistic view of learning and its derived first pedagogical
principle of the socioemotional nature of learning and teaching processes. For
instance, depending on the social and *cultural distance* between the young, diverse
children and the target language and culture, they may experience some socioemotional processes such as *cultural adaptation* and its expressions through *culture
shock* and *language shock.* Cultural distance is defined as the degree of similarities or
differences that exist between two cultural behaviors and products (e.g., child rearing cultural practices, food habits, dress code, cultural styles of thinking and using
language, and communication patterns). In the BPDC, we observed that the
Hispanic preschoolers experienced culture shock because of the cultural distance of
differences in food habits and child rearing practices for feeding between the school
and home environments. Young, Hispanic children wanted to sit on the lap of their
teachers, and they expected to be cuddled and fed liked their mothers did at home.
In fact, many Hispanic youngsters called their teachers "mama" (mother), and their
mothers sent their bottles to school for the children to drink their milk from.

Obviously, teachers and parents' cultural expectations for child rearing acceptable behaviors for three- and four-year-olds were very different. There was a big cultural distance or gap between the Hispanic home culture of dependence of children on adults and the mainstream school culture of independence of children and mastery of self-help skills at young ages.

Another example of cultural distance observed in the BPDC was the difference in dress codes between the mainstream school culture and the Hispanic parents. At the beginning of the school year, most Hispanic children (especially girls) were sent to school in their best Sunday clothes, with uncomfortable shoes and accessories that did not allow children to play in the gym and on the playground or to go to the restroom on their own. Some children also expressed some fear of messing up their best clothes while playing because their parents had explicitly told them "don't get messy" (no te ensucies). Teachers had to explain to Hispanic parents that children needed to be dressed in more simple and comfortable clothing that could be washed.

Cultural adaptation processes are complex and require immigrant, diverse children and their families to undergo some stages that take *developmental time* (from a few months to as many as eight years, depending on individual and contextual factors). Teachers need to be aware of the characteristics of these *cultural adaptation stages*, the socioemotional cost for the individual, the impact on L2 proficiency levels, and necessary developmental time for young, diverse children. According to Adler (1975), *cultural adjustment* requires the immigrant child to go through a progressive sequence of three maturational stages of personality changes and coping skills, including (1) *identifying self in relation to the home culture* behaviors and values, (2) *identifying self during the transition between the home and the host culture* and experiencing some conflicts in cultural values and behaviors and feelings of "living between two cultural worlds" (culture shock and language shock can occur at this stage), and (3) *identifying self in relation to the host culture* in which individuals compare and contrast similarities and differences between cultures and becoming aware of cultural meanings in their host culture, allowing for intercultural communication.

Culture shock is an expression of the second adaptation stage, in which the minority child experiences anxiety, fear, disorientation, and confusion when previous adaptation or coping strategies used successfully in the native home or culture do not work for solving problems in the second culture or environment (i.e., the school classroom). The minority child experiences a transitional phase in which new adaptation strategies need to be learned (i.e., reorganize values and beliefs, change behaviors, and ultimately change personality characteristics based on new cultural experiences) to become *transcultural* or *bicultural*. Individuals need to negotiate how to integrate home-country values with new host-country values and behaviors, with conflicts arising when cultures are in opposition or do not complement each other. This process takes developmental time and a nurturing environment with the presence of caring teachers and parents who can serve as role models for the new adaptation strategy.

A particular Guatemalan girl, Paula, comes to mind as an example from the BPDC illustrating the second cultural adaptation stage of transition and conflict between cultural values. Paula was three years old and monolingual-Spanish when she came to us, and she was delayed in her oral-language proficiency.

After about six months in the BPDC, Paula strongly identified with her bilingual (Spanish/English) preschool teacher, she improved significantly in her Spanish proficiency, and she mastered a large number of phrases in English, which led to a beginning communicative-competence level. At this point, Paula started to express cultural value conflicts typical of a transitional second-cultural adaptation stage. Paula was becoming aware of her growing biculturalism and bilingualism, which was highly valued at school by her bilingual teacher, and by contrast, she articulated her preoccupation in the fact that her mother could only speak Spanish at home. As part of the parental involvement emphasis of Head Start, we had also started a parents' English program, so Paula's mother was starting to learn a few English phrases to use at home. Paula was overjoyed one morning when she shared with her bilingual teacher that her mom, for the first time, spoke to her in English at home. Her mom said, "Paula, go to bed." That simple phrase had finally solved Paula's cultural conflict of the value of being bilingual at school. Now, she could identify with bilingualism through her most important role models—her mother and her teacher. Culture shock was observed in the BPDC Hispanic children when they first experienced the school menu. Items like chicken nuggets and peanut butter and jelly sandwiches were not part of their home experiences. Hispanic children first reacted with surprise and lack of interest in trying unfamiliar food. An effort was made to bring parents in to school to learn with their children, to stimulate independent behaviors at the table, and to learn to prepare and eat the typical foods of mainstream school menus. At the same time, an effort was made to incorporate familiar Hispanic household items in the school menu, such as tacos and beans. By the end of the school year, many Hispanic children enjoyed moving from typical American foods to their beloved Hispanic food, becoming transcultural, and transcending their initial cultural distance and culture shock. In fact, socioemotional learning and cultural adaptation are very much related to academic achievement in young, diverse children. Nurturing the integration of successful socioemotional development in both cultures supports young, diverse children and their families in adapting successfully to the school culture by becoming bicultural or transcultural.

Language shock involves an emotional stage of confusion and frustration that monolingual speakers of languages other than English experience when entering an environment where only English is used. It is related to the first stage or *silent period* of L2 learning, in which diverse children may start using their native language until they become frustrated and enter a silent period that may be short or long lasting. The second stage is the *nonverbal period,* in which gestures, body language, and symbolic behaviors (i.e., drawings, symbolic play, role-play, imitation) are used to communicate, while remaining active listeners trying to decipher meanings in the L2 based on contextual clues and formulaic speech that they will repeat and memorize.

An observation from a BPDC bilingual (English/Spanish) teacher, Sarah, very well illustrates these first and second stages of L2 learning with an interaction of socioemotional factors on an ESL child's *selective* silent period. Sarah was proud of her accomplishments as a teacher during the first few months of school, when she realized that she had very few anecdotal notes on one particular ESL Hispanic child, Pedro. As Sarah reflected about Pedro's behavior in the classroom, she began noticing a pattern of silence. This was not the typical silent period of ESL children that she was noticing, for she had one nonverbal student who fit this typical pattern. The silence that Pedro was demonstrating was more of a selective silence. Sarah turned to Pedro's mother, then to her adviser and professor (i.e., the author of this book), and later to her books for answers, but could not find any easy solutions to this dilemma.

Pedro had been in the Head Start center for two years, but this was his first year in the bilingual classroom. Pedro had an older brother who was in third grade, but his mother reported that they only used Spanish at home. What confused Sarah was that she often had heard Pedro speaking with many of the monolingual-English children. So why did Sarah have no observational notes on Pedro's class-room interactions? In her reflections, Sarah noticed that she often tried to use Spanish with this child during play, but she received no response. Pedro often looked at Sarah over his glasses with a grin on his face. He was a very compliant, quiet child who did not cause any trouble. He was never the root of a tattle by another child. For the next week, Sarah tried to intentionally play and make con-versation with him in Spanish. Sarah was only responded to with a look and a grin. The next week, Sarah tried speaking in English with him. This time Pedro responded, but only with "yes" and "no" answers. Judging from her observa-tions, Sarah realized that Pedro had no language or intellectual impairments, but he just seemed to not want to speak—to her. She was dumbfounded.

Throughout the course of the year, Pedro eventually began speaking to Sarah and even began participating openly in circle time and offering his opinions dur-ing reading. He became an outgoing child who sometimes did cause trouble and, on occasion, screamed angrily. In her reflections written for her adviser, Sarah openly confessed that she did not know what changed. She never found one par-ticular tactic that worked with Pedro. She tried using very specific targets, which she knew would interest him, to try to draw him out of his shell. Pedro would dab-ble with the objects Sarah was showing him, but he did not fully engage while she was around. Then, Sarah tried being nonchalant with Pedro's participation or conversation at meals, but he was equally or even more silent than before.

Pedro did not change in one day, but the good news is that he gradually, and over the course of months, starting coming out of his silence. He spoke of trips to Mexico to see his sister and of visits to jail to see his dad. This information opened Sarah's eyes and provided an answer for her queries: This child was preoccupied with *social and emotional experiences* that were difficult and traumatic for him and his family. The holistic developmental approach of *interaction between cognition and language, and social and emotional developmental areas* resonated as truthful in Pedro's case. It was only when Pedro could incorporate his real-life stories and journeys into his play and drawings that he was *developmentally ready* to speak to his teacher. As Pedro's nonverbal expressions through stories and drawings came to Sarah's atten-tion, she was able to use Pedro's authentic expressions of his thoughts and emotions as assessments of his language, social, emotional, and cognitive development. Sarah, of course, had to use the mandated standardized tests, but she gained little more than his typical look and grin when administering them to Pedro. Sarah found that as Pedro developed, he showed her what he knew in the context and scope of the classroom. Extra props and measures were unnecessary, actually useless, and prompted Pedro to hide more in his shell, or selective silence. This is a wonderful real-life story that helps teachers understand the powerful influence of socioemotional, real-life experiences on young, diverse children's learning processes.

The third stage is the *telegraphic and formulaic speech period*, in which children may use content words without function words or morphological markers. That is, instead of saying full sentences (e.g., "please give me a cookie"), children just use single words to convey meaning (e.g., "cookie"). Children may also memorize and appropriately use chunks of language, strings of words, or routine phrases. I will never forget a young Asian boy, Michael, at the BPDC whose first utterance in English in the classroom was used to assert his needs to another competing child. Michael exclaimed, "This book is mine!" This memorized phrase served a social-communication purpose and was appropriately used to express his feelings and needs. As this example clearly illustrates, the teacher had served as a role model to socialize the child to use language in an appropriate social manner. Michael was not really imitating his teacher but had internalized the phrase and used it meaningfully in a different but appropriate situation.

The fourth stage is the *productive language use period*, in which the children construct their own full sentences, following morphological and syntactic rules. These are newly produced combinations of language, which can show overgeneralizations and misuse of linguistic rules but are used in appropriate social contexts and are successful in conveying meaning. These four sequential developmental stages of L2 learning are supported by literature (McLaughlin, Blanchard, & Osanai, 1995; Saville-Troike, 1987; Tabors & Snow, 2001).

Thus, as illustrated by the examples from real-life children who attended the BPDC, the first pedagogical principle of the ethnic-educator approach highlights the socioemotional dimensions of teaching and learning processes among young, diverse children. Cognitive and language development interact with the cultural adaptation stages that diverse immigrant children go through. So it is important for educators to be aware of language shock and culture shock experiences, as well as stages of L2 learning when serving immigrant ESL children. It is also important for educators to endorse transculturation models that support maintaining ESL children's L1 and cultural heritage while learning the English culture and language. Transculturation results in *bicognitivism* (i.e., the ability to think and form concepts in both languages), *bilingualism* (i.e., the ability to articulate thoughts into two linguistic systems), and *biculturalism* (i.e., the maintenance of two cultural identities and cultural adaptation processes).

EXAMPLES OF PRINCIPLE 2
The Holistic View of Learning Considers Internal and External Factors in Resilience and At-Risk Conditions

Early childhood educators endorsing an ethnic-educator perspective need to stimulate young, diverse children to participate actively in learning activities so that they can develop their potential for learning and problem-solving abilities, such as concept formation. Then, as endorsed by the second philosophical and pedagogical principles, it becomes important for teachers to differentiate between external and internal factors affecting development and learning in young, diverse children. That is, educators must fully understand the impact that low-SES factors and cultural and linguistic differences (all external factors) can have on intelligence, development, and learning (internal or psychological factors—including L1 and L2 learning). The impact of external factors may result in diverse, low-SES children needing extra developmental time and *individualized instruction.*

Thus, educators must understand similarities and differences between mainstream, middle-class students' learning and developmental needs and diverse students' unique educational needs. Some examples of unique educational needs of young, diverse children include extra developmental time needed for language learning (i.e., readiness for reading and writing, difference between social and academic English-language proficiency, the role of having L1 other than English in learning), cultural differences in learning styles, and curriculum and assessment accommodations for cultural and linguistic diversity. That is, bilingualism or speaking a minority variety of English per se does not put children at risk. But SES factors associated with poverty (common in minority groups, such as Hispanics and African Americans), place diverse children at risk of underachievement and developmental delays, hence the needed extra developmental time and curriculum accommodations. The problem arises when the same developmental standards and achievement expectations are applied to mainstream, middle-class, and low-SES minority children. Young, diverse children who are at risk for learning difficulties and developmental delays because of poverty need to be exposed starting in their preschool years (and even birth) to high-quality and nurturing classroom environments. Educators need to adopt a wait-and-see approach (providing them with extra developmental time), giving the benefit of the doubt to the child, while observing his or her *potential for learning* across time and providing high-quality and appropriate education.

Another example of differences between mainstream and young, diverse students' relates to cultural factors affecting children's language learning processes. Educators need to understand that a topic-centered academic language cannot be the only acceptable normative style in school for young, diverse learners. *Using language in diverse cultural ways for social and academic interactions needs to be validated in the classrooms for young, diverse children.* Young, diverse children bring to school the real-life language they have learned in their minority homes and social communities, which probably use more *topic association,* but it is also perfectly appropriate for expressing abstract academic concepts.

For instance, when I have observed diverse, preschool children from low-SES backgrounds in the BPDC, I have found that their concept formation is expressed through vocabulary commonly used in real life, which also conveys categories and abstract use of concepts and language. That is, diverse, low-SES preschool children may not be able to identify elephants as mammals that live in the Sahara desert and have a specific diet, as the typical response of middle-class, mainstream children would because they have been schooled and raised in a mainstream family. However, a diverse child can demonstrate abstract knowledge by engaging in analogical reasoning, as she can compare how the parts of an elephant relate to familiar objects from different category domains (e.g., the elephant's ears are like giant leaves that are moved by the wind, like a rug because they are flat, and also like a tortilla because besides being flat they are also round). The diverse child can also demonstrate flexibility of thinking, creativity, awareness of real-world knowledge and ability to elaborate based on networks of prior knowledge, and the use of assimilation as a learning strategy. Based on this example, a teacher has the choice of focusing on the weak aspects of the diverse child's development, such as lack of academic vocabulary and topic knowledge according to age level, or on the child's strengths showing his or her potential for learning, such as the diverse child's strength for concept formation processes at or above age level when using real-life experiences.

Unfortunately, many teachers choose to have a single pedagogical register and purpose for educating all children, in an equal but unfair manner, with no respect for differences and unique educational needs, such as children who come from diverse language and cultural backgrounds (e.g., African American, Asian, Hispanic, and Appalachian). In such schools, the *standard* language is only English, representing a middle-class, mainstream school culture, and the curriculum is preplanned and prepackaged, in which minority languages and minority varieties of English have no value. The ideal school setting for diverse children needs to value children's genuine way of using language (whether minority or mainstream). In these ideal educational settings, diverse children are allowed to talk and express their different cultural identities, interests, and experiences with language, which do not fit the homogeneous curriculum of the mainstream school culture. For instance, child-centered, literature-based, real-life communication situations can be used by teachers of diverse children to talk, write, and read about real events and objects in culturally and linguistically familiar environments. Then, the use of play interaction in culturally appropriate ways and the cooperation of teachers and parents as social facilitators of learning are key for the academic success of young, diverse children.

By gaining cultural awareness, early childhood teachers can develop positive attitudes and intrinsic motivation for supporting their young, diverse students' learning, development, and academic achievement. As endorsed by the second philosophical and pedagogical principles, high-quality educational support requires teachers to take a holistic perspective to the instruction and assessment of young, diverse students. The ethnic-educator position endorsed in this book supports a holistic vision for young, diverse students' educational and teachers' professional development. Teachers need to educate the *whole* child, encompassing not only academics but also social and affective development, general mental and physical health and safety. Furthermore, this book endorses the position that the professional development of teachers needs to infuse in them a holistic vision of education that aims to develop cognitive, ethical, and moral abilities in ESL students. Curriculum areas (i.e., language arts, mathematics, social studies, and science) are integrated with all developmental areas (i.e., cognitive, linguistic, social, and emotional) into a *spiral curriculum* to meet the educational needs of young, diverse children in a holistic manner.

The ethnic-educator approach defines a spiral curriculum as the integration of themes and topics that present concepts at different developmental levels throughout the school year with teachers modeling the application of critical-thinking and problem-solving skills across developmental and content areas. In this way, children are exposed to learning experiences that reinforce the same concepts but with different representations that transform their application to different content and levels. For instance, the kindergarten curriculum can use the concept of categorization in sorting leaves by colors in science and sorting words that rhyme in language arts. Content areas, themes, and topics can also represent cultural and linguistic concepts and products that validate the diversity of young children (such as cultural traditions to celebrate holidays—clothing, food, symbols, cards, and decorations). For instance, classroom discussions and storytelling can be centered on contrasting the celebration of the new year in different cultures represented in the classroom. Parents can be invited to share their cultural traditions with stories and bring objects symbolizing their culture in a show-and-tell scenario. Some parents can share how they celebrate the Chinese New Year, such as the colors and symbols associated with decorations, the food served, the presents offered, the family gatherings, and its cultural meaning.

Our experience at the BPDC can illustrate how teachers can have a holistic vision of education and their curriculum implementation when serving young, diverse children. Joyce's reflections about her teaching in the BPDC relate to the implementation of a wholistic curriculum. The first curriculum unit that Joyce implemented was called "All About Me," and it was focused on validating each child as an individual. The children brought in "me boxes" full of things that represented who they were. Some children brought in a favorite stuffed animal or book, while others brought in family pictures or a new backpack. Each child had a story to share and illustrated it using their objects, and everything was done in their home language. Joyce's teaching assistant, Becky, often repeated the children's story in English, making sure that she clarified the details with the same focus that the children had given to their story in their L1. Joyce and Becky felt that this was a good way to introduce the children's minority languages and their cultural and family backgrounds. Joyce and Becky focused on all children getting to know one another's names, both verbally and in print. They worked on developing strong self-concepts, and besides asserting the children's home cultures and languages, they also valued one another as individuals. Joyce, Becky, and their students looked at themselves in their imaginary mirrors every morning and said, "Hey, good looking! How are you doing today?" ("Hola, guapo! Como estas hoy dia?"). The children began imitating the praising behaviors with one another and began repeating some of the common phrases that they heard their teachers saying in both languages used in the classroom—Spanish and English. This was a fun activity that stimulated children's cognitive, language, and socioemotional development in a truly holistic curriculum.

The ethnic-educator curriculum also uses different instructional materials, such as verbal and nonverbal stimuli, for example, from children's exposure to actual real-life experiences (picking leaves in the park) to pictures of leaves, plastic leaves, and words used to categorize leaves by color. In addition, different formats of delivery are used, stemming from individual teacher-child interactions and child-to-child interactions to small- and large-group interactions for discussing lived experiences and categorization activities. In this way, different forms of social interactions and active learning nurture the child's learning potential. Curriculums represent genuine cultural, linguistic, and social products that are used as socialization methods or tools for teaching concepts and stimulating young, diverse children's learning potentials. For instance, cognate words across languages (e.g., English and Romance languages such as Spanish, French, Italian, Portuguese; *elephant* in English is *elefante* in Spanish) are used to reinforce concepts of animals and sorting and categorization skills and abilities. Another example is the use of family values as curriculum content when they share similarities with school culture, such as cooperation and sharing, and can be translated into useful teaching strategies, such as storytelling. In sum, the ethnic-educator curriculum uses integration as "massed" experiences across developmental and content areas, themes, topics, verbal and nonverbal instructional materials, and delivery formats. In this way, the individual differences in development (e.g., interests, maturational levels, and stages) and cultural and linguistic differences are respected and used as an enrichment strategy for the early childhood curriculum.

EXAMPLES OF PRINCIPLE 3
Pluralistic and Transcultural Perspectives Include Culture and Language in Assessment and Instruction

Developmental time needed sometimes is extensive, but should at least encompass six months to one year for conducting a performance-based assessment of progress in learning and *potential for learning* in a longitudinal manner. Educators also need to take into account that academic language proficiency takes from five to eight years in any child and is a dynamic and individual learning process that is highly influenced by external educational factors. That is, educators need to provide developmental time and different kinds of learning opportunities for young, diverse children to acquire concepts and content. Educators need to focus on what children *can do* and on gains made while high-quality educational opportunities have been provided for developing their potential for learning.

In an ethnic-educator approach, the objective for assessment is to value the unique characteristics of individuals and to respect their cultural and linguistic differences. Systematic records of performance-based assessment linked to instruction need to be collected across developmental (i.e., cognitive, language, and socioemotional) and content areas (i.e., language arts, mathematics, social studies, and science). I fully support the possibility for teachers to become advocates of young, diverse students by contributing to and collecting classroom-based authentic assessment evidence that documents classroom performance across content and developmental areas. Early childhood teachers assume an advocacy role for young, diverse children when they act as role models and introduce change in the educational system by using alternative assessments and instructional practices.

Potential for learning refers to the child's ability to learn and relates to the maturational level at which the child can think and construct concepts related to sociocultural experiences. Then, potential for learning must be differentiated from the amount of knowledge acquired by children in a particular sociocultural setting. The point is that young, diverse children develop in different cultural, linguistic, and SES contexts and, therefore, actualize or develop their learning potential differently than mainstream counterparts. During assessment, the comparison of amounts of knowledge acquired between individuals (i.e., a focus on *products*) is not an interest of the ethnic-educator approach, but the priority is to identify the individual's developmental milestones and stages achieved (i.e., a focus on *process*).

Alternative assessments focus on measuring *learning processes*, such as the strategies students use for learning, their developmental stage, and particular expression of students' *learning potential* as a certain ability or skill level in a specific educational environment. Some examples of alternative assessments are developmental problem-solving tasks; unstructured observations of students across contexts; surveys, questionnaires, and interviews with parents and teachers; teacher-made, criterion-referenced measures, such as rating scales and rubrics; and portfolio assessments. Some standardized tests can also be used in an ethnic-educator perspective, but not with the objective of comparing between individuals (a product approach). Instead, standardized tests can be used to identify an individual's strengths and weaknesses to individualize instruction to meet the educational needs of young, diverse students.

Teachers in the BPDC program were very sensitive to representing children's individual, cultural, and linguistic diversity through a thematic curriculum. One BPDC teacher's account relates to her goal of adapting the curriculum to children's interests. As the beginning of the year unfolded, Allison realized that the children quickly let her know through their play what topics they were interested in. Based on the children's preferences, Allison selected some themes for the curriculum. Some of the curriculum units that Allison used were based on environmental factors, such as changes in the weather, seasons, and seasonal activities. Allison's curriculum went through such topics as "Camping" (complete with gear and a make-believe fire for cooking meals), "Harvest Time" (with a farmer's market and growing vegetables), and an "Arctic Zone" (with an ice-cream shop and balloons representing "ice" in the sensorial table). Each unit used thematic centers that had interrelated content and integrated developmental areas (from cognition, to language, to socioemotional skills). The children quickly noticed the similarities across content represented in themes and were soon making connections across their experiences in the classroom and in the outside world.

As the anecdote documents, Allison was thrilled to observe the power of *individualizing* a thematic curriculum to the children's interests in real-life topics. By *individualizing instruction*, the students' interests and motivation for learning can be validated, and the curriculum can be enriched. Individualization of instruction also allows for nurturing the *whole* child, as all aspects of the student's personality can be stimulated including cognitive, linguistic, social, and emotional areas. The student's strengths and weaknesses are identified to nurture their learning potentials and to stimulate the development of skills and abilities at higher levels.

EXAMPLES OF PRINCIPLE 4
Teachers as Advocates and Cultural Mediators

I have always been an advocate for the role of teachers as cultural mediators, resource people, and collaborators with parents and school personnel for developing mentor relationships with diverse students and their families. I perceive that the role of teachers as cultural mediators or liaisons is to help diverse children and their families adapt to the school and community cultural environment. In addition, committed teachers are advocates (as partners with parents) for the best interest of diverse children in three important ways: (1) they understand federal and state educational policies that apply to their children, (2) they learn about community resources for meeting the children's health needs, and (3) they refer students and parents to the appropriate community agencies or school personnel who can assist them further with their individual needs (e.g., application to the free-lunch programs, medical and dental care).

My experience with Hispanic parents is that, in some situations, school personnel had to help them find appropriate housing (e.g., moving from an unsafe neighborhood that had created anxiety and stress in their children as they witnessed robbery, assault, and other signs of violence), find clothing for cold weather (sometimes a new experience such as snow is not common in Latin American, Asian, and African subtropical and tropical regions), prepare to take the driver's license exams, fill out papers to register their children in school, learn how to use bank accounts, learn how to buy a car and apply for a loan, learn how to read bus route maps, and other similar tasks. In general, educators and school personnel become cultural mediators for helping their students and their families adapt to their new daily routines and school and cultural realities, which demand the development of new social knowledge and skills (e.g., learning a new language) for which they are ill prepared (e.g., their literacy levels may not be up-to-level to the reading skills necessary to take a driver's license exam even in their L1).

In addition, I believe that intervention strategies used by educators and parent-teacher liaisons, such as parent educators, need to take into consideration the diverse families' values and cultural patterns present in educational goals and child-care practices. Understanding the particular idiosyncratic characteristics of the community and family in which the child lives is necessary because minority groups vary widely between different cultures (e.g., Hispanics, Asian Americans, and Native Americans) but also in ethnic groups. For instance, some factors affecting ethnic diversity are as follows: (1) different countries of origin and regions make a difference in cultural heritage (e.g., Puerto Ricans have unique characteristics different from Mexican Americans and other Central American and South American groups; Koreans are very different from Japanese and Chinese groups); (2) SES factors make a difference between and in minority groups (low-SES, immigrant, diverse children are at risk of underachievement but not middle- and upper-class, diverse children); (3) number of generation also makes a difference for cultural adaptation levels (e.g., degree of proficiency of the minority and the English language).

At the BPDC, we found that teachers reported that their experiences with diverse families were very rewarding. Minority parents were very willing to become involved, once given the opportunity. Trueba and Delgado-Gaitan (1988) reported the desire of immigrant families to be participants in their child's education, but as we found out by our experience in the BPDC, they often did not know how. Teachers at the BPDC often encounter families whose desire to participate in school activities was there, but they had a multitude of barriers to overcome (Chrispeels & Rivero, 2001). It was in these circumstances that BPDC teachers became the liaison between school, home, and community for better serving diverse families.

For instance, we had to arrange for mothers to come to the preschool by riding with their child on the school bus, as they lacked transportation and had no idea of how to use public bus routes. Reading a map was a new experience and a "foreign" concept for many diverse, low-SES parents. At the beginning of the school year, we also had to reach out to parents by making phone calls in their native language and inviting the whole family to come to open house activities at school. We found out, through experience, that if we only sent a flier home, even if it was written in their home language, parents would not respond. We learned that in many minority cultures personal contact through spoken language, such as a phone conversation, would make a big difference for establishing a trusting social relationship between parents and teachers. Some minority parents were socialized in oral-language traditional cultures in which social contact had to be established through informal conversations and gatherings. Another barrier was the low literacy level that many diverse, low-SES parents had in their native language. Once parents learned to trust the teachers, they would come back to participate in classroom activities.

Another central idea of the fourth principle, the need for teachers to become advocates for diverse children and their families, is that family and school provide social experiences and nurture the child's development of thinking and language. Interactions with adults and other children in family and school settings socialize the child's potential for learning into skills and abilities that are culturally and linguistically loaded. Social interactions provide nurturing opportunities for the child to observe, imitate, internalize, and transform creatively social experiences into images, symbols, and concepts that take a verbal and nonverbal form. For instance, social experiences provide the child with cultural immersion into language, religious values, habits, traditions, and, in general, with the social products of culture. That is, "Cultural and linguistic experiences are celebrated as diversity, through subject, actual experiences and activities, and learning about self" (Gonzalez et al., 1997, pp. 86–87). That is, this quote emphasizes that instructional activities need to specifically celebrate the cultural identity of young, diverse learners.

A BPDC, bilingual, mainstream teacher, Joyce, relates her experience of collaboration with diverse parents. In her reflections about her teaching, Joyce explained that many times the BPDC children would request a book or story that was familiar to them. Joyce quickly requested the help of some parents to visit the classroom to tell stories from their own childhoods to increase parent involvement, as well as pull more authentic, diverse materials into the curriculum. Many of the immigrant parents brought in books that they had read as a child in their home country. Joyce was delighted when her Arabic families brought in Arabic folktales to share with the children. Because the BPDC children were so used to hearing other languages, they sat silently on the carpet as Arabic parents read stories during their weekly classroom visits. Once, some children giggled as a father read a story in Arabic, but all children were still able to listen and pay attention. After the Arabic father finished the story, he related its meaning in English. Joyce was sure to translate the story into Spanish and relate it to a familiar Mexican fairytale to help the Hispanic, monolingual-Spanish children understand the story. Joyce was grateful for the parents' willingness to share a piece of their culture with her class. Parents reported satisfaction at becoming useful to their children's teachers and had an opportunity to increase their understanding of the curriculum used for educating their children.

Thus, for educators to become committed advocates of diverse children and their families, they need to learn about the ethnic background of students and to develop a habit of sociocultural observation for understanding idiosyncratic cultural patterns and avoiding stereotypes and overgeneralizations. By attending community events, such as festivals or local ethnic restaurants, educators can understand firsthand their students' experiences as they occur in the genuine cultural and linguistic environments. The challenge for educators is to link the personal lives of their diverse students with their experiences at school. Thus, I believe that by becoming cultural mediators, educators become mentors who can offer meaningful interfaces between their diverse students' cultural identities associated with their home lives and their school experiences.

The Ethnic-Educator Pedagogical Model

Chapter 2 presents a pedagogical model that follows the ethnic-educator approach, which is based on research evidence (Carnegie Task Force on Learning in the Primary Grades, 1996; National Research Council, 1999a, 1999b). This ethnic-educator pedagogical model has been pilot-tested with young, diverse children in the Bilingual Preschool Development Center (BPDC). This pedagogical model is holistic, as it integrates developmental areas (i.e., cognition, language, social, and emotional) with content areas (i.e., language arts, math, science, and social studies) across concepts represented by themes and topics in the curriculum.

Following an ethnic-educator approach, the most important tool for instruction is the teacher's personality, encompassing his or her cultural values and beliefs, attitudes, prior knowledge about learning and instruction, and their level of familiarity with diverse children's cultural and linguistic backgrounds. Then, in the first section of Chapter 2, we discuss teachers' personality factors affecting the delivery of instruction for young, diverse learners. Once teachers reflect on their personality influence on instruction, they are ready to consider the adoption of the curriculum model endorsed by the ethnic-educator approach. Then, the second section of Chapter 2 presents a socioconstructivistic pedagogical model that integrates developmental and content areas.

HOW TEACHERS' PERSONALITIES AFFECT THEIR ASSESSMENT AND INSTRUCTIONAL DECISIONS

The ethnic-educator approach urges teachers to undergo an "awakening" experience to become aware of how much their personalities affect their instructional and assessment decisions and practices with young, diverse learners. Following one of the main philosophical and pedagogical principles of the ethnic-educator philosophy, we consider that *teachers' individual differences reflected in their personalities result from the interaction between internal and external factors.* Teachers are

exposed to different sociocultural environments that shape their personal and professional backgrounds, such as family, ethnic community, schooling, and teacher-
training programs.

Educators' personal and professional backgrounds reflected in their personalities are the most important tool for delivering instruction to and performing
evaluations on young, diverse learners. Educators' personality factors affecting
their educational decisions encompass three main areas: (1) their individual differences, such as attitudes, cultural values, and beliefs; (2) their prior knowledge
of educational constructs and theories used for assessment and instruction; and
(3) their level of familiarity with the diverse cultural and linguistic backgrounds
of their students. Following another main philosophical and pedagogical principle of the ethnic-educator approach, we consider that *socioemotional processes affect
teachers' delivery of instruction through their personalities.* Then, it is important for
educators to understand the subjectivity involved in their instructional decisions
and to try to become conscious of their attitudes and other socioemotional
processes.

Attitudes include bias and beliefs and are based on previous experiences.
Baker (1992) defined attitudes as encompassing cognitive components (i.e.,
thoughts and beliefs), affective components (i.e., feelings toward an object or
subject), and behavioral components (i.e., a readiness for action). Thus, the cognitive component of educators' attitudes refers to beliefs and the knowledge of
particular theories and practices they have acquired through professional training, teaching experiences, and their personal cultural and linguistic backgrounds.
The second component of attitudes refers to socioemotional processes that shape
teachers' preferences or attitudes toward certain components of their instruction.
The presence of individual differences in teachers' personalities, their interaction
with internal and external factors, and the importance of socioemotional
processes in teaching behaviors are highlighted by two of the main philosophical
and pedagogical principles of the ethnic-educator approach. For instance, specific
students' characteristics, such as their individual interests in content areas, interact with teachers' preferences for certain teaching methodologies, themes, and
topics and other characteristics of teachers' personalities that shape the socioemotional processes through which they deliver their instruction.

Moreover, it is through their personalities that teachers create a social environment of interactions among teachers, students, and peers. Teachers model, for
young children, the use of specifically chosen linguistic and cultural behaviors,
concepts, values, and beliefs in relation to content and concepts in the curriculum.
For instance, teachers may choose to represent only the mainstream culture and
language of schooling. Or yet, following an ethnic-educator approach, teachers
may choose to represent, in their social classroom interactions, the diverse cultural
and linguistic heritages of the children as an enrichment and validation approach
to the curriculum.

An example that comes to mind from my experience at the BPDC relates to
the importance of representing the diverse children's culture in the curriculum to
accelerate their social adaptation to the new classroom setting. During the start of

the academic year, young, diverse preschoolers who had had no previous school experience felt uneasy about entering the classroom and adjusting to their new teachers and a new classroom routine. A bilingual lead teacher, Claudia developed a wonderful strategy for making children feel at home. Claudia took the initiative to find traditional nursery rhymes and music representing the minority cultures of the children, and she played these tunes as a "welcome" activity as children entered the classroom. Children reacted enthusiastically to the music, showing positive emotions and feelings (i.e., socioemotional aspects of attitudes) that increased their classroom participation and interactions with peers and teachers (i.e., behavioral aspects of attitudes). Children's behaviors clearly showed that they felt more comfortable with the familiar environment created by the music representing their home culture.

The following example comes from my experience as a mother of a Hispanic child. Even though it does not pertain to preschool-age children, it very clearly illustrates the potential negative (and probably unintentional) impact of teachers' lack of awareness of their biased attitudes toward minority cultures and their diverse students' bicultural identities. Recently, my then fifth-grade child came home from school complaining about his teacher's comment that "Spaniard *conquistadores* were bad settlers in America." As a Spanish speaker, descendant of Spaniard immigrants to Peru and Costa Rica, and with a strong bicultural, Hispanic American identity, my 11-year-old resented his teacher's comment. In her class comments, his teacher had declared her preference for "English as good settlers because they cared about farming and building cities," in contrast to "Spaniards, who only cared about fighting the Indians and searching for treasures."

My child also resented the quick class review that his teacher had made about Hispanic heritage in America, pointing out some cultural products, such as food, in narrow ways. The teacher had only referred to Mexican food as tortillas and tacos, in a rather stereotypical way. Having enjoyed recurrent exposure to his Peruvian and Costa Rican cultural heritage and many trips to visit relatives in these Latin American countries, my child declared that he knew better. He tried to clarify to his teacher and fellow classmates that there is much more to Hispanic food than tacos and tortillas. But he was sad because they did not want to listen or understand his point. He asked me to prepare some food so that they could try his favorite Hispanic dishes—ensalada de col (cabbage salad, very different from the American coleslaw, prepared with tomatoes and vinegar), which he always enjoys in Costa Rica, my arroz con leche (rice pudding but with a very different twist from the American version), and las sopas de abuelita (grandma's soups, prepared from scratch, very rich, and uniquely Peruvian), which he enjoys in Lima.

I could feel my child's frustration and resentment. As far as he remembered, he had lived in Ohio and had attended school in this district. This was the first time he had become keenly aware of a teacher's biased perception of his beloved Hispanic cultural heritage. Previously, biased perceptions of teachers had been expressed in a more implicit manner and in a way only his parents were aware of. My child's recent experience resonated with me. Knowing the sweet and caring personality of his teacher, I realized that this stereotypical view that she had presented in her social studies lessons about the Spaniard conquistadores could not have been intentionally negative or directed to hurt the feelings of her Hispanic student. Instead, the teacher's subjectivity and mainstream cultural values and beliefs were expressed subconsciously and in a natural and matter-of-fact manner, as part of her mainstream cultural heritage and traditional teacher training in the Midwest. This particular teacher had been in the public schools for about 30 years, and unfortunately, the textbook approved by the Ohio State Department of Education supported her biased perceptions of conquistadores.

This example illustrates the powerful impact of the lack of representation and value of a child's bicultural identity in the curriculum in an authentic manner. Teachers' biased, subtle behaviors can make diverse children experience *cultural dissonance* between home and school experiences. At least, at my child's age, with the help of his parents, he can process this socioemotional experience. Eventually, he will overcome the stage of cultural dissonance unintentionally created by his teacher. But we definitely do not want to expose young preschoolers to cultural dissonance experiences in the classroom and curriculum because their socioemotional, cognitive, and language developmental levels make it more difficult to process and transcend stereotypes and negative attitudes (Trawick-Smith, 2006). Instead, they may internalize biased perceptions of their minority cultures, resulting in a negative self-concept and self-esteem and a negative and stereotypical attitude toward their minority culture and language.

To prevent the experience of cultural dissonance among young, diverse children, educators can follow the recommendations of Banks and McGee Banks (1993). They suggested teachers become aware and develop knowledge about the diverse cultural and linguistic backgrounds of their students. Ideally, teachers should have some knowledge of foreign languages and exposure to other cultural realities. But teachers' understanding of most important cultural and linguistic similarities and differences between the mainstream school culture and English language and their diverse students' backgrounds would make a big and positive difference in the education of diverse students. For instance, teachers can use information from the Internet, books, instructional materials, pictures, videos, and visits to local and regional ethnic communities to create a positive image of different cultures and languages represented in their students. Teachers in the BPDC were required to conduct home visits at the beginning of the school year, an experience that proved to be eye-opening and helped them to better understand the sociocultural reality in which their young, diverse students lived at home. Teachers were also encouraged to participate in community events, such as local ethnic festivals, where they would be exposed to different languages and cultural experiences (e.g., food, music, dances, clothing, art, handcrafts, and authentic cultural celebrations).

In addition, minority parents can become major resources for teachers to provide their diverse students with exposure to genuine cultural and linguistic experiences. A minority parent can bring rich traditional stories to add to storytelling time in the pluralistic classroom and can teach some words, phrases, and concepts of his or her native culture and language to the teacher and children. In a pluralist classroom, young, diverse children would feel valued and empowered by the integration of their language and cultural heritage through the collaboration and partnership between their family members and teacher. In this manner, the holistic development of children would also be completely integrated across cognitive, linguistic, and socioemotional developmental areas with mainstream and minority languages and cultures.

Educators select subjectively different instructional approaches and theories and a variety of evaluation measures that represent their beliefs, values, philosophies, and theories that they endorse. Considering the difficulty of accurately assessing young children and the scarcity of valid measures and appropriate instructional programs for young, diverse children, early childhood educators face a challenging task. According to the ethnic-educator approach, assessment of young, diverse children demands deep knowledge of the constructs being evaluated as well as awareness of the influence of cultural and linguistic factors on developmental and learning processes (Gonzalez, Bauerle, & Felix-Holt, 1996; Gonzalez, Bauerle, Black, & Felix-Holt, 1999). An ethnic educator values idiosyncratic characteristics of children and respects cultural, linguistic, and socio-economic-status (SES) differences to validate and enrich the schooling experience of young, diverse children in a pluralistic classroom environment. The issue of the accurate assessment of young, diverse children's classroom performance is discussed extensively in Chapter 6. The ethnic-educator approach asserts that similar instructional and assessment procedures can be used very differently by educators who hold contrasting philosophical and theoretical positions. Then, it is of central importance for educators to build a pluralistic classroom setting that nurtures and values the bicultural identity of young, minority children.

Thus, as discussed in this section, the teacher following an ethnic-educator approach is open to creating a pluralistic classroom environment to model, for young, diverse learners, multiple and equally valid cultural and linguistic patterns of social behaviors and learning processes. Pluralistic classroom environments nurture creativity in young children and a healthy, multicultural identity and support a bridge with real-life experiences in minority family and community settings. Therefore, ethnic educators have a moral responsibility to act as committed advocates of young, diverse children and their families by validating their idiosyncratic, cultural, and linguistic differences.

A SOCIOCONSTRUCTIVISTIC PEDAGOGICAL MODEL SUPPORTING THE ETHNIC-EDUCATOR APPROACH

The National Research Council published two documents titled *How People Learn* (1999a) and *Improving Student Learning* (1999b). These important documents identify major principles of teaching and learning, derived from contemporary research in cognitive and developmental psychology and cognitive science, which can improve our educational practice. The philosophical and theoretical principles listed and discussed next integrate mainstream (National Research Council, 1999a, 1999b; Teachers of English to Speakers of Other Languages [TESOL],

2005) research in a socioconstructivistic perspective for developmental, learning, and teaching processes.

Four main pedagogical principles are derived from contemporary-mainstream and ethnic-minority research following a socioconstructivistic framework. These four main pedagogical principles are derived from the four main philosophical principles of the ethnic-educator approach discussed in Chapter 1. Table 2.1 shows the connection between the four main philosophical principles and the embedded pedagogical principles.

Table 2.1   Main Philosophical and Pedagogical Principles for Learning and Developmental Processes

Philosophical Principles	*Pedagogical Principles*
Principle 1 *Developmental and Humanistic View of Learning*	*Socioemotional Nature of Teaching and Learning Processes*
• A **holistic developmental perspective** for learning across cognitive, linguistic, and socioemotional developmental and academic areas (i.e., language arts, mathematics, science, and social studies)	• **Developmental and humanistic** view of learning processes and academic achievement • View of teaching and learning processes as a *social and affective experience* • Central role of prior knowledge in learner-centered classrooms, such as culturally and socially loaded preconceptions
Principle 2 *Holistic View of Learning and the Curriculum*	*Internal and External Factors Affect Resilience and At-Risk Conditions*
• **Socioconstructivistic** theoretical perspective with the interaction of internal and external factors in developmental and learning processes	• Learning and developmental processes are affected by the **interaction of internal factors** (i.e., maturational, psychological, and biological) and **external factors** (i.e., cultural, social, schooling, and family settings) o *Internal and external factors* affecting low-socioeconomic-status (SES), young, diverse children can support or hinder their *academic achievement* (i.e., becoming resilient or at risk of underachievement) o Two complementary processes occur—learning assimilation (i.e., positive transference of concepts) and accommodation (i.e., formation of new sociocultural concepts)

(Continued)

Table 2.1 (Continued)

Philosophical Principles	Pedagogical Principles
	• Teachers need to help young, diverse children develop *conceptual frameworks* (or abstract learning principles and higher-level cognitive strategies) that can be transformed and become relevant to other knowledge and problem domains and that can be connected to real-world experiences • All students need to develop conceptual competence (i.e., principles that can be transformed into higher-level learning strategies and critical-thinking skills) and be able to apply it to factual knowledge gained in multiple academic-content and real-world situations • All students need to develop concepts through inquiry-based learning (i.e., active and discovery learning, learner-centered) • Developing higher-learning skills provides insight into self-regulation and independent thinking and learning processes • Teachers need to use thematic curriculums that intersect developmental and content areas through common topics and core concepts
Principle 3 *Pluralistic and Transcultural Perspectives*	*Culture and Language Represented in Assessment and Instruction*
• **Pluralistic pedagogical approach** because it celebrates cultural and linguistic diversity as an asset enriching the developmental and learning potential of young, diverse children into multicultural and multilingual minds and spirits	• Language is a conceptual tool for learning and representing sociocultural, affective, and emotional processes (i.e., cultural and bicultural identity) • Indissoluble connection between language and cognition, both influenced by sociocultural processes • Language as a conceptual tool that provides developmental continuity of the *index, symbolic, and sign learning processes* for three- to five-year-old children • Language learning is a cultural process in which children need to acquire sociocultural competence and new cultural knowledge • Schools use language to socialize children to use reading and writing as major learning tools • Language is used by parents as a socialization tool in relation to sociocultural factors (i.e., social class, ethnicity, topic, purpose, value and belief systems, cultural thinking and interpersonal-communication styles)

Philosophical Principles	Pedagogical Principles
	• Learning and academic achievement are influenced by external family, community, and school conditions • Language learning is a process that takes developmental time and effort (5–8 years) • Teachers need to develop alternative pedagogical approaches that link assessment to instruction
Principle 4 Teachers as Advocates and Cultural Mediators	
• **Advocacy position** that calls teachers to raise their cultural awareness and develop *personal connections* between their family history and their students' sociohistorical backgrounds	• Teachers need to develop *nurturing learning communities* in which young, diverse children can maintain collaborative relations, participate actively, and have a sense of belonging and intrinsic motivation • Teachers need to act as *cultural bridges or mediators* between the mainstream school culture and the minority family environments • Teachers need to act as *mentors* for developing *rapport* with diverse children and *partnerships* with parents to establish mutual trust and respect for cultural and linguistic diversity and idiosyncratic differences

Pedagogical Principle 1 describes a holistic developmental perspective for teaching and learning processes in relation to subject matter, grade level, and purpose of instruction. Teachers following an ethnic-educator approach need to educate the *whole* child, by stimulating learning across cognitive, linguistic, and socioemotional developmental areas and across content areas (i.e., language arts, mathematics, science, and social studies). Language and cognitive development need to be stimulated using simultaneous and authentic methodologies. Teachers need to act as mediators to help children understand why, when, and how factual knowledge and abstract learning principles (or conceptual frameworks) can be transferred or transformed and can become relevant to other content areas, knowledge domains, and real-world experiences.

Pedagogical Principle 2 describes the interaction between internal and external factors in learning and developmental processes and academic achievement in young, diverse children. Developmental delays resulting from external factors need to be differentiated from genuine handicapping conditions or disabilities, especially among diverse children (for a more extended discussion of this topic see Gonzalez, Brusca-Vega, & Yawkey, 1997; Gonzalez, 2001a). Teachers need to respect and nurture children's individual biological (i.e., temperament, physical growth rates, maturation), psychological (i.e., learning styles, learning potential, interests, motivation, personality traits, developmental time), and sociocultural differences (i.e., SES of parents, related to levels of education and literacy, level of cultural adaptation, mental health, quality of parent-child relationship, ethnicity, language differences, such as varieties of English and English-as-as-second-language [ESL] background) in a learner-centered, pluralistic classroom environment.

Pedagogical Principle 3 states that teachers must use a pluralistic pedagogical approach, which celebrates cultural and linguistic diversity and includes alternative pedagogical strategies that link assessment and instruction. Young, diverse children's developmental and learning potential needs to be nurtured in a multicultural classroom setting.

Pedagogical Principle 4 describes the important role of teachers as sociocultural instructional mediators to develop cultural adaptation and higher academic achievement levels in young, diverse children. Teachers need to become committed mentors, role models, and empathic advocates for helping young, diverse children become resilient learners and achievers in the U.S. public school system.

In sum, these four major pedagogical principles emphasize an integrative approach that interfaces developmental areas across cognitive, language, and socioemotional domains with content areas across all subjects. Important educational implications of these four pedagogical principles for improving learning and academic achievement in young, diverse children are discussed in relation to examples from the BPDC.

THE FOUR PEDAGOGICAL PRINCIPLES FOR LEARNING AND ACADEMIC ACHIEVEMENT

Next, we discuss the four main pedagogical principles and their educational implications for increasing academic achievement and stimulating learning in young, diverse children. These pedagogical principles are (1) supported by the ethnic-educator philosophical principles from which they are derived, (2) recommended as best research-based educational practice for all children by the National Research Council (1999a, 1999b), and (3) presented across developmental (i.e., cognitive, language, and socioemotional domains) and content areas (i.e., language arts, mathematics, science, and social studies). Figure 2.1 shows the interaction between developmental and content areas, as stated by the first pedagogical principle. Examples from the BPDC project are used for illustrating the pedagogical principles.

Pedagogical Principle 1: Socioemotional Nature of Learning and Teaching Processes

The first pedagogical principle endorses a humanistic and developmental view of learning processes and academic achievement. In addition, teaching and learning processes are conceptualized as a social and affective experience. An empathic and caring teacher needs to build a nurturing classroom environment

Figure 2.1   Representation of the Interaction of Developmental Areas With Content
              Areas in an Ethnic-Educator Model

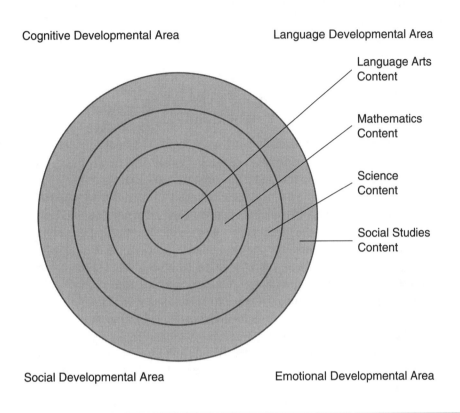

Cognitive Developmental Area   Language Developmental Area

Language Arts
Content

Mathematics
Content

Science
Content

Social Studies
Content

Social Developmental Area   Emotional Developmental Area

for young, diverse children to feel respected and valued as members of minority
cultures. Teachers need to represent ethnic diversity throughout content areas in
the curriculum by incorporating authentic representations of diverse language
and cultures as instructional materials. In this manner, prior real-world knowledge learned by young, diverse children in their homes can be transferred and
validated in the learner-centered classroom. Prior knowledge has a central role
in learning processes in young, diverse children (Carnegie Task Force on Learning
in the Primary Grades, 1996; National Research Council, 1999a, 1999b). Classrooms
need to be learner-centered, in which teaching and learning processes consider
students' culturally loaded preconceptions about specific real-world, topic,
content, or subject-matter knowledge.

An illustration of how teachers can include authentic cultural and linguistic materials in the curriculum refers to how themes and topics in BPDC classrooms can help to validate and make connections to diverse children's prior
knowledge (Feldman, 1999; García & Beltrán, 2003; Gauiento & Morley, 2001).
For instance, a popular theme in the curriculum is "The Restaurant," with symbolic play areas set up with props and menus containing favorite dishes that
children eat at home, representing different cultures and languages. Some of

these favorite dishes are also prepared for classroom celebrations by parents and included in teachers' food preparation demonstrations in the classroom. Different content and developmental areas are stimulated through these symbolic play and food preparation activities, such as oral-language skills—naming and defining, preliteracy skills, verbal and nonverbal concept formation, and math skills—counting and measuring.

Pedagogical Principle 2: Internal and External Factors Affect Resilience and At-Risk Conditions

The second philosophical principle endorses a socioconstructivistic theoretical perspective that supports a holistic view of development and the curriculum. The pedagogical principle states that internal and external factors affect resilience and at-risk conditions in diverse children. That is, external factors, such as high-quality education, can help promote learning and development. Then, teachers need to help young, diverse children develop *abstract learning principles* (or *conceptual frameworks*) and *higher-level cognitive strategies* (i.e., critical-thinking, cognitive, *metacognitive,* and *metalinguistic* skills) that can be (1) transformed and become relevant to other knowledge and problem domains and content areas (Carnegie Task Force on Learning in the Primary Grades, 1996; National Research Council, 1999a, 1999b) and (2) connected to real-world experiences and recurrent topics and themes across the curriculum (Feldman, 1999). By presenting a thematic curriculum, students can use multiple thinking skills and strategies for applications and transformations to other problem and knowledge domains (National Research Council, 1999a, 1999b).

The reflections of a bilingual (English/Spanish), BPDC teacher, Joyce, provide an example of how teachers can decide to implement a thematic curriculum and stimulate the development of conceptual frameworks for enhancing both their teaching and their students' learning processes. Joyce stated,

> As I began my classroom setup, and general outline of what we might cover throughout the year, I wanted to be sure that my schedule allowed for flexibility, based on how the educational needs of the children evolved with time. I found this difficult, as I am a planner, but I knew that developing this flexibility would be useful because each class that I would encounter throughout my teaching career would be different. I used this belief, keeping in mind that children are more intrinsically motivated when they are interested in the subject matter. I also felt that this flexibility would provide a prior-knowledge foundation for making connections with future teaching experiences. I structured my general thoughts in a unit format, centered on themes and topics, hoping that it would give me the necessary context to create these connections in and across teaching years.

As Joyce explained, the use of a thematic curriculum can help learners built connections across developmental and content areas. Children need to be stimulated to develop *conceptual competence* (i.e., understanding of knowledge structures) in *factual knowledge* (i.e., topic and content knowledge). In addition, as supported by educational research compiled by the National Research Council (1999a, 1999b), young, diverse children need to be stimulated *to learn how to learn and learn how to think* (both cognitive and metacognitive skills) and *learn how to think about language* (metalinguistic skills). Young, diverse children can develop conceptual competence and factual knowledge by applying concepts to multiple examples of real-world problems across content areas, relating prior and new knowledge, and engaging in multiple cognitive, metacognitive, and metalinguistic processes (i.e., comparison, evaluation, categorization, using feedback, elaboration).

Thus, based on the second pedagogical principle, the focus of instruction is on concept development through inquired learning, such as active and discovery learning, learner-centered classrooms, and collaborative problem-solving activities that lead to flexibility of thinking and creativity (Carnegie Task Force on Learning in the Primary Grades, 1996; National Research Council, 1999a, 1999b). Then, young, diverse children need to develop greater insight into their thinking and learning processes (i.e., cognitive and metacognitive strategies) to become independent thinkers with self-regulation. It is considered important to stimulate young, diverse learners to generate new concepts so that not only *assimilation* of concepts is achieved, but also *accommodation* of concepts occurs for the generation of new knowledge.

Pedagogical Principle 3: Culture and Language Are Represented in Assessment and Instruction

The third pedagogical principle supports a pluralistic view of learning and teaching processes. It celebrates cultural and linguistic diversity as an asset to enriching the developmental and learning potential of young, diverse children into multicultural and multilingual minds and spirits (Fang, 1999; Nieto, 2004; Ovando, Combs, & Collier, 2006). Language provides young, diverse children the ability to move from perceptual to concrete, abstract, metacognitive, and metalinguistic levels of thinking (Gonzalez, Yawkey, & Minaya-Rowe, 2006). That is, through internal symbolic thinking, children can detach from immediate time and space and manipulate and transform reality into nonverbal and verbal mental symbols in unique ways through engaging in problem solving, concept formation, active learning, creativity, and flexibility of thinking. For instance, through language, children can engage in intrapersonal thinking via verbal thoughts or interpersonal thinking via group brainstorming, instructional conversations, dialogue, and inquiry-based learning (Araujo, 2002; Brown, 2000; Piper, 2003).

Language development provides an example of developmental continuities across age groups in preschoolers (Gonzalez et al., 2006). Three- to four-year-olds use *index learning processes,* in which they represent images of three-dimensional objects through actions, manipulations, and real-life experiences. Four- to five-year-olds use *symbolic learning processes,* in which two-dimensional representations of images (such as drawings and sketching) are used as direct and indirect examples of objects. Five- to six-year-olds use *sign learning processes,* in which figural or one-dimensional representations of abstractions represent verbal and nonverbal concepts (such as in phonemic-awareness skills). Figure 2.2 shows a

Figure 2.2   Representation of Developmental Continuity Across Alignment of
Developmental Milestones for Three Age Groups

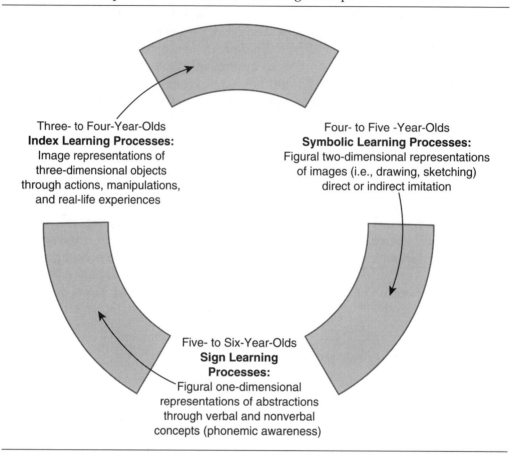

Three- to Four-Year-Olds
Index Learning Processes:
Image representations of
three-dimensional objects
through actions, manipulations,
and real-life experiences

Four- to Five -Year-Olds
Symbolic Learning Processes:
Figural two-dimensional representations
of images (i.e., drawing, sketching)
direct or indirect imitation

Five- to Six-Year-Olds
**Sign Learning
Processes:**
Figural one-dimensional
representations of abstractions
through verbal and nonverbal
concepts (phonemic awareness)

representation of the developmental continuity of the index, symbolic, and sign
learning processes for three age groups of preschoolers.

Moreover, language has a central role for initializing young children in the
school culture. Language is used to socialize children to be literate through a cultural
and social orientation toward using reading and writing as major tools for learning
(Heath, 1983; Piper, 2003). Young, diverse children need to gain *rhetoric* competence
(i.e., academic language proficiency) so that they have the discourse needed to
understand and communicate about conceptual competence and factual knowledge
in specific content areas.

A pluralistic classroom environment that provides exposure to authentic
instances of diverse cultures and languages enhances the cognitive, linguistic, and
socioemotional development of young children. For the case of language-minority
children (i.e., Hispanics, Asians, Pacific Islanders, and Native Americans), it is
important to continue developing their first language because it is a conceptual tool
for learning and for representing sociocultural, affective, and emotional processes.
That is the reason cultural identity needs to be nurtured because it mediates other

important socioemotional and sociocultural developmental processes (i.e., self-concept, self-esteem, attitudes, belief and value systems, and motivation for learning), which significantly influence learning and academic achievement.

Moreover, language and cognitive development are indissoluble, culturally loaded processes. Language acquisition occurs through meaningful and significant use and interaction in a *natural* sociocultural environment. Language is used in real-world experiences as a tool for communication and learning from social interactions with role models and cultural mediators (i.e., parents, caretakers, and teachers). Therefore, language is a tool for the socialization of (1) thinking in culturally appropriate ways by implicitly transmitting cultural values, sociocultural styles of thinking, and verbal and nonverbal interpersonal communication styles; and (2) emotional and affective processes, such as religious and spiritual beliefs and value systems and attitudes and cultural perceptions. Then, early language learning in the family and community context is a culturally loaded process. Young children acquire linguistic patterns and structures that vary across cultures and reflect differences in values, norms, and beliefs about social roles and relationships. Language provides sociocultural conventions that can be used as symbolic tools (semantic development or academic language) for communicating nonverbal and verbal thoughts, concepts, ideas, and meanings. Thus, during the early stages of language development, young children also acquire sociocultural competence and new cultural knowledge that is particular to their culture and language of origin.

Young, diverse children have the double task of developing academic language proficiency to be successful in the school culture and social language proficiency to be successful in their sociocultural community of origin (Hadaway, Vardell, & Young, 2002; Johnson, 1981; Peregoy & Boyle, 2005). This double task requires young, diverse children to invest extra effort and developmental time, which is in contrast to young, mainstream children who come to preschool with the advantage of having been exposed to home settings that stimulate the more rapid and earlier acquisition of academic and social language. Therefore, on entrance to preschool or kindergarten, it might take from five to eight years of schooling for young, diverse children to develop academic and social competence necessary to become literate and achieve in the mainstream school culture (Cummins, 1991). In contrast, young, mainstream children might only need three to four years of schooling for developing academic and social language competence necessary to become literate and achieve in school (Cummins).

Then, teachers following a pluralistic pedagogy supported by the ethnic-educator approach need to develop alternative instructional strategies and curriculums, linked to alternative assessments, that meet the unique cultural and linguistic educational needs of young, diverse children (Gonzalez et al., 1997). Teachers need to provide young, diverse children with extra developmental time and authentic instructional and assessment methodologies necessary to acquire academic and social language competence so that language can be used as a tool for learning and achieving in school.

The case of a Hispanic child attending the BPDC can illustrate the importance of using alternative strategies to link assessment and instruction when serving young, diverse children (Gonzalez & Riojas-Clark, 1999). Juanita is a five-year-old Spanish-speaking child who attended the BPDC for approximately seven months by the time classroom observations were reported by teachers. She has had approximately 150 hours of combined Spanish and English instruction at the BPDC, where instruction emphasizes preliteracy across content areas. Juanita has two older brothers, and she speaks both English and Spanish at home. She is active and well liked by her peers, and she seems to enjoy school.

Classroom observations of Juanita's social, emotional, cognitive, and language development made by her teachers provide important information about her learning potential. Juanita is considered by her teachers as one of the most capable students in her class. She demonstrates interpersonal intelligence as shown by her attention to classmates' feelings and her attempts to console or distract classmates who are upset. For instance, Juanita shows sensitivity to remarks made by other children, such as, "I don't want to be your friend anymore." She is very vocal and switches freely from Spanish to English, as the situation requires. She speaks English with her English teacher, Spanish with her Spanish teacher, English with her English peers, and so on. She even translates from Spanish to English when one of her classmates is having trouble communicating in English, sometimes stopping in mid-translation to check for understanding in Spanish with the classmate.

Juanita's example illustrates the value of using a pluralistic pedagogy for nurturing a diverse child's learning potential across developmental areas. Juanita's diversity is celebrated and valued by her teachers; her bilingual skills are especially valued by her teachers as an asset for enhancing her metalinguistic and metacognitive skills, interpersonal intelligence, and socioemotional maturity. The use of classroom observations helps Juanita's teachers learn from her classroom performance and to identify her strengths to individualize her curriculum (Igoa, 1995).

Pedagogical Principle 4: Teachers as Advocates and Cultural Mediators

The fourth pedagogical principle calls for teachers to assume an advocacy position. Teachers who endorse the advocacy position need to raise their cultural awareness and develop personal connections between their family history and their students' sociohistorical backgrounds (Gonzalez, 2001a; Gonzalez et al., 2006). Teachers need to *develop nurturing learning communities*, in which young, diverse children can maintain collaborative relations, participate actively, and have a sense of belonging and intrinsic motivation. Teachers also need to act as cultural bridges or mediators between the mainstream school culture and the minority home and family cultural environments.

Moreover, teachers need to act as mentors for developing rapport with young, diverse children and partnerships with their parents to establish mutual trust and respect for cultural and linguistic diversity and idiosyncratic differences. The reflections of a BPDC bilingual (English/Spanish) teacher, Theresa, provide an illustration of how teachers can make a personal connection to enhance their teaching experience. Theresa stated,

> Even though I had been a second-language learner in Mexico as a child, my early undergraduate training in early childhood education had focused primarily on serving mainstream children. My personal experience as a child living in a foreign country helped me in the beginning of my first year of teaching to develop rapport with the minority children attending the BPDC. However, I needed to develop content knowledge in theories and educational practice of how to teach and evaluate ESL, young students. My knowledge grew with my classes in the masters Teaching-English-as-a-Second-Language (TESL) Program I was attending, and I was able to implement more solid theories into my teaching as the year went by. Using my classroom experience to shape my personal educational philosophies while serving young, diverse children, I was able to experiment with teaching and assessment practices, build relationships with minority, low-income parents, and develop outreach community partnerships and find some resources to help diverse children and their parents. Reflecting, I cannot think of a single moment that I regret accepting this challenging position, during my first year of teaching. There are things that I know could and should have been done differently, but I know that I will have these learning experiences every year of my teaching career. I hope that I encounter such children and such families as I continue to work with the immigrant population.

Theresa discussed the value of reflecting on the connections between her personal experience of living in a foreign culture and building rapport with her young, diverse students and their families. Theresa also understands that she needs to continue building on her teaching experiences with diverse children and their families. She acknowledges the challenges of her first year of teaching, but she also accepts the commitment and social responsibility and welcomes the privilege of serving diverse children.

Thus, in Chapter 2, emphasis has been given to the discussion of teachers' personality factors (especially attitudes, values, and beliefs) affecting their instructional and assessment decisions when serving young, diverse children. Once we discussed the powerful effect of teachers' socioemotional process on learning processes, we discussed a pedagogical model endorsed by the ethnic-educator approach. Four pedagogical principles were defined and explained through examples, which are supported by contemporary socioconstructivistic research in cognitive and developmental psychology and cognitive science (Carnegie Task Force on Learning in the Primary Grades, 1996; National Research Council, 1999a, 1999b). In Chapter 3, the discussion of the curriculum model and pedagogical principles supported by the ethnic-educator approach will be extended to include standards recommended by Head Start and TESOL (2005) and derived pedagogical strategies and samples of lesson plans.

PART II

Educational Applications of the Ethnic-Educator Approach

3

Teaching Strategies

Chapter 3 presents four main clusters of pedagogical strategies that follow the ethnic-educator pedagogical model presented in Chapter 2, which are research-based and meet the educational needs of young, diverse children. Then, Chapter 3 translates the core theme of this book, the ethnic-educator approach with its philosophical principles, into an actual praxis or clusters of pedagogical strategies that build a curriculum. Examples of teachers using the ethnic-educator pedagogical strategies at the Bilingual Preschool Development Center (BPDC) are provided to portray the unique educational needs of young, diverse children.

STRATEGIES SUPPORTING
THE ETHNIC-EDUCATOR APPROACH

In this section, four clusters of ethnic-educator pedagogical strategies are discussed in light of research-based instructional guidelines provided by the National Research Council (1999a, 1999b) and research-based instructional strategies recommended for improving the academic achievement of young, diverse children by a number of authors (e.g., Collier, 1994, 1995; Collier & Thomas, 2001, 2004; Gonzalez, 1999, 2007; Gonzalez, Brusca-Vega, & Yawkey, 1997; Gonzalez, Yawkey, & Minaya-Rowe, 2006; Ovando, Combs, & Collier, 2006; Tharp, 1997, 1999; Tharp, Estrada, Dalton, & Yamauchi, 2000; Tharp & Gallimore, 1998; Thomas & Collier, 2003; Waxman & Padrón, 2002). See Table 3.1 for a representation of the alignment of the philosophical and pedagogical principles endorsed by the ethnic-educator approach with the four clusters of pedagogical strategies discussed in this chapter.

The four clusters of pedagogical strategies endorsed by the ethnic-educator curriculum include the following:

1. Thematic and Holistic Curriculum

This describes an integrated and holistic developmental curriculum that aligns content and developmental areas with the cultural, linguistic, and idiosyncratic needs of young, diverse children. The first cluster of pedagogical strategies discussed includes the alignment of the curriculum across content and developmental areas through using themes and topics and the individualization of the curriculum to themes and topics of interest to the children.

2. Stimulation of Critical-Thinking Skills

This describes a curriculum supported by theory and research following a socioconstructivistic perspective, which represents the interaction of internal and external factors on young, diverse children's developmental and learning processes. The second cluster of pedagogical strategies discussed includes a learner-centered approach, the stimulation of critical-thinking skills (cognitive, metacognitive, and metalinguistic strategies, instructional conversation, and inquiry-based learning), and the connection of concepts learned and content areas taught with young, diverse children's prior sociocultural knowledge and real-world experiences in particular sociocultural settings.

3. A Pluralistic Pedagogy Stimulating Connections to Prior Sociocultural Knowledge and Real-Life Experiences

This describes a curriculum that follows a pluralistic pedagogical approach, which values cultural and linguistic diversity as an asset enriching the developmental and learning potential of young, diverse children. The third cluster of pedagogical strategies discussed includes the use of additive language (i.e., first and second language [L1, L2]) as a method of instruction and a socialization tool for stimulating critical-thinking and socioemotional abilities and the use of classroom-based alternative assessments linked with instruction that represents cultural and linguistic diversity.

4. An Advocacy Position for Teachers

This describes an advocacy position that calls teachers to raise their cultural awareness and to develop personal connections between their family history and their students' sociohistorical backgrounds. The fourth cluster of pedagogical strategies discussed includes the need for teachers to develop commitment and rapport, and serve as cultural mediators or bridges between the school culture and diverse children and their families.

FIRST CLUSTER OF PEDAGOGICAL STRATEGIES
Thematic Curriculums

Thematic and topical presentations of instructional materials can be used to connect young, diverse children's cultural and social prior knowledge and real-life, daily experiences with content and developmental areas represented across the

(Text continued on page 44)

Table 3.1 Alignment of Philosophical and Pedagogical Principles and Pedagogical Strategies Endorsed by the Ethnic-Educator Approach

Philosophical Principles	Pedagogical Principles	Pedagogical Strategies
Principle 1 *Developmental and Humanistic View of Learning*	*Socioemotional Nature of Teaching and Learning Processes*	
• **A holistic developmental perspective** for learning across cognitive, linguistic, and socioemotional developmental areas and academic areas (i.e., language arts, mathematics, science, and social studies)	• **Developmental and humanistic** view of learning processes and academic achievement • View of teaching and learning processes as a social and affective experience	• Integrated and **holistic developmental curriculum** that aligns content and developmental areas and connects concepts learned through the school year across **themes and topics** • Connection of concepts learned and content areas taught to **children's interests in particular themes and topics** that are related to their idiosyncratic differences and sociocultural backgrounds and experiences • Need to develop a **personal rapport**, and familiarity and knowledge of the sociocultural background of young, diverse children and their families
Principle 2 *Holistic View of Learning and the Curriculum*	*Internal and External Factors Affect Resilience and At-Risk Conditions*	

• **Socioconstructivistic** Theoretical perspective with the interaction of internal and external factors in developmental and learning processes	• Learning and developmental processes are affected by the **interaction of internal factors** (i.e., maturational, psychological, and biological) and **external factors** (i.e., cultural, social, schooling, and family settings)
	   ○ **Internal and external factors** affecting low-socioeconomic-status (SES) young, diverse children can support or hinder their **academic achievement** (i.e., becoming resilient or at risk of underachievement)
		• **Individualizing the curriculum** to young, diverse children's learning and developmental needs resulting from the interaction of internal and external factors
		   ○ *Strengths and weaknesses (related to maturational and developmental processes, individual differences, and sociocultural experiences (degree of schooling and early stimulation, literacy and education levels at home)*
		   ○ *Assimilation and accommodation processes are affected by similarities and differences between cultural and linguistic factors in young, diverse children*

	○ Two complementary learning processes take place: **assimilation** (i.e., positive transference of concepts) and **accommodation** (i.e., formation of new sociocultural concepts) • Teachers need to help young, diverse children develop **conceptual frameworks** (or abstract learning principles and higher-level cognitive strategies) that can be transformed and become relevant to other knowledge and problem domains and that can be connected to real-world experiences ○ *Teachers need to use thematic curriculums that intersect developmental and content areas through common topics and core concepts*	○ *Use of active learning strategies such as cooperative learning* ○ *Development of critical-thinking skills in the form of metalearning (learning how to learn), metacognitive, and cognitive strategies (learning how to think and monitor thinking skills), and metalinguistic strategies (learning how to think about language and improve language skills)* ○ *All students need to develop conceptual competence (i.e., principles that can be transformed into critical-thinking skills and be able to apply it to factual knowledge gained in multiple academic content and real-world problem situations* ○ *All students need to develop concepts through **inquiry-based learning** (i.e., interactive dialogue and instructional conversations, cooperative learning, storytelling, reading stories, scripts)* ○ *Developing **critical-thinking skills** provides insight into self-regulation and independent thinking and learning processes* • Connection of concepts learned and content areas taught to prior sociocultural knowledge and real-world experiences in particular sociocultural settings in learner-centered classrooms
Principle 3 *Pluralistic and Transcultural Perspectives* • **Pluralistic pedagogical approach** because it celebrates cultural and linguistic diversity as an asset enriching the developmental and learning potential of young, diverse children into multicultural and multilingual minds and spirits	*Culture and Language Represented in Assessment and Instruction* • Language is a conceptual tool for learning and representing sociocultural, affective, and emotional processes (i.e., cultural and bicultural identity) • Indissoluble connection between **language and cognition**, both influenced by **sociocultural processes**	• **Additive stance toward language and culture** (value of maintaining and developing native language and culture in addition to English language and mainstream-American culture) • **Teaching all content areas interconnected with the four integrated components of language development** (i.e., listening, speaking, reading, and writing)

(Continued)

Table 3.1 (Continued)

Philosophical Principles	Pedagogical Principles	Pedagogical Strategies
Principle 3 *Pluralistic and Transcultural Perspectives*	*Culture and Language Represented in Assessment and Instruction* • **Language as a conceptual tool** that provides developmental continuity of the *index, symbolic, and sign learning processes* for three- to five-year-old children • **Language learning is a cultural process** in which children need to acquire sociocultural competence and new cultural knowledge • **Language is used by schools to socialize children to be literate** and use reading and writing as major tools for learning • **Language is used by parents as a socialization tool in relation to** sociocultural factors (i.e., social class, ethnicity, topic, purpose, value and belief systems, cultural thinking, and interpersonal communication styles) • **Language learning is a process that takes developmental time and effort** (5–8 years during early childhood) • **Learning and academic achievement are influenced by external family, community, and school conditions** that may be at risk for disadvantaged, diverse children	• **Use language as a method of instruction**, in which verbal concepts are used as symbolic tools for developing critical-thinking skills (metacognitve, cognitive, and metalinguistic strategies) • Use of **cultural styles of learning and thinking** for representing diverse cultures and languages in the **curriculum** (e.g., storytelling, through instructional conversations, collaborative learning, and sheltered instruction) • Use of the **language experience approach for teaching reading and writing skills**, such as the use of dialogue journals, reading aloud, picture books, artwork, filmstrips for making a story, and in general writing stories for a real-life audience at school, at home, and in the community • **Stimulate learning potential** of economically disadvantaged, young, diverse children, providing them with developmental time to show learning progress and high-quality curriculums with grade-level expectations for success • Use **alternative assessments** that measure **potential for learning** instead of performance (i.e., amount of knowledge and degree of skills developed resulting from exposure to stimulation, bias indicators for disadvantaged, diverse children)

	• Teachers need to develop alternative **pedagogical approaches that link assessment to instruction**	• Use of **nonverbal and verbal classroom measures** to link assessment and instruction across content and developmental areas • Use of alternative assessment measures that **represent cultural and linguistic diversity**

Principle 4   Teachers as Advocates and Cultural Mediators

• **Advocacy position** that calls on teachers to develop cultural awareness and *personal connections* between their family history and their students' sociohistorical backgrounds	• Teachers need to **develop nurturing learning communities** for young, diverse children to develop intrinsic motivation for learning, maintain collaborative relations, participate actively, and having a sense of belonging • Teachers need to act as **cultural bridges or mediators** between the mainstream school culture and the minority home and family cultural environments • Teachers need to act as **mentors for developing rapport** with young, diverse children and *partnerships* with their parents so that teachers can build mutual trust and respect for cultural and linguistic diversity and idiosyncratic differences	• Role of teachers as **sociocultural mediators or bridges, advocates, mentors, and role models** for young, diverse children and their families • Teachers need **to integrate diverse cultures and languages in the curriculum**, value and use as an enrichment the diverse cultural and linguistic backgrounds of students, and model appropriate attitudes and behaviors to develop social adaptation to the mainstream school culture and American general society • Success in academic achievement needs to be considered by teachers as resulting from a **socioemotional process of cultural adaptation** in which diverse children need to learn how to behave, think, and talk to bridge their school, home, and community sociocultural settings

curriculum. Themes and topics need to represent the cultural and linguistic backgrounds of young, diverse children and serve as vehicles to introduce them to the mainstream school culture and the American general culture. In this way, the curriculum can help young, diverse children develop cultural adaptation and a bicultural identity, resulting in higher academic achievement.

Offering choices is one way of adapting the thematic curriculum to the idiosyncratic interest, developmental needs, and linguistic and cultural characteristics of young, diverse children. Offering choices in the classroom environment, such as "alternate activities, alternate channels of learning, and alternate assignments . . . presents real learning opportunities for decision-making, social participation, and successes" (Gonzalez et al., 1997, p. 160). By allowing students to make learning choices, teachers foster diverse children's motivation, self-esteem, and self-concept. In this manner, young, diverse children become independent thinkers who experience affective and cognitive involvement in their success in task completion. Teachers can also encourage young, diverse children to have personal initiative in making choices, follow through on a decision with persistence in task completion, and have better understanding of their potential as learners.

Another way to individualize instruction is by using *thematic interdisciplinary instruction* because by using themes that connect to children's prior cultural knowledge, teachers can create classroom environments that motivate young children to engage in the learning activity. Themes can develop intrinsic motivation for young children to become actively engaged in learning, thinking, and applying concepts to their social and cultural reality. Thematic instruction creates a meaningful context for exploring multiple content areas to stimulate cognitive, language, and socioemotional development and, ultimately, increase academic achievement. Moreover, themes can be used as media through which young children explore their senses, perception, memory, and stored conceptual knowledge. That is, themes can be used as conceptual tools to integrate content areas (such as literacy skills, math, social studies, and science) and as symbolic representational tools for learning and thinking.

Specific instructional strategies for using thematic curriculums to stimulate learning processes and academic achievement in young, diverse children include the following:

1. Use thematic curriculums to expose young children to *repetition of concepts* throughout the academic year, with the use of a variety of instructional activities and materials.

2. Allow *overlearning through extended periods of practice* for the assimilation of new content. The presence of a thematic curriculum will allow for *continuity* of topics and concepts stimulated across content areas. Use *mass experiences*, or continuous and different experiences, as a strategy for extending concepts across content areas and for learning situations and applications.

For instance, a BPDC teacher with experience serving young, diverse children, explained in a reflection:

> I like to create interdisciplinary theme units. This type of unit helps students develop a better understanding of a concept, its meaning, and its use in different content areas. Because I serve diverse children from age three to five in a mixed-age group, I am used to making accommodations to meet all my students' developmental needs and learning styles. I always try to include nonverbal cues like visual aids (big books, posters, hand puppets) and body language when explaining a concept or idea. I also like to include as many hands-on and cooperative-group activities as possible. Children learn from each other while interacting. I think it is good to include drama, partner reading, choral reading, dialogue journals, show-and-tell, and a variety of scaffolding nonverbal activities (e.g., create comic books, make collages about topics, select music for stories) as part of our curriculum. I also believe that teachers need to provide young, diverse children with many opportunities for social interactions with their mainstream peers. Diverse children not only need to learn to speak, listen, read and write in English, but they also need to learn cultural behavior in real-life social situations (e.g., taking turns in a conversation, following a script for going to a restaurant or grocery store), and mainstream peers are the best role models.

In sum, as the teacher's reflection points out, young, diverse children can benefit from a variety of verbal and nonverbal instructional activities that repeat across content areas in the curriculum. Teachers who provide extensive exposure to the same concepts and content areas through repetitive themes and topics in the curriculum facilitate developmental and learning processes in young, diverse children. Thematic curriculums also provide a holistic developmental approach that interfaces the stimulation of cognitive, language, and socioemotional learning and adaptation processes in young, diverse children.

FIRST CLUSTER OF PEDAGOGICAL STRATEGIES
Holistic Developmental Curriculums

Several instructional strategies that interface cognitive, language, and socioemotional developmental processes are recommended for increasing the development of social and academic language in young, diverse children. These strategies include storytelling, reading stories, interactive dialogue, and instructional conversations based on children's prior knowledge and real-life experiences in sociocultural settings. These strategies will be described in relation to examples in the BPDC.

Storytelling

This pedagogical strategy can help young, diverse children make a connection between prior knowledge and real-life experiences and new content learned.

Young children can, with the help of teachers, develop a *script* (i.e., story or verbal narrative) based on real-life experiences in their home, family, and community environments. The development of a script can start by helping children re-create real-life experiences in the classrooms through nonverbal and verbal behaviors. When teachers engage in talking about lived experiences at home and then assist children in re-creating their memories in the classroom through symbolic play, young children can develop their oral-language skills, conceptual development, and socioemotional processes. Then, young children can transform lived experiences and symbolic play into scripts or verbal narrations for developing their identity and socioemotional processes. Besides symbolic play, young, diverse children can also benefit from using real objects or props (i.e., nonverbal manipulative materials) to facilitate the verbal expression and recreation of lived experiences. For instance, puppets, a flannel board, and other props, such as costumes and concrete representations of objects and other referents (e.g., plastic food, doll, store, purse), can facilitate the creation of scripts or verbal narratives in young children.

Storytelling is a pedagogical strategy that is traditionally associated with content-based language learning. According to Diaz-Rico (2004),

> The use of stories is probably the most important means by which teachers can develop oral and written language in young children. Stories come naturally to children, and in the telling and retelling, they gain vocabulary enrichment, sensitivity to audience, and mastery over oral language. The same holds true for written stories as they learn to read. (p. 148)

As described by Diaz-Rico (2004), storytelling is a valued skill in many traditional cultures, and many young, diverse children will be familiar with the cultural use of stories for both teaching and entertaining. Using a broad definition of a story, one can say that storytelling encompasses much of everyday speech. A story may be a factual narrative about someone's daily routine, or it may be a fantastic imaginary tale that happens only in one's dreams. We use stories to explain who we are and where we are from, and we ask for stories when we inquire about others' experiences. Moreover, stories clearly provide a natural context for oral-language production that can take a written form. For writing, authenticity may translate as having a *real* reason and a *real* audience (Diaz-Rico, 2004, p. 167). This may take the form of requesting something, thanking someone for a gift, writing to a pen pal, writing directions for how to get to a park in the community, or myriad other purposes for writing that involve authentic communication.

Stories also offer an engaging context for grammar study, spelling practice, and reading fluency development, among many other literacy-related skills. In the form of written literature as language input, stories have the potential to teach young, diverse children new cultural and linguistic information as well as affirm their cultural diversity (Nieto, 2004). In a spoken or written form, stories have the potential to give young, diverse children *a voice and a space* in which they can safely explore their cultural identities as they acquire literacy (Igoa, 1995). Finally, stories can also be used as pedagogical strategies to convey concepts across content and developmental areas. History comprises collections of stories, and the realms of literature and history very often overlap. Science experiments can be told in story format, and even the steps taken to complete a math problem can become stories (also called algorithms).

Reading Stories

The pedagogical strategy of reading stories needs to be used by teachers as an opportunity for making connections and generalizing concepts across content in a thematic curriculum. Presenting new concepts to learners in meaningful contexts that make links with prior sociocultural knowledge is an effective instructional strategy for all students (August & Hakuta, 1997). Books can be a very good way to learn the *rhetoric* (i.e., script or verbal narrative) of talking about lived experiences at home and in the classroom. That is, reading stories can be used by teachers for making connections between prior sociocultural knowledge and the language necessary to express such knowledge in the form of text. Young, diverse children need to develop preliteracy skills, such as awareness of the connections between print and meaning and real-life experiences and verbal representations.

Moreover, young, diverse children need to understand the usefulness of books and literacy skills in general as tools for fulfilling many daily life needs, such as reading a recipe, reading a map for finding the location of an unknown place, and reading an invitation or ad. Young, diverse children also need to understand the power of literacy skills as a tool for learning concepts across content areas, as well as to socialize their minds to particular sociocultural ways of thinking, talking, and behaving. Ultimately, young, diverse children need to understand the usefulness of literacy skills to succeed in school and improve their academic achievement and to succeed in real-life contexts, such as work and real-life situations in the general society.

In sum, the classroom can become a real-life scenario for understanding the symbolic and social nature of talking, telling and reading stories, and developing prewriting skills. Together, the teacher and young, diverse children can follow a recipe by reading through the sequence of steps involved in the preparation of cupcakes and experiencing together the value of literacy. In the same manner, a map can be drawn by children to show understanding of the location of any real space (e.g., the playground, the supermarket, the mailbox down the street) in relation to their classroom. Any of these real-life experiences can generate concrete "anchors" for children to understand conceptually the symbolic functions of language and the use of telling and reading stories for conveying social and culturally valued meanings in school and in real-life scenarios.

Example of Using Scripts and Storytelling in Thematic Curriculums

Teachers can use *natural scripts*, acted out by young children in their symbolic play through nonverbal behaviors, for creating *verbal scripts* (or stories). For instance, three Hispanic, preschool girls are engaging very eagerly in the home symbolic-play area in their BPDC classroom. They are very actively gathering some food to prepare for dinner. One is washing the vegetables in the sink while the other is cutting the vegetables, and the third girl is setting the table. Once they have finished preparing dinner, they sit together at the table and use their napkins and utensils to eat their food. Immediately after they are done eating, they again cooperate in doing the household duties. One little girl picks up the dishes from the table and gets busy washing dishes in the sink. The other little girl goes off to do the laundry and very carefully folds clothes. The third little girl hears the babies crying and runs to attend to their needs.

As an observer of this pretend household scenario, I am delighted to see cooperative play and vicarious imitation in full swing. It is obvious to me that the three little girls are reliving daily life experiences and that they come from pretty organized and harmonious family environments. Their play is very organized and unfolds in a natural collaboration that is *unspoken*, as they just engage in collaborative activities. Their unspoken script is enacting common daily life experiences that follow a natural sequence. The teacher can help these three little girls translate their symbolic play from actions (or nonverbal script) into a written story (or narrative). This script can be shared with peers, illustrated through drawings, and discussed in relation to peers' real-life experiences and prior sociocultural knowledge. Thus, the teacher can assist these three little girls in pushing their oral-language and literacy development by showing them how to re-create the action of lived experiences into oral scripts and written narratives.

In conclusion, the use of stories in the classroom offers endless possibilities for the implementation of sound language-learning pedagogy for young, diverse children. First, stories in the form of carefully selected published literature and student-produced work (both written and oral as storytelling) can affirm diverse children's real-life experiences and sociocultural background knowledge. Stories can also present young, diverse children with concepts across content areas needed to succeed in school. Moreover, activities involving telling, reading, writing, and sharing stories lend themselves to independent learning, individualized instruction and boost young, diverse children's intrinsic motivation and cultural identity. Finally, books provide opportunities to stimulate the four language skills (i.e., speaking, listening, reading, and writing) in a naturally integrated manner, as natural language is embedded in the rich, authentic, and meaningful context of stories.

SECOND CLUSTER OF PEDAGOGICAL STRATEGIES
Stimulating Critical-Thinking Skills

A main focus of the ethnic-educator curriculum is to stimulate young, diverse children to develop conceptual knowledge that can be transformed and applied to multiple instances of problem-solving situations across academic content areas (National Research Council, 1999a, 1999b). The emphasis is on young, diverse children gaining general principles of learning and thinking that can help them abstract and generalize conceptual frameworks, such as metacognitive, cognitive, and metalinguistic strategies.

An illustration of cognitive and metacognitive strategies is the use of analogical reasoning, or syllogistic reasoning, and other more abstract forms of verbal logic and reasoning strategies. In turn, an illustration of the use of analogical reasoning is the ability to transpose knowledge across different content domains, such as a four-year-old at the BPDC making a comparison between his body sounds and musical instruments, by saying, "My stomach makes noises like a piano." Another illustration of the use of analogical reasoning is for children at the BPDC to interact with peers through collaborative problem-solving activities. Peers can help learners broaden self-centered perspectives to flexible-thinking processes. For instance, young, diverse children engaged in learning how water converts into ice can depart from their own real-life experiences with rain and snow, make hypotheses and predictions, engage in the actual experience of manipulating different elements, and discover what happened and why. Finally, they can learn the language expressions necessary to articulate their thoughts.

Specific critical-thinking, pedagogical strategies that can be used in early childhood classroom settings include the following:

1. Use instructional activities for stimulating abstract-conceptual knowledge, topic knowledge, and problem-solving abilities. Teachers can help children develop *adaptive expertise* in learning strategies for how to think (metacognition), how to think with language (metalinguistic awareness), and how to learn (metalearning) when facing daily life and problem-solving situations. For instance, children can learn applications and transformations of conceptual knowledge in in-school and out-of-school contexts through problem-solving activities and can learn to apply these strategies in a creative and flexible manner.

2. Emphasize the formation of new concepts through *discovery and exploration* and the stimulation of assimilation and accommodation learning processes. *Inquiry-based learning* strategies using student-centered, active learning, discovery of concepts, and critical-thinking skills (i.e., cognitive, metacognitive, and metalinguistic strategies) need to be modeled by teachers. *Interactive dialogue and instructional conversation strategies* can be modeled in relation to specific content areas because thinking and learning strategies are not generic (e.g., articulating observations and making deductions and elaborations in relation to specific concepts and topics).

3. Build concrete "anchors" or authentic sociocultural experiences for stimulating higher levels of learning (from index, to symbolic, to sign levels) across content areas.

4. Develop awareness in young, diverse children of their characteristics as learners (i.e., learning styles, interests, strengths, and weaknesses) so that they use appropriate metacognitive, cognitive, and metalinguistic strategies to enhance the learning process.

Application of all four critical-thinking, pedagogical strategies in an integrated manner is used in the BPDC preschool classroom. The critical-thinking, pedagogical strategies endorsed by the ethnic-educator approach provide young, diverse children the opportunity to learn from their teachers high-level critical-thinking skills, including how to think (metacognitive strategies), how to think with language (metalinguistic awareness), and how to learn (metalearning strategies). Together, teachers and young, diverse children can engage in inquiry-based activities, such as brainstorming, elaboration, the use of trial and error for problem solving, and the use of language as a vehicle for thinking aloud and asking explanatory questions (of the what, how, when, and why nature). In this way, teachers can serve as role models for young, diverse children learning how to use language as an internal mental tool for thinking by modeling critical-thinking strategies, such as analysis, synthesis, elaboration, comparison, imagery, transformation, abstraction, generalization, and deduction.

Teachers acting as models for inquiry-based learning promote an active and learner-centered classroom environment. The inquiry-based learning approach promotes intrinsic motivation for learning in young, diverse children, stimulates creative and flexible thinking, and develops conceptual understanding; and in general, it creates the ideal environment for stimulating independent problem solvers. The use of a conceptual approach also helps young, diverse children focus on similar topics across content areas and use language as a symbolic tool for learning, resulting in the stimulation of language competence at a faster rate.

The result is an emphasis on the process of learning (rather than on the product) and on conceptual learning and the development of critical-thinking skills (rather than on memorization of information). The development of critical-thinking skills will provide young, diverse children with the mental abilities for learning topic and content knowledge at a faster rate because they have developed the mental tools necessary for transforming topic knowledge into general conceptual principles and networks. For instance, numbers are no longer isolated pieces of information that need to be memorized in a string of words through a song. Instead, numbers become concepts attached to prior experiences and conceptual knowledge that provide the ability to engage in one-to-one correspondence when using counting for solving a real-life problem. That is, helping the teacher and classmates follow a recipe by reading first how many eggs are needed for making cupcakes and then by breaking the exact number of eggs that the recipe calls for: Six! No less and no more.

In sum, teachers act as facilitators, mentors, role models, and social mediators for engaging in cooperative discovery with young children and modeling critical-thinking, pedagogical strategies. As recommended by Ovando, Combs, and Collier (2006), children share with teachers the responsibility for learning and integrating real-life experiences, prior and cultural knowledge, and new content learned in school. We will explore how the curriculum can be connected to young, diverse children's prior sociocultural knowledge and real-life experiences in the next section.

SECOND AND THIRD CLUSTERS OF PEDAGOGICAL STRATEGIES

A Pluralistic Pedagogy Stimulating Connections to Prior Sociocultural Knowledge and Real-Life Experiences

The ethnic-educator curriculum celebrates cultural and linguistic diversity as an asset and enrichment for multilingual and multicultural children. This pluralistic curriculum centers on the development of the potential for learning of young, diverse children, by using their strengths and cultural and linguistic thinking style for enriching the curriculum and classroom experiences. The active, inquiry-based classrooms encourage young, diverse children to use their prior sociocultural knowledge to create meaningful learning (National Research Council, 1999a, 1999b). When diverse children do not share the same cultural knowledge as the school culture, teachers need to create learning opportunities in the classroom to build life experiences that anchor the formation of new cultural knowledge.

Young, diverse children usually find themselves struggling not only with the task of comprehending a new language but also with sociocultural background knowledge they have not been exposed to. This new knowledge includes all the belief systems, practices, and shared experiences that members of that culture often take for granted but that may in fact be quite foreign to young, diverse children. Success in school too often depends on students' familiarity with mainstream sociocultural knowledge (Gonzalez et al., 2006; Nieto, 2004). Thus, it becomes the task of the teacher to explicitly teach background knowledge that is culturally relevant to a mainstream school context. However, teachers must be careful not to adopt a deficit stance regarding diverse children's prior experience and background knowledge. Diverse children bring with them extensive experiences and knowledge grounded in their native language and culture, and teachers must find ways to first familiarize themselves with students' experiences and background knowledge and then to creatively capitalize on students' prior knowledge to introduce new mainstream cultural knowledge (Heath, 1983; Igoa, 1995; Nieto, 2004).

The ethnic-educator curriculum stimulates language development through using meaningful sociocultural experiences and authentic texts that represent the actual reality of young, diverse children at home and at school. For instance, diverse preschool children in the BPDC, who are growing up in the Midwest while listening to a story about what happens in the fall, need to develop new cultural experiences with the English language and the American concepts of pumpkins, scarecrows, leaves changing colors and falling from trees, and squirrels piling up nuts and acorns. When teachers just read this kind of *culturally loaded* book, young, diverse children just listen to strings of words with *empty* sociocultural meanings. But when teachers bring out leaves of multiple colors and sizes and ask preschoolers to count the leaves, sort them by color and size, and then demonstrate the spatial concept of "up and down" by dropping the leaves, young, diverse children engage in the activity and build meaningful life experiences that can anchor their newly formed cultural concepts.

Another instructional strategy for connecting learning to prior knowledge is to use the children's L1 and L2 as methods of instruction, resulting in a *spiral curriculum* that can represent languages by teacher, by content area, or by time scheduled. By using both languages as symbolic tools for learning content and concepts, young, diverse children can transfer their prior verbal and non-verbal, sociocultural knowledge (acquired through their L1 and native culture) to learning new content in their L2 (i.e., English). In the BPDC, the use of both languages for instruction results in faster language learning and higher levels of academic achievement for young, diverse children learning English as a second language.

Yet another instructional strategy for connecting prior sociocultural knowledge and real-life experiences to the content learned in the curriculum is to teach the four language skills in an integrated manner. That is, listening, speaking, reading, and writing language skills should reflect their natural use—integrated with one another and situated in authentic and meaningful contexts. Traditionally, language has been taught in a segmented manner in which listening, speaking, reading, and writing have been artificially isolated from one another (Diaz-Rico, 2004; Ovando et al., 2006). Such an approach robs children of the excellent learning opportunities available in the natural sociocultural context, overlapping-language environment that occurs in real life. One can observe how children seem to learn their L1 so effortlessly. They do not sit down at a desk for a predetermined amount of time each day to practice talking or listening. Rather, they learn as they go about their normal routines of playing with siblings and friends and participating in family activities. Similarly, diverse children learning ESL do better when both languages are situated in real and meaningful social and instructional interactions—as in the BPDC. Piper (2003) warned against a tendency to believe that children need a rehearsal period initially before moving on to real communication. Instead, young, diverse children should be encouraged and guided to engage in authentic interaction from the very first day of school.

High-quality, early childhood curriculums, such as the ethnic-educator approach, encourage connections to real-world experiences by emphasizing *active learning*. Student-centered learning at the BPDC allows children to actively develop conceptual knowledge through discovery and dynamic interaction with meaningful instructional materials representing different content areas and objectives. Children engage in inquiry-based learning by constructing new meanings and concepts, creating original uses of language and information, and engaging in authentic communication and dialogue with peers and teachers.

A student-centered approach is highly motivating and validates students' ownership of the learning process. According to Piper (2003), although there are some factors that teachers can control, such as materials and methodology, the idea that teachers can determine students' learning is actually an illusion. Therefore, we need to let students guide their own learning. The descriptions of Igoa's classroom in her book *The Inner World of the Immigrant Child* (1995) offer a powerful argument for placing the responsibility for learning in the hands of students. In a child-centered classroom, students learn to establish their own goals for learning, and they choose the specific daily tasks that will best help them achieve those goals. At the BPDC, children assist one another, work at their own pace, and are highly motivated as they are given the freedom and the supportive environment that they need to become independent learners.

Other specific instructional strategies used at the BPDC for stimulating young, diverse children to make connections between prior sociocultural knowledge, real-life experiences, and new concepts across content areas include the following:

1. Select developmentally appropriate and linguistically and culturally authentic instructional materials. In addition, provide classroom opportunities to develop lived experiences so that the curriculum represents young, diverse children's sociocultural prior knowledge and links it to opportunities to construct new mainstream sociocultural knowledge. In this manner, teachers value the home language and cultural experiences (e.g., dialect and cultural values) for affirming young, diverse children's cultural identity and motivate them to build conceptual links to new mainstream sociocultural knowledge. *Interactive dialogue* or *instructional conversations* can be used as individual and group strategies for children to talk about lived experiences (e.g., real-life, daily events like eating lunch at the school cafeteria and recalling the menu) and to provide verbal descriptions and explanations of the sequence of events. Community and sociocultural contexts are ideal authentic experiences for providing authentic learning opportunities for oral-language and literacy development in young, diverse children.

2. Use *sheltered instruction* (i.e., the integration of language and content instruction), in which teachers use pedagogical strategies that adapt to the needs of ESL learners (e.g., using nonverbal materials such as manipulative materials and pictures, speaking slowly and clearly, using repeated patterns of language, building on prior sociocultural knowledge and real-life experiences). The sheltered instruction strategy also works for diverse, mainstream, or monolingual-English children who come from low-income households and show delays in language development (in comparison to middle- or upper-class mainstream peers).

3. Use *learner-centered, high-quality teaching* to help children increase their intrinsic motivation for learning, such as instructional activities that are varied, engaging, and socially relevant to real life (authentic and project oriented) and develop experiential knowledge, build linguistic and cultural competence, and involve cooperative and collaborative learning. High-quality teaching can also stimulate the formation of high self-expectation and high self-esteem while learning, through instructional activities representing children's interests and by teachers' modeling a positive attitude diverse cultures and languages. A learner-centered classroom stimulates active

and inquiry-based learning that motivates learners to become independent and successful.

4. Use *individualized instruction* to represent the multiple learning needs of young, diverse children, including their idiosyncratic interests, learning pace, strengths and weaknesses (across cognitive, linguistic, and socioemotional developmental areas), and learning styles (e.g., visual, auditory, kinesthetic). Teachers can individualize instruction by offering choices in the classroom, such as alternative activities, various teaching and learning strategies, and a variety of assignments. By individualizing instruction, teachers can set developmental prerequisites needed for maximizing success and minimizing failure in the educational process of young, diverse children.

According to Gonzalez, Brusca-Vega, and Yawkey (1997), *active learning* requires that ESL "students must interact or come in contact with their environments in some fashion . . . [and] must be provided [with opportunities for] . . . emphasis on process and concrete object manipulation" (p. 158). Thus, for young, diverse children, the availability of multiple objects that they can touch, smell, see, and manipulate to sort, seriate, order, and use for symbolic play and problem-solving activities generates opportunities for developing conceptual mental abilities. For example, for young, diverse children at the BPDC to discover why autumn is also called fall, they need to manipulate actual leaves of different colors, shapes, and sizes and understand what happens when they drop them into a table or pail of water. Young children can discover, by *doing*, that the season *fall* is named after the many leaves that *fall* from trees, by engaging in collaborative learning with peers through instructional conversation activities that require critical-thinking and problem-solving processes, such as probing, trial and error, deduction, prediction, elaboration, and the use of prior knowledge.

Another example of BPDC curricular activities that stimulate language development through exposing young, diverse children to authentic sociocultural experiences is providing concrete anchors for developing concepts. Almost every primary-level class starts with a group time for describing the weather and identifying the date and month. When young children are asked to repeat strings of words, even in the context of a song, language becomes empty of meaning. Most young children disengage from learning weather concepts because they are presented without concrete, experiential anchors. Instead, when BPDC preschoolers are provided with manipulative materials to develop connections to real-life experiences, such as creating lived experiences in the classroom, they can attach language to these experiences and motivation for learning increases dramatically among young, diverse children. A good source of manipulative anchors may be representations of clouds in the form of cotton balls falling from the sky that preschoolers need to catch in a basket in the context of small groups. Then, with the help of a BPDC teacher as a mediator, children can engage in counting, adding, and subtracting quantities in relation to how many clouds their group and other groups of children were able to gather. The actual prior real-life experience of catching clouds provides young children the opportunity to build connections between prior and new knowledge across content areas and develop conceptual understanding of the abstract concept of "cloudiness," having had the opportunity to develop meaning for a previous empty label. Then, coming back to the singing activity about how the weather is today, young children can experience that words in the song are meaningful because they had an opportunity to develop prior conceptual knowledge through exposure to real-life social and cultural experiences. Young children now become engaged, happy singers, who are actively learning the meaning of language. You can tell by their happy faces and their body language!

Another instructional strategy used at the BPDC to emphasize the connection of school with real-world experiences is to use *cooperative learning*. It is one of the best instructional strategies for helping young, diverse children acquire conceptual knowledge and increase their academic achievement and their language skills. In the context of an ethic-educator curriculum, peers can use cooperative learning to model learning and thinking strategies and to act as mentors and mediators or social resources for one another. Young peers can act as resources for one another because they have different strengths and weaknesses across content and developmental areas. Then, through the use of cooperative learning strategies, teachers can use the help of peer groups to increase conceptual learning, to integrate prior knowledge to subject and topic learning, and ultimately, to increase academic achievement. The participation in teams also helps young children improve emotional and social developmental skills, such as self-esteem self-concept, identity, trust, mutual respect and support, and a sense of synergy. Roles of group members should be rotated so that every student becomes responsible for different tasks and actively engages in all aspects of the learning tasks. For instance, some roles suggested by Ovando, Combs, and Collier (2006) for group members are captains, timekeepers, cheerleaders, presenters, recorders, and bilingual facilitators.

The diversity in young children's ethnic and cultural backgrounds, language-proficiency levels, achievement levels, learning styles, personalities, and developmental strengths and weaknesses can increase team group productivity and can enhance the utility of cooperative learning as a successful teaching strategy. Groups should be formed based on heterogeneous characteristics of students and should be rotated to maximize exposure to a diverse array of peer characteristics. Always, team or group work should avoid tracking of students by level of academic achievement or language proficiency background. In fact, it is beneficial for young, diverse children to be exposed to peers achieving at higher levels, in both academic and language proficiency. By experiencing exposure to the diverse backgrounds of peers, students can improve their attitudes toward mainstream and diverse groups and improve their communicative and cultural competence.

FOURTH CLUSTER OF PEDAGOGICAL STRATEGIES
An Advocacy Position for Teachers

Teachers need to develop classroom environments in which they act as mentors, advocates, role models, and cultural mediators for fostering caring, collaborative, nurturing, and motivated learning communities. Teachers of young, diverse children need to become cultural mediators or bridges between their students' home culture and language and the mainstream school culture. This means that teachers need to adapt instructional strategies and the curriculum to the unique cultural and linguistic educational needs of diverse children. What works for mainstream students will not necessarily match the learning and developmental needs of young, diverse children. Thus, teachers need to become role models of instructional strategies that meet the cultural and linguistic diversity of their students.

Traditional mainstream education in U.S. public schools reflects the values and attitudes held by mainstream-American families, and it does not make allowances for diverse backgrounds. Thus, many diverse children and their families find themselves alienated from and confused by the norms and expectations of schools. The burden rests almost completely on the diverse children and their families to adapt to the way things are traditionally done at school. This can be exceptionally challenging for young, diverse children because while they are busy trying to deal with the cultural and linguistic dissonance they experience, they are missing valuable opportunities for learning academic subject matter, often with detrimental effects on their academic achievement. Children bring their cultural and linguistic background with them to school, as part of their personality. When a child's culture and language become part of their curriculum, the entire schooling process become more meaningful. Support in both school and home settings is beneficial and essential for the academic success of young, diverse children.

Therefore, to better serve diverse children, teachers need to become advocates and value their unique cultural and linguistic backgrounds as assets for their learning and developmental processes. For instance, BPDC teachers help young, diverse children make connections between what they already know (i.e., concepts in their L1, such as numbers and colors) and concepts and subject matter they are learning at school. Another example is that BPDC teachers use a variety of instructional strategies to try to match the different cultural learning and thinking styles, as well as the individual learning styles and topics of interest of their diverse students. Peer collaborative interactions in the BPDC classroom provide opportunities for young, diverse children to make connections with real-world experiences and prior sociocultural knowledge and use peers as role models for engaging in critical-thinking processes. When interacting with peers, language can be used as a tool for conveying concepts and new meanings (i.e., instructional conversations and interactive dialogue).

Teachers of young, diverse children also need to act as mentors and involve parents in the educational process. For instance, BPDC teachers help engage diverse parents in collaborative activities and open house events at school and in workshops and orientation sessions about the school culture. An important benefit of teacher-family collaboration is that it can also serve to empower parents through validation of their cultural and language heritage (i.e., child-rearing and socialization practices, communication styles, and cultural values toward education). This is very important for diverse families, who may often feel isolated from mainstream institutions like schools. Through these partnerships, parents' expertise and cultural backgrounds can be utilized by making them feel valued and respected as players in their child's education. Thus, care must be taken by teachers to develop collaborative partnerships with immigrant minority parents, which need to be based on empathy and trust (Pease-Alvarez, García, & Espinosa, 1991).

Teachers can also facilitate diverse parent involvement by doing home visits and making phone calls to better understand their students' educational needs. By learning about the home and community environments of their diverse students, teachers become educated about their students' cultural and linguistic backgrounds and can make the educational context more equitable and meaningful. Then, the advocacy position of the ethnic-educator curriculum is that teachers need to be educated not only about the learning and instructional process but also about their diverse students' cultural backgrounds. Although clearly a time-consuming process, taking the time to learn about students' cultural backgrounds and home cultures is an essential aspect of providing more equitable educational opportunities for young, diverse children.

A major challenge for educators seeking to develop conceptual links for diverse children has been the practical task of identifying their prior sociocultural knowledge. It is becoming increasingly clear that diverse parents can play a crucial role in this identification process. A parent possesses invaluable insight into a child's prior knowledge because of the intimate and long-term nature of the relationship they hold with each other. A parent's thorough understanding of a child's household, community, and cultural environments also contributes to this expertise. Unfortunately, many barriers can exist between educators and diverse parents that inhibit sharing this understanding and applying it to the classroom. One of the barriers is that educators hold misperceptions of diverse parents. For instance, one common misconception is that immigrant parents hold low educational aspirations for their children or are uninterested in participating in their education.

An important step for teachers in coming to understand the cultural backgrounds of diverse children and their families is assessing their attitudes, beliefs, and related misconceptions and misperceptions of diverse children and their families. Teachers must realize that their personalities are the most important tool for instruction; they need to acknowledge their own beliefs and prejudices as well as determine how their particular cultural and linguistic backgrounds affect the way they conduct instruction. A BPDC teacher summed up very well how the experience of using an ethnic-educator curriculum had affirmed her commitment to better serve diverse children.

> My teaching experience has affirmed my belief that educators must take the initiative to inform others about the many wonderful differences in our world. The curriculum should be multicultural, giving students the opportunity to learn about all people and respect differences in our world. This will give students the chance to understand and respect all people, regardless of their social or economic status, race, gender, age, or religion, and make lifelong contributions for a better world.

In sum, as the reflection of the BPDC teacher illustrates, serving young, diverse children is a demanding and challenging task that requires advocacy and commitment. Teachers need to act as role models of respect and value for multi-culturalism and as mentors and cultural bridges for facilitating the cultural adaptation of young, diverse children and their families.

SUGGESTIONS FOR APPLYING THE STRATEGIES

These recommended pedagogical strategies can be used to interface content with developmental areas across the curriculum. Then, while the teacher stimulates young, diverse children to develop their language (with emphasis on additive L1 and L2 development), critical-thinking, and socioemotional skills, children can acquire verbal and nonverbal concepts in math, science, and social studies.

1. Teachers may use the language-experience approach (LEA), in which children tell their teacher or a more capable peer a story in their own words. Then, the teacher transcribes the story and reads it back to the students. With guidance, children eventually begin to read the text on their own. This can help connect children's words, personal stories, and experiences with print, and it supports the development of phonemic awareness (Diaz-Rico, 2004; Hadaway, Vardell, & Young, 2002).

2. Dialogue journals can be excellent and flexible follow-ups to reading a text. Typically, there is no established topic, and the teacher responds but does not evaluate or correct children's early attempts to write (Diaz-Rico, 2004). This strategy can be adapted for beginning writers by creating *frame sentences*, which are based on the initial text and present fill-in-the-gap key words for children to complete.

3. Reading aloud (listening to the teacher read or audiotapes of stories) is an excellent practice that provides students with "big words and literary sentences" (Hadaway et al., 2002, p. 168).

4. With the help of the teacher, children can work in small groups to respond to wordless picture books. Children can be stimulated to engage in discussions with peers of what they think will happen in the story, telling the story as they see it in the illustrations, or writing the events depicted in the pictures (Hadaway et al., 2002).

5. Children can be stimulated by teachers to respond to stories by drawing and then labeling key points of the illustrations with words and phrases (Hadaway et al., 2002; Igoa 1995). Together, children can compose the text for a big book. Each child is assigned a page of the book to illustrate, and then each of the pages is bound together to create the big book (Diaz-Rico, 2004).

6. Igoa (1995) described children's *filmstrip-story making*, in which they transform their own stories into a simple filmstrip. Children write their stories, and then they divide the text of the story into sections to accompany each film slide and record themselves reading the text. This becomes the narration for the film. Next, the child creates the graphics by creating a series of illustrations on a long strip of paper, which will be fitted to a reel for viewing. Finally, classmates are gathered around to listen to the story, offer constructive feedback, and decide together on sound effects. After they practice the sound effects, the film is viewed again with the audience providing the sound effects.

7. Teachers need to observe children carefully to discover their interests. Then, teachers locate texts that support the children's interests with the goal of motivating them to read and showing them that reading is related to their lives (Diaz-Rico, 2004).

Therefore, by using the pedagogical strategies endorsed by the ethnic-educator curriculum, teachers of young, diverse children can facilitate their academic achievement across content areas by stimulating their language, cognitive, and socioemotional development. By using language and literacy skills as tools for thinking, teachers empower young, diverse children to communicate verbal and nonverbal meanings across content areas in a socially appropriate manner.

4

Linking the Teaching Strategies With Academic Content Standards

Chapter 4 integrates the pedagogical strategies of the ethnic-educator approach with academic content standards for young, diverse children. The first section of this chapter explains how pedagogical strategies link assessment to instruction through *classroom-based assessments* (observations and evaluation tasks) that represent academic content standards endorsed by Head Start and Teachers of English to Speakers of Other Languages (TESOL, 2005). The second section of this chapter discusses the instructional purposes of assessment and presents the rationale explaining why classroom-based assessments are alternative measures that are more valid and reliable when assessing young, diverse children. The third section of Chapter 4 presents an integration of the ethnic-educator approach with TESOL academic content standards in the Bilingual Preschool Development Center (BPDC) curriculum. In the fourth section of this chapter, weekly sample lessons of the curriculum used in the BPDC are presented as examples of integration of the ethnic-educator curriculum with TESOL academic content standards and links to classroom-based observations.

LINKING ASSESSMENT TO INSTRUCTION THROUGH CLASSROOM-BASED OBSERVATIONS

The main pedagogical principle of the ethnic-educator approach proposes a holistic developmental perspective for stimulating developmental and learning processes across content areas. Teachers need to act as mediators to help children understand why, when, and how factual knowledge and abstract learning principles can be transferred and transformed and can become relevant to other content areas, knowledge domains, and real-world experiences. So the following two tables represent the BPDC curriculum that translated the holistic pedagogical principle of the ethnic-educator approach by clustering the Head Start academic standards. Table 4.1 shows a representation of the alignment of clustered developmental milestones by cognitive, language, social, and emotional developmental areas with Head Start academic standards across content areas (i.e., language arts, mathematics, social studies, and science) in the BPDC curriculum. Table 4.2 represents this same alignment of Head Start academic standards across content areas by quarter.

An alignment of milestones by developmental area with content standards by age group is provided in Table 4.3. That is, academic standards cluster the cognitive development area through the concepts of vocabulary, number, space, time, and classification. In the same manner, the language development area includes preliteracy skills with the acquisition of the following concepts: vocabulary knowledge, phonemic awareness, letter recognition, handwriting, and eye-hand coordination.

As proposed by Gonzalez, Yawkey, and Minaya-Rowe (2006), language and cognitive development and preliteracy skills show three levels of learning processes that are acquired in a developmental sequence: (1) the *index level* with three- to four-year-old children needing perceptual experiences with nonverbal, concrete, tridimensional objects present in real-life experiences; (2) the *symbolic level* with four- to five-year-old children needing symbolic experiences with nonverbal or graphic two-dimensional stimuli (e.g., pictures, photos, rebus symbols, art, and imagery); and (3) the *sign level* with five- to six-year-old children needing verbal signs or one-dimensional stimuli (e.g., sounds in a printed format such as making connections between phonemes, graphemes, and words—defined as phonemic awareness). The sign level of learning requires children to make an abstract connection between the real-life experience with an object, idea, or situation with the sound or print. For instance, the development of phonemic awareness requires young children to acquire the ability to pair up real-world sounds with cultural conventions, such as onomatopoeic sounds and language, the ability to recognize words that rhyme, and the ability to identify the first or ending sounds or graphemes of words (Breznitz, 1987; Fountas & Pinnell, 1996; Snow, Burns, & Griffin, 1998). This developmental sequence is represented in the BPDC curriculum as a continuum of developmental milestones and content standards at the three learning process levels.

Finally, the socioemotional developmental area includes the concepts of prosocial behavior, sense of self, and responsibility. Prosocial behaviors are defined as the sense of being comfortable when engaging in social interactions with familiar and new adults and children. Prosocial behaviors include the sense of feeling close to others, receiving acceptance and respect, and feeling connected with positive bonds or rapport, such as receiving, giving, loving, and caring behaviors (Shore, 2004). Sense of self is defined as self-esteem, self-respect, and self-concept emerging from their social experiences with parents, other adults, and children in their home and school environments (Green & Piel, 2002). When children's experiences are positive, their sense of self improves, and they perceive themselves as competent, successful, valued, and respected individuals. Responsibility is defined as the child's capacity to feel competent to make decisions and direct their actions (Hall & Barongan, 2002). When children feel emotionally secure, and have a sense of

(Text continued on page 73)

Table 4.1 Alignment of Clustered Learning Processes and Milestones With Head Start Academic Content Standards Across Developmental and Subject Areas

Clustered Learning Processes and Milestones by Head Start Academic Content Standards	Socioemotional Developmental Area (Affective Nature of Teaching and Learning Processes)	Cognitive Developmental Area (Concepts Learned in Math, Social Studies, and Science)	Language Developmental Area (Language as a Tool for Socialization and Learning)
Three- to four-year-olds index learning processes Image representations of *three-dimensional* objects through actions, manipulation, and real-life *experiences* (e.g., using blocks to build a house, classifying objects by color)	• Egocentric perception of social interaction (monologues, collective monologues, not a good listener, focuses on own perspective) • Centers attention on here-and-now social experiences • Inconsistent use of some social conventions (communication, politeness) • Responds to name • Makes eye contact **Sense of self** • Centered in own feelings, desires, and perspective • Needs adult prompting to continue working on familiar and new tasks and situations; tries single approach	**Classification skills** • Needs to manipulate three-dimensional objects to learn (actions and real-life experiences) • Perceptual dominance (need to see, hear, touch, smell, and do to learn) • Egocentricity of thought **Concept of number** • Can see only one side of experiences (only his or her perspective), one dimension of concepts (only color, only shape, but cannot coordinate attributes of objects) • Can apply daily life experiences to similar situations	**Listening and speaking skills** • Grammar becomes more complex (e.g., use of past tense, present progressive, plurals, possessives) • Begins using full sentences with more than one clause (joined by conjunctions, e.g., and, but, because) • Mastery of many single phonemes and some consonant blends • Uses more simple phonemes for advanced phonemes (/t/for/th/) • Can respond to questions when prompted by teachers **Vocabulary skills, prereading, and prewriting skills** • Can label common daily life objects • Can follow one-step simple directions

Four- to five-year-olds' symbolic learning processes Figural *two-dimensional* representations of images, such as drawing, sketching, and finger painting, which could use *direct or indirect imitation* (model present or absent) through pantomime or sociodramatic play (make-believe or fantasy)	**Responsibility** • Still learning to be responsible for actions and self well-being, can use self-help skills with adult prompting **Prosocial behavior** • Self-centered in own rights, may care for objects and others with adult prompting	• Can interact with real objects in pretend play • Uses numbers for counting but may not be in correct sequence or cannot use one-to-one correspondence **Vocabulary skills** • Can use concepts of time and position across one dimension (i.e., present, inside)	• Recognizes that words are made up of letters (e.g., uses mock letters to write name, recognizes fewer than 10 letters, can identify first letter of name) • Can identify matching sounds in real life, but cannot associate sound to letter—no phonemic awareness • Can recognize environmental print
	• Can recognize that others have different feelings and perspectives from own (e.g., may accept taking turns after child's request) • Wants to continue working on familiar and new tasks even after difficulties, tries different approaches **Responsibility** • With some adult prompting takes responsibility for actions and self well-being, uses self-help skills	• Egocentricity of thought continues **Classification skills** • Need to manipulate two-dimensional objects to learn (actions for direct and indirect imitation, use of pantomime and sociodramatic play) • Perceptual dominance (need to engage in *action* to learn) **Concept of time** • Can see two-dimensions of concepts (can coordinate up to two attributes of objects—e.g., classify by color *and* shape; can form patterns up to two dimensions)	**Listening and speaking skills** • Added complexity in syntax and semantics (e.g., can use adjectives indicating space concepts—in, on, under, over, into) • Can use sentences with more than one clause (joined by more complex adverbs—however, then, so) • Responds to series of verbal commands calling for pointing to pictures, objects, and actions **Phonemic awareness** • Continues mastery of more complex phonemes and consonant blends (less need to use phonological processes to simplify sounds)

(Continued)

Table 4.1 (Continued)

Clustered Learning Processes and Milestones by Head Start Academic Content Standards	Socioemotional Developmental Area (Affective Nature of Teaching and Learning Processes)	Cognitive Developmental Area (Concepts Learned in Math, Social Studies, and Science)	Language Developmental Area (Language as a Tool for Socialization and Learning)
	Prosocial behavior • With some adult prompting shows respect for self and others' rights, and may care for objects and others	• Can engage in prompted direct and indirect imitation (model present or absent) through nonverbal actions • Can apply experience and learning to a new contexts and situations • Can use objects, drawings, pictures, acting out, and gestures to represent real objects and stories • Uses one number per object when counting, uses one-to-one correspondence for comparing up to two sets of objects **Concept of time** • Can use concepts of time across two dimensions (i.e., present, past, or future; day, night; yesterday, last week)	
Five- to six-year-olds' sign learning processes Figural *one-dimensional* representations of *abstractions* through verbal and nonverbal	**Sense of self** • Can recognize and respond to others' feelings, desires, and perspectives	**Classification skills** • Transition from figural to concrete level of thought • Can decenter and take the perspective of another person (e.g., listener)	**Listening and speaking skills** • Can elaborate and use complex syntax (e.g., use of pronouns—himself/herself, they/them; interrogative forms—who, where, how;

concepts (*onomatopoeia*— sounds of animals, *phonemic awareness*— beginning and ending letters in words, and *pragmatics*) • Shows persistence, flexibility, or adaptation when approaching familiar and new tasks and situations **Responsibility** • Takes responsibility for actions and self well-being, can use self-help skills **Prosocial behavior** • Shows respect for rights of self and others, cares for objects and others • Can use passive voice	• Can think about three dimensions of attributes (can classify by color, shape, and size) and verbally explain underlying reasoning for classifications and concept **Classification skills** • Can think with concepts (verbal and nonverbal), can think with language (no need to do to learn), can use multiple verbal and nonverbal representations for ideas (e.g., actions, writing, singing) • Can engage in self-initiated direct and indirect imitation (presence and absence of model) through verbal actions • Can apply knowledge and concepts learned to a new context (makes comparisons—similarities and differences, uses comparative words across three dimensions related to number, size, shape, texture, weight, color, speed, volume)	negative forms and contractions—won't, don't) • Can actively participate in and start conversations in relation to own experiences and thoughts • Increased complexity of semantics (uses advanced verbal concepts) • Responds to series of questions asking to define or describe objects **Phonemic awareness vocabulary, prereading, and prewriting skills** • Can engage in metalinguistic reasoning (i.e., meanings of words, can explore cause-effect relations, goes beyond literal meanings, understands meanings of new words from context and pictures, predicts stories) • Masters phonemes in most positions of the word, classifies objects beyond perception (by sounds, beginning or ending letters)

(Continued)

Table 4.1 (Continued)

Clustered Learning Processes and Milestones by Head Start Academic Content Standards	Socioemotional Developmental Area (Affective Nature of Teaching and Learning Processes)	Cognitive Developmental Area (Concepts Learned in Math, Social Studies, and Science)	Language Developmental Area (Language as a Tool for Socialization and Learning)
		• Can compare and predict story events, can retell a story with many details and draw connections between story events **Concepts of time and number** • Connects number words and symbols to objects counted, knows that last number is the total, uses one-to-one correspondence for comparing over two sets of objects even in real-life problems (can form patterns over two dimensions) • Can use concepts of time across three dimensions (past present, and future—e. g., when I was a baby)	• Can use conventional writing for name, recognizes environmental prints • Can relate own experiences to text and retell stories, participates in shared readings, uses print in play in complex ways • Can engage in dialogue, decenters from own perspective, talks about more than one dimension of objects **Listening and speaking skills** • Can follow three-step directions • Can use passive voice • Can use stress and intonation for meaning when talking and reading

Table 4.2 Alignment of Head Start Academic Content Standards by Developmental Areas per Academic Quarter

Academic Content Standards Aligned by Developmental Areas	Fall Academic Quarter (September, October, November, and December)	Winter Academic Quarter (January, February, and March)	Spring Academic Quarter (March, April, and May)
Language Developmental Area			
Phonemic awareness	• Discriminates natural and environmental sounds	• Identifies rhyming sounds in familiar words	• Relates sounds to letters
Vocabulary	• Uses labels for daily life objects and experiences • Responds to questions when prompted by teacher	• Learns new words from stories and images	• Learns advanced words, categories and subcategories
Listening and speaking skills	• Mastery of single phonemes and some consonant blends	• Mastery of complex phonemes and many consonant blends	• Mastery of most phonemes in most positions
Prereading skills	• Interest in books and stories • Recognizes that words are made up of letters • Can understand questions • Recognizes fewer than 10 letters • Uses mock letters to write own name	• General knowledge of print • Gains information from images • Asks questions and makes comments • Recognizes more than 10 letters • Uses conventional letters to write own name	• Asks and answers questions and makes comments • Uses emerging reading skills to make meaning from print • Recognizes more than 15 letters • Uses conventional letters to write own name and spells some letters of familiar words
Prewriting skills	• Recognizes some environmental print • Understands print concepts and purpose of writing • Can scribble mock letters	• Recognizes own name and some familiar words • Identifies letters in own name and familiar words • Can use mock letters to write own name and familiar words	• Recognizes new and familiar words • Identifies letters in familiar and new words • Can use letters to write own name and some familiar words

(Continued)

Table 4.2 (Continued)

Academic Content Standards Aligned by Developmental Areas	Fall Academic Quarter (September, October, November, and December)	Winter Academic Quarter (January, February, and March)	Spring Academic Quarter (March, April, and May)
Cognitive Developmental Area			
Concept of number	• Across one dimension	• Across two dimensions	• Across three dimensions
Concept of time and space	• Counting may not be in correct sequence • Cannot use one-to-one correspondence	• Counting is in correct sequence • Counts up to 10 • Uses one-to-one correspondence	• Counting is in correct sequence • Counts up to 20 • Uses one-to-one correspondence
Classification	• Can sort and use patterns by one dimension • Uses perception to learn from experiences and manipulations of objects • Compares based on one perceptual dimension only	• Can sort and use patterns by two dimensions • Compares across two functional dimensions • Can make and interpret figural representations • Engages in pretend roles and symbolic play • Needs to do to learn (figural thinking)	• Can sort and use patterns by three dimensions • Compares across three abstract dimensions • Can make and interpret abstract representations • Engages in elaborated pretend roles and symbolic play • Uses abstractions to learn
Egocentricity	• Egocentricity of thought • Uses single approach for tasks	• Starts to decenter when prompted shows task persistence • Can think flexibly • When prompted can explore cause and effect	• Can decenter • Applies knowledge and experiences to new contexts • Shows task persistence and flexibility of thinking • Has own interest to explore cause and effect

Social and Emotional Developmental Areas

Sense of self	• Responds to name • Makes eye contact	• Uses simple forms of polite requests • Understands only literal meanings of messages	• Uses feedback, engages in dialogue • Uses complex polite forms and variations in style • Understands indirect speech and passive voice
Responsibility	• When prompted can use self-help skills • Is still learning to be responsible for actions and well-being • Shows appropriate trusts, in adults • Can follow classroom routines and rules	• When prompted uses self-help skills • Is still learning to take responsibility for actions, objects, others' and own well-being • When prompted can be independent and use self-direction • Follows classroom routines and rules	• Uses self-help skills, takes responsibility for actions, objects, others' and own well-being • Shows social adaptation to new tasks and situations • Demonstrates self-direction and independence
Prosocial behavior	• Egocentric perception of social interactions • Parallel play and monologues • Attention to present social experiences • Self-centered in own rights • Learning to read own feelings and uses behaviors to express feelings	• Egocentric speech but starts to decenter by understanding that others may have different perspectives or feelings • Can read own feelings and use language to express feelings • Uses collective monologues	• Can decenter and engage in dialogue • Can read own feelings • Uses language to express feelings • Can read and respond verbally to others' feelings • Uses thinking skills and negotiation to resolve conflicts

Table 4.3 Evaluation Tasks: Alignment of Milestones by Developmental Area With Head Start Academic Content Standards Across Subject Areas

Language and Fine Motor Areas: Evaluation Tasks

Milestones by Developmental Area	*Content Standards for Three- to Four-Year-Olds: Index Level*	*Content Standards for Four- to Five-Year-Olds: Symbolic Level*	*Content Standards for Five- to Six-Year-Olds: Abstract Level*
Letter recognition Reading Handwriting Eye-hand coordination	Children will recognize up to 10 letters, use mock letters to write own name, and form scribbles with mock letters	Children will recognize over 10 letters, use real letters to write own name, and can recognize and write familiar words	Children will recognize over 20 letters, use real letters to write familiar and new words
Phonemic awareness	Child will name natural and environmental sounds	Children will match an object with a picture that has its initial letter sound	Children will make the sound of the target letter presented in a card

Cognitive Area: Evaluation Tasks

Milestones by Developmental Area	*Content Standards for Three- to Four-Year-Olds: Index Level*	*Content Standards for Four- to Five-Year-Olds: Symbolic Level*	*Content Standards for Five- to Six-Year-Olds: Abstract Level*
Classification	Children will sort tangrams by **one** characteristic (e.g., color)	Children will sort tangrams by **two** characteristics (e.g., size and color)	Children will sort tangrams by **three** characteristics (e.g., shape, color, size)

Vocabulary Reading	Children identify, define, and describe (at a perceptual level) realia of familiar words	Children identify, define, and describe (at a functional level) pictures of familiar and new words	Children identify, define, and describe (at a conceptual level: categories and subcategories) pictures of advanced words
Concept of number	Children will count objects in correct sequence	Children will count objects and match them with pictures (one-to-one correspondence)	Children will identify the number that represents the objects and pictures counted (i.e., quantity)
Concept of time	Children will categorize events of a story heard by time sequence including **one dimension** (i.e., present)	Children will categorize events of a story heard by time sequence including **two dimensions** (i.e., present and past)	Children will categorize events of a story heard by time sequence including **three dimensions** (i.e., present, past, and future)
Concept of space	Children will place objects in space including **one dimension** (i.e., inside/outside)	Children will place objects in space including **two dimensions** (i.e., inside/outside *and* top/bottom)	Children will place objects in space including **three dimensions** (i.e., inside/outside, top/bottom, *and* right/left)

(Continued)

Table 4.3 (Continued)

Socioemotional Area: Evaluation Tasks			
Milestones by Developmental Area	*Content Standards for Three- to Four-Year-Olds: Index Level*	*Content Standards for Four- to Five-Year-Olds: Symbolic Level*	*Content Standards for Five- to Six-Year-Olds: Abstract Level*
Sense of self	Children will respond to name and make eye contact	Children will make **simple** polite requests based on role-playing situations	Children will make **complex** polite requests based on role-playing situations
Responsibility	Children will follow a few classroom rules	Children will have self-direction on a task	Children will have social adaptation to a new task
Prosocial behaviors	Children will have egocentric perception of social situations	Children will identify verbally own feelings for a story	Children will identify verbally own feelings for a story and start to understand characters' perspectives and feelings

Product Samples
Copying or drawing geometric figures and letters: Draw or copy these figures the best you can.
Human figure: To measure fine motor skills: Draw yourself the best you can. Draw your family the best you can.
Name writing: Write your name the best you can.

belonging to a family and school community, then they can direct their learning and take charge of their actions to care for objects, themselves, and other individuals in their social environment.

These three components of the socioemotional developmental area (i.e., prosocial behavior, sense of self, and responsibility) are closely connected with language and cognitive development in an ethnic-educator, holistic curriculum that is child-centered and stimulates active learning. The holistic curriculum also creates a nurturing classroom that provides many opportunities for young, diverse children to engage in meaningful social interactions. One of the pedagogical principles of the ethnic-educator approach stresses the affective nature of learning processes and the significant role that social and emotional scaffolding experiences play in learning processes, especially during the sensitive periods of early childhood. With the support of the scaffolding role of teachers and peers (e.g., verbal directions, physical assistance, probing questions), young children can understand a task at higher developmental levels, resulting in growth, learning new skills, and knowledge.

Moreover, Tables 4.4, 4.5, and 4.6 provide weekly sample lesson plans that implement the BPDC curriculum through instructional activities that interface academic standards across developmental and content areas. The three samples of weekly lesson plans span across three quarters of the academic year (i.e., fall, winter, and spring) and provide clusters of Head Start academic content standards following a holistic and thematic curriculum. The three themes sampled are "Falling Leaves" for the fall quarter, "Valentine's Day" for the winter quarter, and "Easter Time" for the spring quarter. The developmental areas clustered with the content areas by age groups are represented in the sample lesson plans throughout instructional activities.

Guidelines for planning instruction included in the sample lesson plans also highlight the main pedagogical strategies of the ethnic-educator curriculum, such as (1) a holistic or thematic curriculum; (2) instructional activities that cluster content standards and developmental areas; (3) the individualization of instruction to accommodate idiosyncratic (i.e., activity level, biological rhythms, adaptability, sensory threshold, mood, temperament) as well as cultural and linguistic (i.e., home language, cultural learning styles, cultural or religious values for child-rearing and educational activities) differences; and (4) the stimulation of skills and content standards at different developmental levels in a continuous manner (i.e., at the index, symbolic, and sign learning processes, as explained later in this chapter in relation to Head Start content standards).

The weekly sample lesson plans represent nine clusters of curriculum objectives throughout instructional activities encompassing all content and developmental areas, including (1) plays well with other children, (2) controls small muscles in hands, (3) controls eye-hand coordination, (4) uses tools for writing, (5) classifies objects, (6) recognizes patterns and can repeat them, (7) demonstrates knowledge of the alphabet, (8) uses emergent reading skills to make meaning from print, and (9) writes letters and words. The sample lesson plans also include guidelines for planning group instruction by dividing days into four units: group time, story time, small-group activities, and special activities. Thus, the sample lesson plans illustrate a truly holistic developmental approach that

(Text continued on page 86)

Table 4.4 Sample Lesson Plan for the Ethnic-Educator Curriculum—Fall Quarter

Weekly Planning Form: Sample for Fall Quarter
THEME: Falling Leaves

Directions: Lesson plans will be written weekly and based on Head Start content standards, selected theme or topic of study, and individual goals for children.

Week: _____

Teacher: _____

Study/Project: _____

Assistant: _____

Part I: Instructional Areas and Activities

Blocks	Dramatic Play	Toys and Games	*Theme: Falling Leaves*
Add props to enhance block play: leaves, sticks, fall colors tissue paper, fall colors felt squares, glue, markers, fall colors construction paper, tape, rakes, and pails	Set up a pretend grocery store with props for making cookies, cash register, grocery ads, coupons, pencils, paper for grocery list **I go to the park activity:** Participate in a script of "going to a picnic" by getting all the food necessary to fill a picnic basket and using coupons at the checkout	• Coupon matching game • Leaves matching game • Leaves pattern game	*Fall Quarter (October)* **Head Start Standards Covered for Instruction** • **Cognitive developmental area:** *Vocabulary, number:* across two dimensions only, space and time; counting may not be in correct sequence; cannot use one-to-one correspondence • **Classification:** Can sort and use patterns by one dimension; uses perception to learn from experiences and manipulations of objects; compares based on one perceptual dimension only; starts from egocentricity of thought, uses single approach for tasks • **Language developmental area:** *Phonemic awareness:* Discriminates natural and environmental sounds; *Letter recognition:* Recognizes some environmental print; *Reading:* Can understand questions, recognizes fewer than 10 letters, can use mock letters to write own name

Art	Library	Discovery	
Necklace activity: Sort and follow color and shape patterns to make a leaves necklace for Mom	**Read a story** about leaves, going to the park, enjoying a picnic, going to the supermarket. **Writing center:** Make cards for friends or parents to invite them to a picnic using writing materials, invitation cards, postcards, envelopes, pretend stamps	**Buried-treasure activity:** Fill sand and water station with assorted real leaves and encourage children to find letters in their first name (first initial and all letters) written on leaf shapes.	*Handwriting:* Can scribble mock letters *Vocabulary:* Learns words from daily life objects and experiences, responds to questions when prompted by teacher *Eye-hand coordination:* Can scribble mock letters • **Socioemotional developmental area:** *Prosocial behavior and sense of self:* Responds to name and makes eye contact *Responsibility:* When prompted can use self-help skills and is still learning to be responsible for actions and well-being; appropriate trust in adults, learning to follow classroom routines and rules
Sand and Water	**Music and Movement**	**Cooking**	
Children can sort leaves (or pinecones, nuts, plastic apples, small pumpkins, or gourds) by color, shape, and size and count leaves using one-to-one correspondence	• Songs with a fall theme • Finger plays • Interactive charts	• Make fall-shape (pumpkins, apples, leaves) cookies and decorate in fall colors in relation to size (e.g., small pumpkin cookies are yellow and larger pumpkin cookies are orange)	

(Continued)

Table 4.4 (Continued)

Computers	Outdoors	Family/Community Involvement
Reading emotions activity: Children reflect about experience of making cookies in relation to "emotion faces" postcards, and then write and mail a postcard to a friend or parent		Parents can participate in activities by sending materials (e.g., collect pinecones, leaves, or acorns with child) and recipes for cookies and by helping during performance of activities

Part II: Planning for Group Instruction During the Weekly Schedule

	Monday	*Tuesday*	*Wednesday*	*Thursday*	*Friday*
Group Time (songs, stories, games, discussions)	Fall or picnic song	Fall or picnic song	Fall or picnic song	Fall or picnic song	Fall or picnic song
Story Time	**Read a story** about going to the park	**Read a story** about picnics	**Read a story** about going to the supermarket		
Small-Group Activities	**Necklace activity**	**Buried-treasure activity**	**I go shopping activity**	**Make cards for friends or parent**	**Read emotions activity:** Write and mail a card to a friend or parent

Special Activities (field trips, special events)	Plan a field trip to the post office to mail cards		Coupon match activity for making cookies

Note: Stimulate children in small-group and free-choice activities in relation to curriculum objectives and content standards.

Curriculum Objectives:

1. Plays well with other children
2. Controls small muscles in hands
3. Coordinates eye-hand movements
4. Uses tools for writing
5. Classifies objects
6. Recognizes patterns and can repeat them
7. Demonstrates knowledge of the alphabet
8. Uses emergent reading skills to make meaning from print
9. Writes letters and words

Guidelines for Instruction:

1. Identify theme for quarter and month
2. Select activities that will cover standards and content across developmental areas
3. Conduct activities in small groups so that you can individualize instruction
4. Stimulate the same skills and content standards across Stages 1, 2, and 3

Table 4.5 Sample Lesson Plan for the Ethnic-Educator Curriculum—Winter Quarter

Weekly Planning Form: Sample for Winter Quarter
THEME: Valentine's Day

Directions: Lesson plans will be written weekly and based on Head Start content standards, a selected theme or topic, and individual goals for children.

Week: _____
Teacher: _____

Study/Project: _____
Assistant: _____

Part I: Instructional Areas and Activities

Blocks	Dramatic Play	Toys and Games	*Theme: Valentine's Day*
Add props for creating a post office, mail boxes, community helpers, mail trucks	Set up a pretend grocery store with props for making cookies, cash register, grocery ads, coupons, pencils, paper for grocery list **I go shopping activity:** Participate in a script of "buying at the supermarket" by getting all the ingredients necessary to make sugar cookies and use coupons at the checkout	• Coupon matching game • Heart matching game • Heart pattern game	*Winter Quarter (February)* **Head Start Standards Covered for Instruction** • **Cognitive developmental area:** *Vocabulary, number:* Across two dimensions only, space and time, counting in correct sequence, counts up to 10, uses one-to-one correspondence • **Classification:** Can do sorting and use patterns by two dimensions, compares across two functional dimensions, can make and interpret figural representations, engages in pretend roles and symbolic play, needs to do to learn, figural thinking, starts to decenter, shows task persistence, can think flexibly, when prompted can explore cause and effect

78

Art	Library	Discovery	• Language developmental area:
Necklace activity: Sort and follow color and shape patterns to make a Valentine's necklace for Mom	**Read a story** about treasures, Valentine's Day, making cookies, going to the supermarket **Writing center:** Make cards for friends or parents using writing materials, valentine cards, envelopes, post cards, heart-shaped paper, pretend stamps	**Buried-treasure activity:** Find letters in first name (first initial and all letters) written on hearts in a treasure box	*Phonemic awareness:* identifies rhyming sounds in familiar words *Letter recognition:* Recognizes own name and some familiar words *Reading:* Asks questions and makes comments, recognizes over 10 letters, can use conventional letters to write own name *Handwriting:* Can use mock letters to write own name and familiar words *Vocabulary:* Learns new words from stories and images *Eye-hand coordination:* Can use mock letters to write own name and familiar words • Socioemotional developmental area:
Sand and Water • Make-believe snow • Make ice cones with food flavors	**Music and Movement** • Right and left movements, top and down movements (for topological space in relation to readings and writing skills, e.g., "b" and "d" have a different right and left orientation, "p" and "b" have different top and down orientation)	**Cooking** • Make letter-shaped cookies	*Prosocial behavior and sense of self:* Uses simple forms of polite requests, understands only literal meanings of messages *Responsibility:* Uses self-help skills and can be responsible for actions, objects, others, and well-being; can be independent and use self-direction, follows classroom routines and rules

(Continued)

Table 4.5 (Continued)

Computers	Outdoors	Family/Community Involvement
Reading emotions activity: Children reflect about experience of making cookies in relation to "emotion faces" postcards, and then write and mail a postcard to a friend or parent	• Collect water from rain and snow (in relation to winter weather)	Parents can participate in activities by sending materials and recipes for cookies and by helping during performance of activities

Part II: Planning for Group Instruction During the Weekly Schedule

	Monday	*Tuesday*	*Wednesday*	*Thursday*	*Friday*
Group Time (songs, stories, games, discussions, etc.)	Valentine's Day song	Valentine's Day song	Valentine's Day song	Valentine's Day song	Valentine's Day song
Story Time	**Read a story** about Valentine's Day	**Read a story** about treasures	**Read a story** about going to the supermarket		

Small-Group Activities	Necklace activity	Buried-treasure activity	I go shopping activity	Make cards for friends or parents	Read emotions activity: Write and mail a card to a friend or parent
Special Activities (field trips, special events)	Plan a field trip to the post office to mail cards			**Coupon match activity for making cookies**	

Note: Stimulate children in small-group and free-choice activities in relation to curriculum objectives and academic standards.

Curriculum Objectives:

1. Plays well with other children
2. Controls small muscles in hands
3. Coordinates eye-hand movements
4. Uses tools for writing
5. Classifies objects
6. Recognizes patterns and can repeat them
7. Demonstrates knowledge of the alphabet
8. Uses emergent reading skills to make meaning from print
9. Writes letters and words

Guidelines for Instruction:

1. Identify theme for quarter and month
2. Select activities that will cover standards and content across developmental areas
3. Conduct activities in small groups so that you can individualize the curriculum
4. Stimulate the same skills and content standards across Stages 1, 2, and 3

Table 4.6 Sample Lesson Plan for the Ethnic-Educator Curriculum—Spring Quarter

Weekly Planning Form: Sample for Spring Quarter
THEME: Easter

Directions: Lesson plans will be written weekly and based on Head Start content standards, a select theme or topic, and individual goals for children.

Week: _____
Teacher: _____

Study/Project: _____
Assistant: _____

Part I: Instructional Areas and Activities

Blocks	Dramatic Play	Toys and Games	*Theme: Easter*
Add props for creating a post office, mail boxes, community helpers, mail trucks	Set up pretend grocery with props for making cookies, cash register, grocery ads, coupons, pencils, paper for grocery list **I go shopping activity:** Participate in a script of "buying at the supermarket" by getting all the ingredients necessary for sugar cookies and using coupons at the checkout	• Coupon matching game • Easter egg matching game • Eastern egg pattern game	*Spring Quarter (April)* **Head Start Standards Covered for Instruction** • **Cognition developmental area:** *Vocabulary and number:* Across three dimensions, space and time, counting in correct sequence, counts up to 20, uses one-to-one correspondence • **Classification:** Can sort and use patterns by three dimensions, compares across three abstract dimensions, can measure, can make and interpret abstract representations, engages in elaborate pretend roles and symbolic play, uses abstractions to learn, starts to decenter when prompted, shows task persistence, can think flexibly, when prompted can explore cause and effect • **Language developmental area:** *Phonemic Awareness:* Relates sounds to letters in news and familiar words

Art	Library	Discovery	Letter Recognition: Recognizes new and familiar words
Necklace activity: Sort and follow color and shape patterns to make an Easter necklace for Mom	**Read a story** about treasures, Easter day, making cookies, going to the supermarket **Writing center:** Make cards for friends or parents for Easter with writing materials, Easter cards, envelopes, postcards, egg-shaped paper, pretend stamps	**Buried-treasure activity:** Find letters in first name (first initial and all letters) written on or placed inside plastic eggs and then place them in an egg carton. Children can match the plastic eggs by color, size, or capital and lowercase letters (or different colors of letters or different sizes of letters—variations according to age of children)	*Reading:* Asks and answers questions and makes comments, uses emerging reading skills to make meaning from print, recognizes more than 15 letters, can use conventional letters to write own name and spell some letters of familiar words *Handwriting:* Can use conventional letters to write own name and some familiar words *Vocabulary:* Learns advanced words in relation to categories from stories read, images, and print
Sand and Water Spring colors sugar (or sand or cotton balls), cups, small bowls, and spoons	**Music and Movement** • Humpty Dumpty and other nursery rhymes • Phonemic awareness in relation to CDs with a spring theme	**Cooking** • Make letters with Jell-O in different flavors and colors (e.g., yellow Jell-O with a lemon flavor, yellow Jell-O with a pineapple flavor for teaching vocabulary of fruits and colors). Children can use multiple senses to learn letters and concepts of fruits and colors (e.g., they can smell, they can see, they can taste the different flavors of Jell-O)	*Eye-hand coordination:* Uses conventional letters to write own name and some familiar words • **Socioemotional developmental area:** *Prosocial behavior and sense of self:* Uses feedback, engages in dialogue, uses complex polite forms and variations in style, understands indirect speech and passive voice *Responsibility:* Uses self-help skills and takes responsibility for actions, objects, others, and well-being; shows social adaptation to new tasks and situations; demonstrates self-direction

(Continued)

Table 4.6 (Continued)

Computers	Outdoors	Family/Community Involvement
Reading emotions activity: Children reflect about experience of making Jell-O in relation to senses (taste/smell, citric/sour taste of lemons; sweet/tart, taste of cherries), then write and mail a postcard to a friend or parent, and make a graph for the colors and flavors of Jell-O that they liked	• Write with chalk of different colors in driveway	Parents can participate in activities by sending materials and recipes for cookies and by helping during performance of activities

Part II: Planning for Groups Instruction During the Weekly Schedule

	Monday	*Tuesday*	*Wednesday*	*Thursday*	*Friday*
Group Time (songs, stories, games, discussions, etc.)	Easter song	Easter song	Easter song	Easter song	Easter song
Story Time	**Read a story** about Easter	**Read a story** about treasures	**Read a story** about going to the supermarket		

Small-Group Activities	Necklace activity	Buried-treasure activity	I go shopping activity	Make cards for friends or parents	Read emotions activity: Write and mail a card to a friend or parent
Special Activities (field trips, special events)	Plan field trip to post office to mail cards			**Coupon match activity for making cookies**	

Note: Stimulate children in small-group and free-choice activities in relation to curriculum objectives and academic standards.

Curriculum Objectives:

1. Plays well with other children
2. Controls small muscles in hands
3. Coordinate eye-hand movements
4. Uses tools for writing
5. Classifies objects
6. Recognizes patterns and can repeat them
7. Demonstrates knowledge of the alphabet
8. Uses emergent reading skills to make meaning from print
9. Writes letters and words

Guidelines for Instruction

1. Identify theme for quarter and month
2. Select activities that will cover standards and content across developmental areas
3. Conduct activities in small groups so that you can individualize the curriculum
4. Stimulate the same skills and content standards across Stages 1, 2, and 3

clusters Head Start standards, content, and developmental areas in relation to the curriculum objectives and content standards.

INSTRUCTIONAL PURPOSES OF ASSESSMENT

Because this book is geared toward early childhood teachers as a main audience, this section discusses the instructional purposes of assessment. The objective is to provide useful information to teachers for implementing alternative assessments in their classroom to improve the learning progress and academic achievement of young, diverse children. Two classroom-based assessment strategies will be discussed in this section—observations and evaluations of developmental tasks, as examples of alternative assessments that provide tools for program evaluation and link assessment to instruction.

Classroom-Based Assessments as Tools for Program Evaluation

Classroom-based assessments can become a tool for accountability provided that early childhood teachers learn how to keep systematic records of children's progress in learning, development, and academic achievement. Systematic records are based on the establishment of criteria or standards—that is, operational or behaviorally defined performance in terms of behaviors and products that are identified based on a set of developmental benchmarks or objectives. These educational or learning objectives or goals are set based on expected developmental outcomes following criteria or standards defined by federal and state agencies and/or professional organizations (e.g., for the case of English-as-a-second-language (ESL) students, we abide by TESOL recommendations).

As well stated by the National Education Goals Panel (1998), "Pressed by demands for greater accountability and enhanced educational performance, states are developing standards for school-age children and are creating new criteria and approaches for assessing the achievement of challenging academic goals" (p. 5). These federal, state, and professional organization standards set minimum performances by grade level that need to be achieved across content areas as evidence or records of meeting standards, which are used as accountability systems for program evaluation and teachers' effectiveness. However, accountability systems are based on assessment programs that need to comply with basic psychometric standards assuring validity and reliability (see Gonzalez et al., 2006, for an extensive discussion of assessment validity issues).

Using alternative assessments is the best strategy for accomplishing the two wide purposes of assessment: (1) to inform instruction, by helping young, diverse children reach higher academic achievement levels, and (2) to document program evaluations and teachers' effectiveness in meeting accountability purposes. The recommended alternative assessment strategies for meeting these two wide assessment purposes are observations and developmental evaluation tasks. These two alternative assessment strategies offer natural and nonintrusive methods of documenting *baseline* (or *formative*) and *progress data* (or *summative* measures) about the individual and group performance of children in relation to demographic and educational factors (*aggregated* and *disaggregated data*) in relation to teachers' ratings, standards, and developmentally appropriate rubrics.

As discussed in this book, in relation to the principles of the ethnic-educator approach, continuous evaluation of progress is key to using alternative assessment feedback to introduce individualization of instruction in teaching and learning strategies, curriculum development, and lesson plans. For the case of young, diverse children, it is important to record learning and *developmental progress* because many diverse children from low-socioeconomic-status (SES) backgrounds are at risk for learning and developmental delays and underachievement. As recommended previously by Gonzalez, Brusca-Vega, and Yawkey, (1997), recording *summative evaluations* at successive established *intervals* (quarters) can help teachers document and demonstrate developmental growth and potential for learning through *qualitative descriptions* and *evaluations of significant changes* (i.e., showing the achievement of milestones and benchmarks) in learning processes and products. Then, classroom-based assessments provide the following:

1. Explicit links to instruction via descriptive, qualitative, and educationally applied feedback (i.e., in the form of analysis of thinking and learning processes, strengths and weaknesses, individual needs and interests)

2. A direct or *authentic* way of evaluating young, diverse children's behaviors in their natural learning environments (i.e., the real classroom setting)

Thus, by using individual data from classroom-based assessments, early childhood teachers can meet the main purpose of assessment (i.e., to link assessment to instruction). In addition, by using group data, educators can meet the second purpose of assessment (i.e., to validly and reliably collect wide-scale accountability data on students' progress in development and academic achievement and a systematic record of program evaluation and teachers' effectiveness).

INTEGRATION OF TEACHING PRINCIPLES WITH TESOL ACADEMIC CONTENT STANDARDS IN THE CURRICULUM

The TESOL (2005) standards complement the ethnic-educator pedagogical principles in terms of a pluralistic view of teaching and learning processes. In a pluralistic classroom environment, committed and caring teachers need to use language as a socialization and methodological tool for stimulating higher learning processes that also nurture the socioemotional development of young, culturally and linguistically diverse children (Gonzalez et al., 1997). TESOL standards and ethnic-educator pedagogical principles, in turn, complement and align with Head Start standards across language arts, mathematics, science, and social studies content areas, including prereading skills (i.e., phonemic awareness), language skills (i.e., vocabulary, listening, and speaking), cognitive skills (i.e., concept formation related to classification, time, and space), and socioemotional skills (i.e., responsibility, sense of self, and prosocial skills). Figure 4.1 shows an illustration of the intersection of TESOL standards, the ethnic-educator pedagogical principles, and the Head Start academic content standards.

As discussed earlier, Head Start academic content standards and their alignment with developmental milestones are analyzed across three age groups of preschoolers (Gonzalez et al., 2006), including (1) three- to four-year-olds using index learning processes, in which image representations of three-dimensional

Figure 4.1   Intersection of National TESOL Standards, Ethnic-Educator Pedagogical Principles, and Head Start Academic Content Standards

National TESOL Standards
- Uses English to communicate for social, intercultural, and instructional pruposes in the school setting
- Uses English to communicate information, ideas, and concepts achieved academically in all content areas: language arts, mathematics, science, and social studies
- To use English in socially and culturally appropriate ways

Pedagogical Principles of the Ethnic-Educator Approach
- Socioemotional nature of teaching and learning processes
- Internal and external factors interact in learning processes and development
- Pluralistic view of learning—uses alternative pedgogical strategies to link assessment to instruction
- Advocacy and commitment in teachers to development partnerships with diverse children and their families

Head Start Academic Content Standards
- Phonemic awareness
- Vocabulary skils
- Listening and speaking skills
- Classification skills
- Concept of time
- Concept of space
- Prereading skills
- Prewriting skills
- Responsibility
- Prosocial skills
- Sense of self

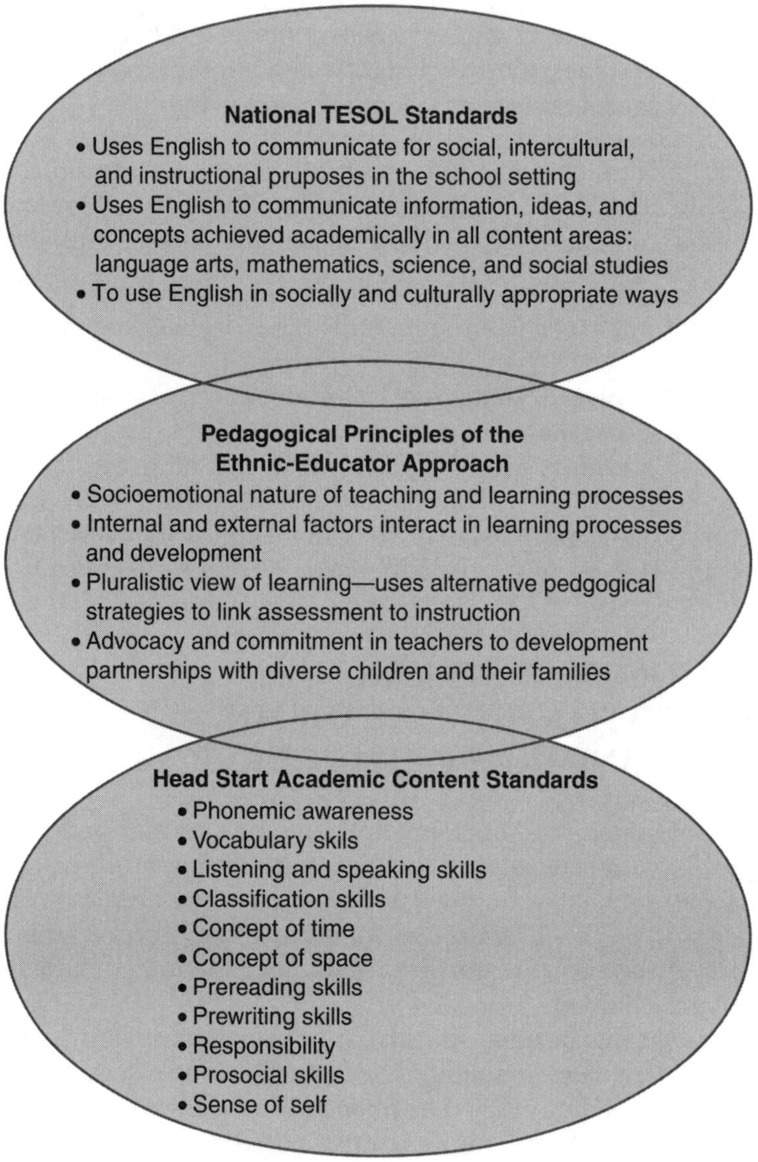

objects are used through actions, manipulation, and real-life experiences (e.g., using blocks to build a house, classifying objects by color); (2) four- to five-year-olds using symbolic learning processes, in which figural two-dimension representations of images (i.e., drawing, sketching, and finger painting) are used for direct or indirect imitation (i.e., model present or absent such as in pantomime or sociodramatic play, make-believe, or fantasy); and (3) five- to six-year-olds using sign learning processes, in which figural one-dimension representations of abstractions are used through verbal and nonverbal concepts (onomatopoeia—sounds of animals, phonemic awareness—beginning and ending letters in words, and pragmatics). Figure 4.2 shows the continuity across developmental milestones for the three age groups. Figure 4.3 shows the alignment of developmental milestones with Head Start and TESOL academic content standards across the three age groups.

In 2005, with the revision of the ESL standards for preK through Grade 12 students, TESOL provided guidelines that can be used by state departments of education and local school districts to develop best educational practices for ESL children. The TESOL standards establish goals and descriptors, progress indicators,

Figure 4.2   Representation of Continuity Across Alignment of Developmental Milestones for Three Age Groups

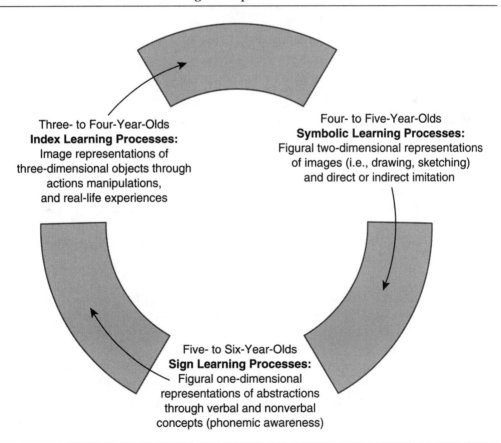

Figure 4.3 Representation of Alignment of Milestones Clustered by Cognitive, Language, Social, and Emotional Developmental Areas With Head Start and TESOL Academic Content Standards Across Subject Areas

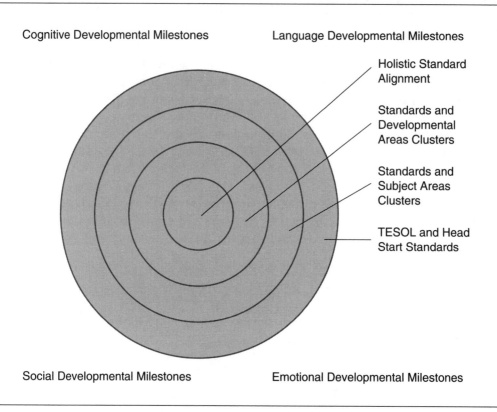

and best classroom strategies across grade levels. The TESOL standards take into consideration other national standards, such as the English language-arts and foreign-language standards. Even though there are commonalties between the TESOL and other standards, it acknowledges the particular needs of ESL children, including (1) the central role of language in learning content and (2) the cultural, linguistic, and developmental factors affecting learning and instruction, such as exposure to limited formal schooling.

The revised TESOL standards center on two main educational recommendations for young ESL children:

1. Use English to communicate in the school setting for social, intercultural, and instructional purposes. Children need to develop sociolinguistic and sociocultural competence (i.e., pragmatics). Language learning is embedded in learning social and cultural competence for understanding contextual uses of language (according to variety, genre, register, audience, purpose, and setting), nonverbal communication (e.g., gestures, physical proximity to people, eye-to-eye contact), and appropriate learning strategies. Cummins (1989, 1991) refers to pragmatics as bilingual interpersonal communication skills (BICS).

2. Use English to communicate information and concepts to increase academic achievement. Children need to use English as a learning tool to encode, process, construct, and express factual and conceptual knowledge across content areas. Children also need to use English as an abstract symbolic tool to engage in critical thinking, problem solving, and active learning. Cummins (1989, 1991) refers to this ability as cognitive, academic language-proficiency skills (CALPS).

According to Piper (2003), BICS refers to the acquisition of social functions of language, including (1) assert and maintain social needs and relations (i.e., make a demand, criticize, and assert identities, opinions, and observations); (2) inform (i.e., to talk about events, to make comparisons and generalizations, to request information, and to communicate past or present events); (3) project into novel situations (i.e., to make-believe roles in their symbolic play and to experience vicariously through other persons' perceptions, observations, thoughts, and feelings); (4) control self and others (i.e., monitor self in actions); and (5) direct attention, memory, and thinking as learning tools (i.e., apply strategies for language or content learning, use language as a cognitive or heuristic tool, discover information, think about causal relations, predict events, make inferences, and so on).

It is important to note that different cultures use diverse social communication styles and norms. For instance, the amount of nonverbal expressiveness or gestures and movement of the hands and body, proximity between speakers, and eye-to-eye contact varies dramatically across users of different languages. Other expressions of affective and emotional variables also differ widely across cultures, such as turn taking between speakers, tone and pitch of voice, fluency or speed of talk, rhythm, volume of voice, and so on. For instance, native Spanish speakers tend to speak very quickly and tend to interrupt one another while in a conversation as the negotiation of turn taking requires intervening in the other speakers' utterances and completing or following their thoughts; it is certainly a cultural art that nonnative speakers find difficult to master.

BICS, or pragmatic development, refers to the use of language for communication purposes in social and real-life situations. Pragmatic development involves the use of prior cultural and social knowledge and results in the development of sociolinguistic and sociocultural competence (Gonzalez et al., 2006). An example of pragmatic competence is the ability to use sociocultural conventions for meeting specific purposes (e.g., the use of active or passive voice to connote suggestions or orders, the use of a specific language to communicate some content to a particular person—this is especially used by ESL children). Therefore, language provides membership in a community by learning the social rules of language use in a social context. Thus, by learning a specific language speakers also learn the rules of effective communication for a large variety of purposes and in many different situations. In the case of young children, they need to achieve a balance between conceptual and language development to be able to express their content knowledge via conversational competence. That is, children need to learn pragmatics (involving terminology and sociolinguistic conventions) so that they can express meaning (achieved via semantic or cognitive academic competence). Then, pragmatic and semantic developmental areas are interconnected, as children need to learn both how to form verbal concepts and how to communicate them in socioculturally appropriate manners by using language.

Children learn pragmatics or conversational competence in natural contexts, such as school and home. Schooling provides the sociocultural context for learning pragmatics to meet the cognitive demands of learning tasks (Piper, 2003). For instance, children learn important pragmatic strategies at school, such as (1) learning to take the listener's perspective into account; (2) becoming sensitive to relevance of topic, content, and useful information; (3) learning to make conversational repairs, such as monitoring their oral and written language; (4) learning how to express their thoughts, opinions, suggestions, and requests in a socially acceptable manner; and (5) becoming socialized to different styles of speech according to cultural factors and contexts (e.g., academic versus social language, jargon, gender-based linguistic differences, accents, and dialects).

CALPS refers to the use of conceptual knowledge as a tool for learning across content areas. That is, competence in CALPS helps ESL students acquire new verbal (or semantic) and nonverbal concepts by using prior knowledge (i.e., assimilation) and the formation of new concepts (i.e., accommodation). Preliteracy and literacy skills emerge when ESL students achieve oral-language maturity and conceptual competence or CALPS. Conceptual competence refers to the ability to (1) use verbal and nonverbal representations to encode, store, and transform ideas, abstractions, generalizations, and categorizations; and (2) express verbal and nonverbal representations in the form of cognitive, metacognitive, and metalinguistic processes and learning behaviors (e.g., identifying attributes, events, and similarities for making comparisons and groupings).

Therefore, authentic language and authentic tasks that represent the daily life experiences of young, diverse children help them develop literacy skills and academic achievement across content areas. Teachers need to provide language stimulation as a natural learning process that requires young, diverse children to be exposed to social learning opportunities that respect their cultural identity and home and community experiences. Language learning needs to be a nurturing process that involves the collaborative partnership of educators, administrators, parents, and the whole community. In sum, the discussed interface of the TESOL and Head Start standards endorses a holistic developmental position that considers preliteracy skills as the interaction of language and cognitive processes in a sociocultural environment.

LINKING ASSESSMENT TO INSTRUCTION THROUGH CLASSROOM-BASED OBSERVATIONS

The sample lesson plans presented earlier in Tables 4.4, 4.5, and 4.6 are extended to links between instructional activities and classroom-based observations for the entire academic year by quarter (see Table 4.7 for fall quarter, Table 4.8 for winter quarter, and Table 4.9 for spring quarter). The milestones by developmental areas clustered with content standards are presented in three continuous age levels: (1) three- to four-year-olds using an index learning process, in which the child

(Text continued on page 111)

Weekly Planning Form: Sample Fall Quarter
THEME: Falling Leaves

Directions: Lesson plans will be written weekly and based on Head Start content standards, a selected theme and topic, and individual goals for children.

Week: _____

Study/Project: _____

Teacher: _____

Assistant: _____

Part I: Instructional Areas and Activities

		Theme: Falling Leaves
Blocks	**Dramatic Play**	*Fall Quarter (October)*
Add props to enhance block play: leaves, sticks, fall colors tissue paper, fall colors felt squares, glue, markers, fall colors construction paper, tape, rakes, and pails	Set up pretend grocery with props for making cookies, cash register, grocery ads, coupons, pencils, paper for grocery list	**Activities/Evaluation Tasks** • Necklace • Coupon match for making cookies • Buried treasures • Read a story about treasures, picnics, making cookies, and going to the supermarket
	I go to the park activity: Participate in a script of "going to a picnic" by getting all the food necessary to fill a picnic basket and use coupons at the checkout *Observe and assess reading skills*	**Standards Covered for Instruction and Assessment**
		• **Cognitive developmental area:** *Vocabulary, concept of number:* Across two dimensions only
Toys and Games • Coupon matching game • Leaves matching game • Leaves pattern game *Observe and assess sorting, patterning, and reading skills*		*Concept of space and time:* Counting may not be in correct sequence, cannot use one-to-one correspondence, *Classification:* Can sort and use patterns by one dimension, uses perception to learn from experiences, and manipulations of objects,
Art **Necklace activity:** Sort and follow color and shape patterns to make a leaves necklace for mom	**Library** **Read a story** about leaves, going to the park, enjoying a picnic, going to the supermarket	**Discovery** **Buried-treasure activity:** Fill sand and water station with assorted real leaves and encourage

(Continued)

Table 4.7 (Continued)

Observe and assess children's sorting and patterning skills	**Writing center:** Make cards for friends or parents to invite them to a picnic with writing materials, invitation cards, postcards, envelopes, pretend stamps.	children to find letters in their first name (first initial and all letters) written on leaf shapes. *Observe and assess phonemic awareness, letter recognition, reading skills*	compares based on one perceptual dimension only, starts from egocentricity of thought, uses single approach for tasks • **Language developmental area:** *Phonemic awareness:* Discriminates natural and environmental sounds *Letter recognition:* Recognizes some environmental print *Reading:* Can understand questions, recognizes fewer than 10 letters, can use mock letters to write own name *Handwriting:* Can scribble mock letters *Vocabulary:* Learns words from daily life objects and experiences, responds to questions when prompted by teacher *Eye-hand coordination:* Can scribble mock letters • **Socioemotional developmental area:** *Prosocial behavior and sense of self:* Responds to name and makes eye contact *Responsibility:* When prompted can use self-help skills and is still learning to be responsible for actions and well-being, appropriate trust in adults, learning to follow classroom routines and rules
Sand and Water • Children can sort leaves (or pinecones, nuts, plastic apples, small pumpkins, or gourds) by color, shape, and size and count leaves using one-to-one correspondence *Observe and assess phonemic awareness, letter recognition, and reading skills*	**Music and Movement** • Songs with a fall theme • Finger plays • Interactive charts	**Cooking** • Make fall-shape (pumpkins, apples, leaves) cookies and decorate in fall colors in relation to size (e.g., small pumpkin cookies are yellow, and larger pumpkin cookies are orange)	

Outdoors	Family/Community Involvement
Computers **Reading emotions activity:** Children reflect about experience of making cookies in relation to "emotion faces" postcards, and then write and mail a postcard to a friend or parent *Observe and assess children's writing skills and fine-motor coordination*	Parents can participate in activities by sending materials (e.g., collect pinecones, leaves, or acorns with child) and recipes for cookies and by helping during performance of activities

Part II: Planning for Groups Instruction During the Weekly Schedule

	Monday	*Tuesday*	*Wednesday*	*Thursday*	*Friday*
Group Time (songs, stories, games, discussions)	Fall or picnic song	Fall or picnic song	Fall or picnic song	Fall or picnic song	Fall or picnic song
Story Time	**Read a story** about going to the park	**Read a story** about picnics	**Read a story** about going to the supermarket		

(Continued)

Table 4.7 (Continued)

	Monday	Tuesday	Wednesday	Thursday	Friday
Small-Group Activities	**Necklace activity** *Observe and assess children's sorting and patterning skills*	**Buried-treasure activity** *Observe and assess phonemic awareness, letter recognition, and reading skills*	**I go shopping activity** *Observe and asses reading skills*	**Make cards for friends or parents** *Observe and assess children's writing skills and fine-motor coordination*	**Read emotions activity:** Write and mail a card to a friend or parent *Observe and assess children's writing skills and fine-motor coordination*
				Coupon match activity for making cookies *Observe and assess children's sorting and reading skills*	
Special Activities (field trips, special events)	Plan field trip to post office to mail cards				

Note: Observe children in small-group and free-choice activities in relation to content standards and checklist.

Curriculum Objectives

1. Plays well with other children
2. Controls small muscles in hands
3. Coordinate eye-hand movements
4. Uses tools for writing
5. Classifies objects
6. Recognizes patterns and can repeat them
7. Demonstrates knowledge of the alphabet
8. Uses emergent reading skills to make meaning from print
9. Writes letters and words

Guidelines for Linking Assessment With Instruction

1. Identify theme for quarter and month
2. Select activities that will cover standards and content across developmental areas
3. Conduct activities in small groups so that you can observe behaviors across standards for evaluation purposes
4. Complete checklist shortly after small-group activities are completed
5. Observe the same skills and standards across Stage 1 (fall), Stage 2 (winter), and Stage 3 (spring)

Checklist

Standards Covered for Instruction and Assessment

Cognitive Developmental Area: *Vocabulary and concept of number, space, time, and classification*

- Sorting and pattern dimensions used ___ color, ___ right/left, ___ size, ___ shape
- The child can count up to number ___
- The child can ___ cannot ___ do a one-to-one correspondence

Language Developmental Area: *Phonemic awareness, letter recognition, reading, and handwriting skills*

- Number of letters identified in name: ___
- Number of letters used for writing postcards: ___

Table Summary for the Skills of Identifying, Defining, and Describing Words, Realia, and Pictures

Words	Realia	Pictures
Familiar	Stage 1	Stage 2
New		Stage 2
Advanced		Stage 3

(Continued)

Table 4.7 (Continued)

Table Summary for Letter Identification

Letter	Name Group 1	Writing
D		
X		
O		
C		
W		
E		
K		
P		

Letter	Name Group 2	Writing
B		
Y		
N		
F		
T		
V		
M		
H		

Letter	Name Group 3	Writing
L		
A		
Q		
G		
S		
U		
I		
R		
J		
Z		

Total number of letters identified: _____

Eye-Hand Coordination
- The child can do _____ simple, _____ advanced, _____ complex eye-hand coordination

Weekly Planning Form: Sample for Winter Quarter
THEME: Valentine's Day

Directions: Lesson plans will be written weekly and based on head start content standards, a selected theme or topic, and individual goals for children.

Week: _____
Teacher: _____

Study/Project: _____
Assistant: _____

Part I: Instructional Areas and Activities

Blocks	Dramatic Play	Toys and Games	*Theme: Valentine's Day*
Add props for creating a post office, mail boxes, community helpers, mail trucks	Set up pretend grocery with props for making cookies, cash register, grocery ads, coupons, pencils, paper for grocery list	• Coupon matching game	*Winter Quarter (February)*
		• Heart matching game	**Activities/Evaluation Tasks:**
	I go shopping activity: Participate in a script of "buying at the supermarket" by getting all the ingredients necessary to make sugar cookies and using coupons at the checkout	• Heart pattern game	• Necklace
		Observe and assess sorting, patterning, and reading skills	• Buried treasures
			• Coupon catch for making cookies
	Observe and assess reading skills		• Read a story about treasures, Valentine's Day, making cookies, going to the supermarket
			Standards Covered for Instruction and Assessment
Art	**Library**	**Discovery**	• **Cognitive developmental area:**
Necklace activity: Sort and follow color and shape patterns to make a Valentine's necklace for Mom	**Read a story** about treasures, Valentine's Day, making cookies, going to the supermarket	**Buried-treasure activity:** Find letters in first name (first initial and all letters) written on hearts in a treasure box	*Vocabulary, concept of number:* Across two dimensions only, *Concepts of space and time:* Counting in correct sequence, counts up to 10, uses one-to-one correspondence
	Writing center: Make cards for friends or parents with writing materials, valentine cards, envelopes, postcards, heart-shaped paper, pretend stamps	*Observe and assess phonemic awareness, letter recognition, reading skills*	*Classification:* Can sort and
Observe and assess children's sorting and patterning skills			

(Continued)

99

Table 4.8 (Continued)

Activities	Developmental area
Sand and Water • Make-believe snow • Make ice cones with food flavors	use patterns by two dimensions, compares across two functional dimensions, can make and interpret figural representations, engages in pretend roles and symbolic play, needs to do to learn, figural thinking, starts to decenter, shows task persistence, can think flexibly, when prompted can explore cause and effect • **Language developmental area:** *Phonemic awareness:* Identifies rhyming sounds in familiar words *Letter Recognition:* Recognizes own name and some familiar words *Reading:* Asks questions and makes comments, recognizes over 10 letters, can use conventional letters to write own name *Handwriting:* Can use mock letters to write own name and familiar words *Vocabulary:* Learns new words from stories and images
Music and Movement • Right and left movements, top and down movements (for topological space in relation to readings and writing skills, e.g., "b" and "d" have a different R and L orientation, "p" and "b" have different top and down orientation)	
Cooking • Make letter-shaped cookies	

100

(Continued)

Eye-hand coordination: Can use mock letters to write own name and familiar words • **Socioemotional developmental area:** *Prosocial behavior and sense of self:* Uses simple forms of polite requests, understands only literal meanings of messages *Responsibility:* When prompted uses self-help skills and is still learning to be responsible for actions, objects, others, and well-being; can be independent and use self-direction; follows classroom routines and rules	
	Family/Community Involvement Parents can participate in activities by sending materials recipes for cookies and by helping during performance of activities
	Outdoors • Collect water from rain and snow (in relation to winter weather)
Computers **Reading emotions activity:** Children reflect about experience of making cookies in relation to "emotion faces" postcards, and then write and mail a postcard to a friend or parent. *Observe and assess children's writing skills and fine-motor coordination*	

101

Table 4.8 (Continued)

Part II: Planning for Group Instruction During the Weekly Schedule

	Monday	Tuesday	Wednesday	Thursday	Friday
Group Time (songs, stories, games, discussions)	Valentine's Day song	Valentine's Day song	Valentine's Day song	Valentine's Day song	Valentine's Day song
Story Time	Read a story about Valentine's Day	Read a story about treasures	Read a story about going to the supermarket		
Small-Group Activities	Necklace activity *Observe and assess children's sorting and patterning skills*	Buried-treasure activity *Observe and assess phonemic awareness, letter recognition, reading skills*	I go shopping activity *Observe and assess reading skills*	Make cards for friends or parents *Observe and assess children's writing skills and fine-motor coordination*	Read emotions activity: Write and mail a card to a friend or parent *Observe and assess children's writing skills and fine-motor coordination*
Special Activities (field trips, special events)	Plan a field trip to post office to mail cards			Coupon match activity for making cookies *Observe and assess children's sorting and reading skills*	

Note: Observe children in small-group and free-choice activities in relation to content standards and checklist.

Curriculum Objectives:

1. Plays well with other children
2. Controls small muscles in hands
3. Coordinates eye-hand movements
4. Uses tools for writing

5. Classifies objects

6. Recognizes patterns and can repeat them

7. Demonstrates knowledge of the alphabet

8. Uses emergent reading skills to make meaning from print

9. Writes letters and words

Guidelines for Linking Assessment With Instruction:

1. Identify theme for quarter and month

2. Select activities that will cover standards and content across developmental areas

3. Conduct activities in small groups so that you can observe behaviors across standards for evaluation purposes

4. Complete checklist shortly after small group activities are completed

5. Observe the same skills and standards across Stage 1 (fall), Stage 2 (winter), and Stage 3 (spring)

Checklist

Standards Covered for Instruction and Assessment

Cognitive Developmental Area: *Vocabulary and concepts of number, space, time, and classification*

- Sorting and pattern dimensions used ____ color, ____ right/left, ____ size, ____ shape
- The child can count up to number ____
- The child can ____ cannot ____ do a one-to-one correspondence

Language Developmental Area: *Phonemic awareness, letter recognition, reading, and handwriting skills*

- Number of letters identified in name: ____
- Number of letters used for writing postcards: ____

Table Summary for the Skills of Identifying, Defining, and Describing Words, Realia, and Pictures

Words	Realia	Pictures
Familiar	Stage 1	Stage 2
New		Stage 2
Advanced		Stage 3

(Continued)

Table 4.8 (Continued)

Table Summary for Letter Identification

Letter	Name	Writing
	Group 1	
D		
X		
O		
C		
W		
E		
K		
P		

Letter	Name	Writing
	Group 2	
B		
Y		
N		
F		
T		
V		
M		
H		

Letter	Name	Writing
	Group 3	
L		
A		
Q		
G		
S		
U		
I		
R		
J		
Z		

Total number of letters identified: ___

Eye-Hand Coordination

• The child can do ___ simple, ___ advanced, ___ complex eye-hand coordination

Table 4.9 Linking Classroom-Based Observations to Instruction—Spring Quarter

Weekly Planning Form: Sample Spring Quarter
THEME: Easter

Directions: Lesson plans will be written weekly and based on Head Start content standards, a selected theme or topic, and individual goals for children

Week: _____

Study/Project: _____

Teacher: _____

Assistant: _____

Part I: Instructional Areas and Activities

Blocks	Dramatic Play	Toys and Games	*Theme: Easter*
Add props for creating a post office, mail boxes, community helpers, mail trucks	Set up a pretend grocery with props for making cookies, cash register, grocery ads, coupons, pencils, paper for grocery list	• Coupon matching game • Easter egg matching game • Easter egg pattern game *Observe and assess sorting, patterning and reading skills*	*Spring Quarter (April)* **Activities/Evaluation Tasks:** • Necklace • Coupon match for making cookies • Buried treasures • Read a story about treasures, Easter, making cookies, going to the supermarket **Standards Covered for Instruction and Assessment** • **Cognitive developmental area:** *Vocabulary, concept of number:* Across three dimensions *Concepts of space and time:* Counting in correct sequence, counts up to 20, uses one-to-one correspondence *Classification:* Can sort and use patterns by three dimensions, compares across three abstract dimensions, can measure, can make and interpret abstract representations, engages in elaborate pretend roles and
	I go shopping activity: Participate in a script of "buying at the supermarket" by getting all the ingredients necessary for sugar cookies and using coupons at the checkout *Observe and assess reading skills*		

(Continued)

Table 4.9 (Continued)

Art	Library	Discovery	
Necklace activity: Sort and follow color and shape patterns to make an Easter necklace for Mom *Observe and assess children's sorting and patterning skills*	**Read a story** about treasures, Easter, making cookies, going to the supermarket **Writing center:** Make cards for friends or parents for Easter with writing materials, Easter cards, envelopes, post-cards, egg-shaped paper, pretend stamps	**Buried-treasure activity:** Find letters in first name (first initial and all letters) written on or placed inside plastic eggs and then place them in an egg carton. Children can match the plastic eggs by color, size, or capital and lowercase letters (or different colors of letters or different sizes of letters—variations according to age of children) *Observe and assess phonemic awareness, letter recognition, reading skills*	symbolic play, uses abstractions to learn, starts to decenter when prompted, shows task persistence, and can think flexibly, when prompted can explore cause and effect • **Language development area:** *Phonemic awareness:* Relates sounds to letters in news and familiar words *Letter recognition:* Recognizes new and familiar words *Reading:* Asks and answers questions and makes comments, uses emerging reading skill to make meaning from print, recognizes over 15 letters, can use conventional letters to write own name and spell some letters of familiar words *Handwriting:* Can use conventional letters to write own name and some familiar words *Vocabulary:* Learns advanced words in relation to categories and subcategories from stories read, images, and print • **Gross-motor area:** *Eye-hand coordination:* Can use conventional letters to write own name and some familiar words • **Socioemotional area:** *Prosocial behavior and sense of self:* Uses feedback, engages in dialogue, uses complex polite forms and variations in style, understands indirect speech and passive voice
Sand and Water • Spring colors sugar (or sand or cotton balls), cups, small bowls, and spoons.	**Music and Movement** • "Humpty Dumpty" and other nursery rhymes • Phonemic awareness in relation to CDs with a spring theme	**Cooking** • Make letters with Jell-O in different flavors and colors (e.g., yellow Jell-O with a lemon flavor, yellow Jell-O with a pineapple flavor for teaching vocabulary of fruits and colors).	

		Responsibility: Uses self-help skills and takes responsibility for actions, objects, others, and well-being; shows social adaptation to new tasks and situations; demonstrates self-direction and independence
	Children can use multiple senses to learn letters and concepts of fruits and colors (e.g., they can smell, they can see, they can taste the different flavors of Jell-O)	
	Family/Community Involvement Parents can participate in activities by sending materials and recipes for cookies and by helping during performance of activities	
Outdoors • Write with chalk of different colors in driveway		
Computers **Reading emotions activity:** Children reflect about experience of making Jell-O in relation to senses (taste and smell, citrus and sour taste of lemons; sweet and tart taste of cherries), and then write and mail a postcard to a friend or parent Children can also make a graph for the colors and flavors of Jell-O that their classmates liked *Observe and assess children's writing skills and fine-motor coordination*		

(Continued)

Table 4.9 (Continued)

Part II: Planning for Group Instruction During the Weekly Schedule

	Monday	Tuesday	Wednesday	Thursday	Friday
Group Time (songs, stories, games, discussions)	Easter song	Easter song	Easter song	Easter song	Easter song
Story Time	**Read a story about** Easter	**Read a story about** treasures	**Read a story** about going to the supermarket		
Small-Group Activities	Necklace activity	Buried-treasure activity	I go shopping activity	Make cards for friends parents	Read emotions activity: Write and mail a card to a friend or parent
	Observe and assess children's sorting and patterning skills	*Observe and assess phonemic awareness, letter recognition, reading skills*	*Observe and assess reading skills*	*Observe and assess children's writing skills and fine-motor coordination*	*Observe and assess children's writing skills and fine-motor coordination*
Special Activities (field trips, special events)	Plan field trip to post office to mail cards			**Coupon match activity for making cookies**	
				Observe and assess children's sorting and reading skills	

Note: Observe children in small-group and free-choice activities in relation to standards and checklist.

Curriculum Objectives

1. Plays well with other children
2. Controls small muscles in hands

3. Coordinates eye-hand movements

4. Uses tools for writing

5. Classifies objects

6. Recognizes patterns and can repeat them

7. Demonstrates knowledge of the alphabet

8. Uses emergent reading skills to make meaning from print

9. Writes letters and words

Guidelines for Linking Assessment With Instruction

1. Identify theme for quarter and month

2. Select activities that will cover standards and content across developmental areas

3. Conduct activities in small groups so that you can observe behaviors across standards for evaluation purposes

4. Complete checklist shortly after small-group activities are completed

5. Observe the same skills and standards across Stage 1 (fall), Stage 2 (winter), and Stage 3 (spring)

Checklist

Standards Covered for Instruction and Assessment

Cognitive Developmental Area: *Vocabulary, concepts of number, space, time, and classification*

- Sorting and pattern dimensions used ___ color, ___ right/left, ___ size, ___ shape
- The child can count up to number ___
- The child can ___ cannot ___ do a one-to-one correspondence ___

Language Developmental Area: Phonemic awareness, letter recognition, reading, and handwriting skills

- Number of letters identified in name: ___
- Number of letters used for writing postcards: ___

(Continued)

Table 4.9 (Continued)

Table Summary for the Skills of Identifying, Defining, and Describing Words, Realia, and Pictures

Words	Realia	Pictures
Familiar	Stage 1	Stage 2
New		Stage 2
Advanced		Stage 3

Table Summary for Letter Identification

Letter	Name	Writing
	Group 1	
D		
X		
O		
C		
W		
E		
K		
P		

Letter	Name	Writing
	Group 2	
B		
Y		
N		
F		
T		
V		
M		
H		

Letter	Name	Writing
	Group 3	
L		
A		
Q		
G		
S		
U		
I		
R		
J		
Z		

Total number of letters identified: _____

Eye-Hand Coordination

• The child can do _____ simple, _____ advanced, _____ complex eye-hand coordination constructs image representations of three-dimensional objects through actions, manipulation, and real-life experiences (e.g., using blocks to build a house, classifying objects by color); (2) four- to five-year-olds using a symbolic learning process, in which the child constructs figural two-dimensional representations of images, such as drawing, sketching, and finger painting, which could use *direct* or *indirect imitation* (model present or absent) through pantomime or sociodramatic play (make-believe or fantasy); and (3) five- to six-year-olds using an abstract learning process, in which the child constructs figural one-dimensional representations of abstractions through verbal and nonverbal concepts (*onomatopoeia*–sounds of animals, *phonemic awareness*–beginning and ending letters in words, and *pragmatics*).

The extension of instructional activities to links with classroom-based assessments is done using the same content standards, instructional areas, and curriculum objectives. In addition, the same guidelines for instruction are extended to links between assessment and instruction through classroom-based observations, including (1) the identification of themes by quarter and month in relation to children's interests and diverse backgrounds, (2) the selection of instructional activities that cover content standards across developmental areas, (3) the implementation of instructional activities in small groups for teachers to observe target behaviors across content standards, (4) the completion of checklists after small-group activities, and (5) the observation of the same skills and content standards during the three quarters across three continuous age levels of learning processes (i.e., at the index, symbolic, and abstract levels).

At the end of Tables 4.7, 4.8, and 4.9, checklists are included, which summarize the particular target behaviors by developmental milestones and content standards. These checklists provide teachers quick tools for summarizing their classroom observations when planning small-group activities that provide links between assessment and instruction. Finally, Table 4.10 presents a checklist in a multiple observation format that facilitates for teachers the recording of classroom observations in the context of small-group activities.

Early childhood teachers can increase the quality of instruction that they provide to young, diverse children by linking assessment to instruction through classroom-based evaluations. The increase in the number of diverse children in American schools should be viewed as a time to reform and restructure early childhood education to foster holistic learning and equal opportunities for education (Barona & García, 1990). Using alternative assessments in the classroom is key for teachers to improve the quality of instruction by becoming active participants in the accurate evaluation of young, diverse children. This chapter presented classroom-based observations as pedagogical strategies for linking assessment to instruction by representing developmental milestones and content standards, individualizing the curriculum, and providing high-quality instruction for young, diverse children intended to develop their learning potential and achieve at higher levels. In the next chapter, we extend the application of pedagogical strategies for linking assessment, instruction, and the use of developmental tasks that represent academic content standards endorsed by Head Start and TESOL. Pedagogical strategies, classroom-based observations, and developmental tasks put into action the ethnic-educator philosophy, pedagogical principles, and strategies that link assessment to instruction.

Table 4.10 Multiple-Format Checklist Linking Assessment to Instruction

Standards	Child 1: Name ___	Child 2: Name ___	Child 3: Name ___
Cognition *Vocabulary concepts of number, space, time, and classification*	• Sorting and pattern dimensions used ___ color, ___ right/left, ___ size, ___ shape • The child can count up to number ___ • The child ___ can ___ cannot do a one-to-one correspondence	• Sorting and pattern dimensions used ___ color, ___ right/left, ___ size, ___ shape • The child can count up to number ___ • The child ___ can ___ cannot do a one-to-one correspondence	• Sorting and pattern dimensions used ___ color, ___ right/left, ___ size, ___ shape • The child can count up to number ___ • The child ___ can ___ cannot do a one-to-one correspondence
Language *Phonemic awareness* *Letter recognition* *Reading* *Handwriting*	• Number of letters identified in name: ___ • Number of letters used for writing postcards: ___	• Number of letters identified in name: ___ • Number of letters used for writing postcards: ___	• Number of letters identified in name: ___ • Number of letters used for writing postcards: ___
Table summary for the skills of identifying, defining, and describing words, realia, and pictures	Words / Realia / Pictures: Familiar — Stage 1, Stage 2; New — Stage 2; Advanced — Stage 3	Words / Realia / Pictures: Familiar — Stage 1, Stage 2; New — Stage 2; Advanced — Stage 3	Words / Realia / Pictures: Familiar — Stage 1, Stage 2; New — Stage 2; Advanced — Stage 3
Hand coordination	The child can do ___ simple, ___ advanced, ___ complex eye-hand coordination	The child can do ___ simple, ___ advanced, ___ complex eye-hand coordination	The child can do ___ simple, ___ advanced, ___ complex eye-hand coordination

Nested "Table summary" grids (same for each child):

Words	Realia	Pictures
Familiar	Stage 1	Stage 2
New		Stage 2
Advanced		Stage 3

Letter identification

Letter	Name	Writing
Group 1		
D		
X		
O		
C		
W		
E		
K		
P		
Group 2		
B		
Y		
N		
F		
T		
V		
M		
H		

Letter	Name	Writing
Group 1		
D		
X		
O		
C		
W		
E		
K		
P		
Group 2		
B		
Y		
N		
F		
T		
V		
M		
H		

Letter	Name	Writing
Group 1		
D		
X		
O		
C		
W		
E		
K		
P		
Group 2		
B		
Y		
N		
F		
T		
V		
M		
H		

(Continued)

Table 4.10 (Continued)

Letter	Name	Writing
	Group 3	
L		
A		
Q		
G		
S		
U		
I		
R		
J		
Z		

Total number of letters identified: _____

Letter	Name	Writing
	Group 3	
L		
A		
Q		
G		
S		
U		
I		
R		
J		
Z		

Total number of letters identified: _____

Letter	Name	Writing
	Group 3	
L		
A		
Q		
G		
S		
U		
I		
R		
J		
Z		

Total number of letters identified: _____

5

Developmental Tasks for Linking Assessment to Instruction

Chapter 5 introduces developmental tasks as pedagogical strategies of the ethnic-educator approach for linking assessment to instruction for young, diverse children. This chapter introduces a collection of *developmental tasks* that represents academic content standards endorsed by Head Start and Teachers of English to Speakers of Other Languages (TESOL; 2005). In a case study, Paula is used to illustrate the application of developmental tasks to evaluate young, diverse children. Paula is a five-year-old, Hispanic, bilingual (English/Spanish) child, who attended the Bilingual Preschool Development Center (BPDC). Paula's performance across developmental tasks in two languages (Spanish and English) is used to illustrate classroom-based assessments that represent cultural and linguistic diversity for young children. These developmental tasks were used in the BPDC and extend curriculum, presented in previous chapters, to link assessment and instruction. The developmental tasks presented in this chapter complement the classroom-based observations presented in Chapter 4, as both are alternative assessments with instructional purposes.

Teachers can adapt developmental tasks to the idiosyncratic and culturally and linguistically diverse characteristics of young children because they are methods of assessment (Gonzalez & Riojas-Clark, 1999). In addition, when teachers use developmental tasks that are also included as regular curriculum activities, instructional materials, and strategies, the accuracy (i.e., validity and reliability) of assessment increases for young children. When teachers record the children's performance on developmental tasks, assessment becomes an authentic record of children's natural behaviors in the classroom. Paula's case study illustrates how teachers can use developmental tasks as authentic or alternative measures that are more valid and reliable for young, diverse children. These later assessment practices follow the *Standards for Educational and Psychological Testing* (American Educational Research Association [AERA], American Psychological Association [APA], and National Council for Measurement and Education [NCME], 1999) and the National Education Goals Panel's *Principles and Recommendations for Early Childhood Assessments* (1998).

CASE STUDY INTRODUCING
INDIVIDUAL DEVELOPMENTAL TASKS

By the time of evaluation, Paula was a five-year-old English- and Spanish-speaking child, who had been enrolled in the BPDC for approximately seven months on a half-day schedule. She had approximately 450 hours of combined Spanish and English instruction at the BPDC, where instruction emphasized preliteracy and content-area skills. Before enrolling in the BPDC, Paula had not received formal schooling. Paula had two older brothers (ages ten and seven at the time of evaluation), and her parents and siblings spoke both English and Spanish at home. Paula's family immigrated to the United States from Guatemala before she was born, and she moved with her family to Cincinnati from Chicago when she was three years old. So Paula was a U.S. citizen, as she was born in Chicago, and she had been exposed to both Spanish and English before attending the BPDC.

Paula's teachers rated her language development as very advanced and considered her as an English-dominant child, with an intermediate level of Spanish proficiency. Paula was a bilingual child with a gift for language development. She was very articulate and could adapt easily to social and cultural situations that required her to use Spanish or English. Paula could communicate using one or two languages with monolingual or bilingual teachers and peers, and she could even translate from one language to the other for her monolingual teachers or peers. Because of Paula's gift in the areas of interpersonal and verbal intelligence, she was chosen as a case study to compare her performance on developmental tasks in language, literacy skills and cognitive and socioemotional areas in Spanish and English languages. Paula's teachers rated her development across languages by the end of the winter quarter. Table 5.1 shows the developmental tasks used to evaluate Paula in small-group situations, including (1) letter recognition, (2) handwriting and eye-hand coordination, (3) vocabulary definition, (4) phonemic awareness, (5) concept of classification, (6) concept of number, (7) concept of space, (8) concept of time, (9) prosocial behaviors, (10) responsibility skills, and (11) sense-of-self skills. The definitions of the developmental tasks across index, symbolic, and sign levels are provided as the evaluation tasks are presented for the case study. Paula was evaluated by her English and Spanish teachers because dual-language administrations across developmental tasks were used. The evaluations were administered in the natural context of Paula's classroom during a two-week interval in the winter quarter. The developmental tasks presented used familiar instructional materials and activities to show amount of learning, and unfamiliar materials were used to show potential for learning (Gonzalez, Brusca-Vega, & Yawkey, 1997; Gonzalez & Riojas-Clark, 1999).

Letter Recognition Developmental Task

Definition (Index Level)

The letter recognition developmental task is at the index level because it represents memorized labels of letters, with no need for the child to identify meanings

Table 5.1   Paula's Performance in Developmental Tasks

Developmental Tasks	Spanish Results	English Results
1. Letter recognition	• 14 out of 26 correct (index level)	• 18 out of 26 correct (index level)
2. Handwriting and eye-hand coordination skills	Task 1 (index level) • 12 out of 28 correct	Task 1 (index level) • 17 out of 26 correct
3. Vocabulary definition	Stage 3 (index, symbolic, and sign levels)	Stage 3 (index, symbolic, and sign levels)
4. Phonemic awareness	• 10 out of 10 correct natural and environmental sounds (index level) • 6 out of 8 correct responses (symbolic level) • 5 out of 8 correct responses (sign level)	• 10 out of 10 correct natural and environmental sounds (index level) • 8 out of 8 correct responses (symbolic level) • 7 out of 8 correct responses (sign level)
5. Concept of classification	Stage 3	Stage 3 (with more detailed verbal explanations)
6. Concept of number	Stage 2 (without mastery of concept of one-to-one correspondence) • 7 out of 10 with correct total number of responses	Stage 3 (with mastery of concept of one-to-one correspondence) • 10 out of 10 with incorrect total number of items
7. Concept of space	Stage 2	Stage 3 (with more detailed verbal explanations)
8. Concept of time	Stage 3	Stage 3 (with more detailed verbal explanations)
9. Prosocial behaviors	Stage 3	Stage 3
10. Responsibility skills	Stage 2	Stage 2
11. Sense-of-self skills	Stage 2	Stage 2

of labels (Gonzalez, Yawkey, & Minaya-Rowe, 2006; Piper, 2003; Valencia, 1994). Letters can be presented to children on small cards and in the same font that they have been exposed to during instructional activities. Clustering letters in three groups allows teachers to segment the task into three units, which helps young children focus their attention and take short breaks between groups of letters. The selected three groups of letters provided in the Recording Form lists letters randomly so that children cannot recall a memorized string of letters from automatic memory.

Instructions (Index Level)

These are the letters of the alphabet. Tell me the name of the letter that I am going to point to (divide the letters in groups of eight). If the child does not respond, tell him or her the letter and move on to the next one. You can come back to the letter and see if the child can remember the letter's name.

Recording Form

Letter	Correct	Incorrect	Letter	Correct	Incorrect	Letter	Correct	Incorrect
Group 1			**Group 2**			**Group 3**		
D			B			L		
X			Y			A		
O			N			Q		
C			F			G		
W			T			S		
E			V			U		
K			M			I		
P			H			R		

Total number of letters identified: ___

Paula's Performance

Paula could identify 18 out of the 26 letters of the alphabet in English and only 14 letters in Spanish. She could identify the same letters in English and Spanish. Besides naming the letters, Paula also attempted to give some examples of words that started with the letters, such as names of classmates and labels for common items (e.g., "This is *B*, as in Bob." "This is *P*, as in pear").

Handwriting and Eye-Hand Coordination Developmental Task

Definition for Task 1 (Index Level)

Task 1 of the handwriting and eye-hand coordination developmental task is at the index level because it requires the child just to copy the letters of familiar words, with no need to identify the meanings of labels (Gonzalez et al., 2006; Witt, Elliott, Kremer, & Gresham, 1994; Wodrich & Kush, 1990). Letters can be presented to children on small cards and in the same font that they have been exposed to during instructional activities. Presenting letters in the context of familiar words allows teachers to link assessment to instruction and record an authentic measure of children's learning (Gonzalez et al., 1997). Teachers should select some words familiar to the children from the ones used during instructional activities. For both familiar and unfamiliar words, teachers should select words that represent all 26 letters of the alphabet, from easy ones (e.g., "A," "P") to more difficult ones (e.g., "W," "H"). For instance, words should represent thematic vocabulary items taught in lessons through reading stories and storytelling activities. The Recording Form includes six different familiar and unfamiliar words so that the child's performance is based on a representative sample.

Instructions for Task 1 (Index Level)

Here we have some cards with some words on them that you have seen before. Each card has a different name. I want you to write these names the best you can.

Example 1

Here is the first card. What are some letters that you know? Can you copy these letters? Do you know what this card says?

Recording Form

Words	Child's Response	Stage

Paula's Performance

Paula could copy most familiar letters of words in English and in Spanish. She could copy 17 letters in English (with 65% of letters copied correctly, 17 out of 26), and 12 letters in Spanish (with 46% of letters copied correctly, 12 out of 26). She could copy the same letters in English and Spanish. While copying the letters, Paula also attempted to name the letters and started sounding some of the letters to decode the familiar words' meanings.

Definition for Task 2 (Index Level)

Task 2 of the handwriting and eye-hand coordination developmental task is at the index level because it requires the child just to copy letters in familiar and unfamiliar words, with no need to identify meanings of labels (Gonzalez et al., 2006; Witt et al., 1994; Wodrich & Kush, 1990). Letters can be presented to children on small cards and in the same font that they have been exposed to during instructional activities. Presenting letters in the context of familiar words allows teachers to link assessment to instruction and record an authentic measure of children's learning (Gonzalez et al., 1997). Moreover, presenting letters in the context of unfamiliar words gives the teacher an opportunity to assess children's potential for learning. Teachers should select some words familiar to the children from the ones used for instructional activities. For both familiar and unfamiliar words, teachers should select words that represent all 26 letters of the alphabet, from easy ones (e.g., "A," "P") to more difficult ones (e.g., "W," "H"). For instance, words should represent thematic vocabulary items taught in lessons through reading stories and storytelling activities. The Recording Form includes six different familiar and unfamiliar words so that the child's performance is based on a representative sample.

Instructions for Task 2 (Index Level)

Here we have cards with some words on them. Each card has a different name, some words you have seen before, and others you have not. I want you to write these letters the best you can.

Example 2

Here is our first card. What are some letters that you know? Can you copy these letters? Do you know what this card says?

Recording Form

Words	Child's Response	Stage

Words	Child's Response	Stage

Paula's Performance

Paula could copy most letters of familiar and unfamiliar words in English and in Spanish. She could copy 17 letters in English (with 65% of letters copied correctly, 17 out of 26), and 12 letters in Spanish (with 46% of letters copied correctly, 12 out of 26), for both languages in the context of both familiar and unfamiliar words. She could copy the same letters in English and Spanish. While copying the letters, Paula also attempted to name the letters but attempted to sound out the letters only of familiar words to decode there meaning.

Vocabulary Definition Developmental Task

Definition (Index Level)

The vocabulary definition developmental task is at the index level because actual familiar objects are presented to the child for providing definitions (Gonzalez et al., 2006; Piper, 2003; Valencia, 1994; Vygotsky, 1986). Examples of different developmental levels of responses are provided so that children can show the developmental level at which they understand concepts modeled. Teachers should select both familiar and unfamiliar words to see whether level of familiarity affects the stage at which children reason with verbal concepts (Gonzalez et al., 1997). Familiar words represent children's authentic performance with regular classroom activities. Unfamiliar words extend children's performance to the assessment of potential for learning. About six words total are suggested to have a sample that represents children's performance. Teachers should select the familiar words from the curriculum activities.

Instructions (Index Level)

Here we have some objects that you have seen before. Each object has a different name. I want you to tell me the name of the object and then tell me all that you know about the object.

Example 1

What is this? This is a pencil. What are pencils? Pencils are long sticks that we use for writing or drawing. Pencils can be long or short and can be of different colors.

Example 2

What is this? This is a banana. What are bananas? Bananas are yellow, long, and are for eating. They are fruits and food.

Recording Form

Words	Child's Responses	Stage
Apple		
Ball		
Book		
Cup		
Rabbit		
Tree		

Scoring

Stages indicate children's level of conceptual understanding of examples. According to socioconstructivistic theory (Gonzalez et al., 2006; Piper, 2003; Valencia, 1994; Vygotsky, 1986), three stages can be identified in children's responses: (1) Stage 1—the child provides definitions of vocabulary based on perceptual attributes of objects (e.g., apples are red but can also be yellow, books can be big or small); (2) Stage 2—the child provides definitions of vocabulary based on functional characteristics of objects (e.g., an apple is for eating, a ball is for playing); and (3) Stage 3—the child provides definitions of vocabulary based on abstract categories of objects (e.g., apples are fruit and also food, rabbits are animals).

Paula's Performance

Paula defined vocabulary items at the Stage 3 level in a consistent manner (five out of six items—a majority of items needs to be defined at the same level for children to be placed in a particular stage). Her performance was also consistent across languages of administration. Paula showed ability to define objects using categories and subcategories and could make relations to her prior sociocultural knowledge and academic knowledge learned at school. For instance, for the item "rabbit," she said in English, "They are little animals that bounce and jump. Rabbits like to eat carrots, radishes, and cabbage. I like the story of *Peter Rabbit* that we read in class the other day." In Spanish, Paula's remarks for this same vocabulary item showed understanding at the conceptual level, with the addition of other acquired sociocultural knowledge. Paula said in Spanish, "Me gustan mucho los conejos, son animalitos muy juguetones. El otro dia vi un conejito blanco, con una colita muy chiquita, que estaba saltando por el parque." (I really like rabbits. They are little animals that like to play around. The other day, I saw a little white rabbit, with a very small tail. It was jumping around the park.)

Definition (Symbolic and Sign Levels)

The vocabulary definition developmental task is at the symbolic and sign levels because graphic representations of familiar objects are presented to the child for providing definitions (Gonzalez et al., 2006; Piper, 2003; Valencia, 1994; Vygotsky, 1986). Examples of different developmental levels of responses are provided for the children so that children can show the developmental level at which they understand concepts modeled. Teachers should select both familiar and unfamiliar words to see whether level of familiarity affects the stage at which children reason with verbal concepts (Gonzalez et al., 1997). Familiar words represent children's authentic performance with regular classroom activities. Unfamiliar words extend children's performance to the assessment of potential for learning. About six words total are suggested to have a sample that represents children's performance. Teachers should select the actual familiar words from the curriculum activities.

Instructions for the Vocabulary Definition Developmental Task (Symbolic and Sign Levels)

Here we have some pictures of objects; some you have seen before while others may be new. Each object has a different name. I want you to tell me the name of the object, and then tell me all that you know about the object.

Example 1

What is this? This is a table. What are tables? Tables can have different shapes such as squares, rectangles, or circles that we use for writing, drawing, eating, and doing many other things. Tables can be big or small and can be different colors.

Example 2

What is this? This is a tortilla. What are tortillas? Tortillas are flat and round and are for eating. They are food.

Recording Form

Words	Child's Responses	Stage
Apple		
Ball		
Book		

Words	Child's Responses	Stage
Camel		
Sunflower		
Coconut		

Scoring

Stages indicate children's level of conceptual understanding of examples. Three stages can be identified in children's responses: (1) Stage 1—the child provides definitions of vocabulary based on perceptual attributes of objects (e.g., apples are red but can also be yellow, books can be big or small); (2) Stage 2—the child provides definitions of vocabulary based on functional characteristics of objects (e.g., an apple is for eating, a ball is for playing); and (3) Stage 3—the child provides definitions of vocabulary based on abstract categories of objects (e.g., apples are fruit and also food, rabbits are pets and are also animals).

Paula's Performance

She maintained her vocabulary definitions at the Stage 3 level for both languages of administration, showing that her abstract level of reasoning with verbal concepts was stable for two-dimensional (pictures) and three-dimensional (objects) stimuli. Even when she could not manipulate actual objects, with the sole presence of pictures, Paula still defined words based on abstract attributes (such as categories and subcategories).

Phonemic Awareness Developmental Task

Definition (Index Level)

The phonemic awareness developmental task is at the index level because instructions and examples represent natural sounds (like an animal) and environmental sounds (like a fire engine) (Gonzalez et al., 2006; Piper, 2003; Valencia, 1994; Vygotsky, 1986). Teachers should select familiar natural and environmental sounds that have been used in instruction (Gonzalez et al., 1997). Familiar words represent children's authentic performance with regular classroom activities. Teachers need to use about ten sounds to have a sample that represents children's performance.

Instructions (Index Level)

Here we have some objects. Each object makes a different sound. I want you to make the sound that the object makes. Objects are divided in two different bags.

Example 1

This is a cat. Cats go "meow."

Example 2

This is a fire engine. Fire engines go "uuuh, uuuhh, honk, honk."

Recording Form

Sound	Natural	Correct	Incorrect
Natural Sounds			
Ruff	Dog		
Oink	Pig		
Moo	Cow		
Chirp	Bird		
Waaah	Baby crying		
Environmental Sounds			
Choo-choo	Train		
Boom	Thunder		
Ding, dong	Door bell		
Vroom, vroom	Cars		
Pom, pom	Footsteps		

Paula's Performance

She could correctly make all natural and environmental sounds (10 out of 10 correct responses) in both languages of administration, as was expected for her age. Paula even made gestures while making the sounds that represented some characteristics of the animals, people, and objects from which the natural and environmental sounds originated. It was very interesting to observe how Paula knew how some animal sounds were represented differently in English and Spanish (e.g., "gua gua" for dogs in Spanish). This ability attested to her metalinguistic awareness, as she knew the sociocultural differences in how sounds are represented in different languages.

Definition (Symbolic Level)

The phonemic awareness developmental task is at the symbolic level because instructions and examples presented to the child use two-dimensional objects, such as pictures (Gonzalez et al., 2006; Piper, 2003; Valencia, 1994; Vygotsky, 1986). Teachers should select words that have been used in instruction. Familiar words represent children's authentic performance with regular classroom activities (Gonzalez et al., 1997). About ten sounds are used in two groups of five cards each so that young children can focus their attention while selecting the card. Ten items are suggested to have a sample that represents children's performance.

Instructions for the Phonemic Awareness Developmental Task (Symbolic Level)

Here we have some cards with pictures on them. Each picture begins with a different letter. I want you to point the card that has the letter I will say.

Example 1

This is a pencil. Pencil begins with the letter "P." Point to the card that has the letter "P."

Correct response: Show all cards to the child. If the child points to the card that has the letter "P" on it, say, "Good job; this is the card that has the letter *P* on it, *P* as in pencil."

Incorrect response: Show all cards to the child. If the child points to the incorrect card say, "This is a pencil. Pencil begins with the letter *P*. This is the card that has the letter *P* on it (show the card to the child paired with the object)."

Example 2

This is a doughnut. Doughnut begins with the letter "D." Point to the card that has the letter "D" on it.

Recording Form

Letter	Object	Correct	Incorrect
Group 1			
P	Pig		
M	Monkey		
N	Nickel		
D	Dinosaur		
B	Bear		
Group 2			
F	Fork		
H	Hippo		
C	Camel		
S	Sugar		
O	Orange		

Paula's Performance

She could understand phonemic awareness at the symbolic level, as she identified correctly eight beginning sounds of objects in English and six beginning sounds of objects in Spanish. Paula even attempted to provide rhyming words by changing the beginning sound (e.g., bear and pear).

Definition (Sign Level)

The phonemic awareness developmental task is at the sign level because instructions and examples use one-dimensional stimuli, such as words (Gonzalez et al., 2006; Piper, 2003; Valencia, 1994; Vygotsky, 1986). Teachers should select words that have been used in instruction. Familiar words represent children's authentic performance with regular classroom activities (Gonzalez et al., 1997). About ten sounds total are used in two groups of five cards each so that young children can focus their attention while identifying the beginning sound of the target word. Ten items are suggested to have a sample that represents children's performance.

Instructions for the Phonemic Awareness Developmental Task (Sign Level)

Here we have some words of objects that begin with a different letter. I want you to sound the beginning sound of each word.

Example 1

This is a pencil. Pencil begins with the letter "P." Make the sound of the letter "P."

Example 2

This is a doughnut. Doughnut begins with the letter "D." Make the sound of the letter "D."

Recording Form

Letter	Object	Correct	Incorrect
Group 1			
P	Pig		
M	Monkey		
N	Nickel		
D	Dinosaur		
B	Bear		

Letter	Object	Correct	Incorrect
Group 2			
F	Fork		
H	Horse		
C	Cat		
S	Soap		
O	Orange		

Paula's Performance

She could understand phonemic awareness at the sign level, as she identified correctly seven beginning sounds of items in English and five beginning sounds of items in Spanish. Paula even attempted to provide other examples of words and classmates' names beginning with the target sounds that were familiar to her (e.g., "F" as in "Frank," and "C" as in "Casey").

Concept of Classification Developmental Task

Definition (All Levels)

The concept of classification developmental task is at all levels (index, symbolic, and sign levels) because instructions and examples presented to the child are unstructured and can trigger groups at any of the three stages (Gonzalez et al., 2006; Mandler, 1989; Markman, 1984; Waxman, 1990). Teachers should select objects for classification that have been used in instruction. Tangrams are suggested as objects because they are a universal set of objects representing three salient characteristics, traditionally used as instructional materials for teaching classification skills to young children.

Instructions (All Levels)

1. Show to the child 15 tangrams of three different colors (five of each color: red, blue, yellow), two different sizes (small and large), and three different shapes (square, circle, and triangle)

2. Say, "Here are figures of different colors, sizes, and shapes. I want you to sort them in different groups that go together."

3. Scoring: How many dimensions did the child used for sorting?

    Color: _____

    Size: _____

    Shape: _____

Scoring

Stages indicate children's level of conceptual understanding of classification concepts. According to sociocconstructivistic theory (Gonzalez et al., 2006; Mandler, 1989; Markman, 1984; Waxman, 1990), three stages can be identified in children's responses: (1) Stage 1—the child sorts by groups showing one dimension of perceptual attributes of objects (e.g., only by color, only by size, or only by shape); (2) Stage 2—the child sorts by groups showing two dimensions of perceptual attributes of objects (e.g., by color and size or by color and shape, forming categories and subcategories); and (3) Stage 3—the child sorts by groups showing three dimensions of perceptual attributes of objects (e.g., by color, size, and shape, forming categories and subcategories).

Paula's Performance

Paula could sort tangrams using three dimensions of attributes of objects (i.e., by color, shape, and size). So Paula's performance for both languages of administration was at Stage 3 because her groups showed categories and subcategories. Besides Paula's ability to sort objects consistently at the nonverbal level, she could also explain verbally why the objects were together. Paula explained, "There are some circles that are yellow, but there are also some squares and triangles that are yellow. Some are big and some are small." Her explanations were more detailed in English, as she seemed to know more vocabulary related to the concepts of color, size, and shape in English than in Spanish.

Concept of Number Developmental Task

Definition (All Levels)

The task is at all levels because objects and pictures presented to the child can be understood at any of the three stages (Gonzalez et al., 2006; Piaget, 1964, 1967, 1970). Crayons were selected as examples because they are common items present in all classrooms. Teachers should select stimuli that have been used in instruction. Familiarity with evaluation items represents children's authentic performance with regular classroom activities (Gonzalez et al., 1997). The use of 10 items is suggested so that young children can focus their attention while pairing up objects and to have a sample that represents children's performance.

Instructions (All Levels)

1. Show 10 crayons to the child and say, "I want you to count these crayons." (Mark only the numbers counted correctly)

   ____ 1

   ____ 2

   ____ 3

___ 4

___ 5

___ 6

___ 7

___ 8

___ 9

___ 10

2. Ask the child to pair the 10 crayons with pictures of the same familiar item (balls, pencils, or cats). Can the child do one-to-one correspondence? ___Yes ___No

3. Ask the child, "How many crayons do we have in total?"

Scoring

Stages indicate children's level of understanding of the concept of number. According to socioconstructivistic theory (Gonzalez et al., 2006; Piaget, 1964, 1967, 1970), three stages can be identified in children's responses: (1) Stage 1—the child can count from 1 to 10, as an automatic memory skill but forms two rows that do not pair up crayons with cards, no concept of one-to-one correspondence, and he or she cannot provide a total of items; (2) Stage 2—the child can count from 1 to 10, as an automatic memory skill and forms two rows that pair up some crayons with some cards but some items are not pair up, emerging concept of one-to-one correspondence, and he or she cannot yet provide a total for the counting; and (3) Stage 3—the child can count from 1 to 10, as an automatic memory skill and also forms two rows that pair up crayons with cards in a consistent manner, established concept of one-to-one correspondence, and he or she can provide a total for the counting.

Paula's Performance

Paula could count crayons and cards up to 10 in English and provided a correct total number of items. Paula's performance in Spanish was lower, as she could count only up to seven and could not provide a total number of items. When counting in English, Paula could form two rows while matching one crayon to one pencil in a consistent manner. So Paula's performance was at Stage 3 in the English language of administration because she could pair up items using the concept of one-to-one correspondence in a consistent manner. Besides Paula's ability to pair up objects consistently at the nonverbal level, she could also explain verbally in English why the objects were together. Paula explained, "Each crayon has one card, and they need to be together." Even though Paula could not count up to 10 in Spanish, she could pair up the two rows of items showing the nonverbal concept of one-to-one correspondence. But Paula could not explain verbally in Spanish the reasoning underlying her groups, with a resulting Stage 2 scoring for her Spanish performance.

Concept of Time Developmental Task

Definition (All Levels)

Even though the story presented to the child used one-dimensional stimuli such as words, children can understand the task at any of the three levels (Gonzalez et al., 2006; Piaget, 1964, 1967, 1970). Teachers should select stories that have been used for instruction and that represent themes and topics included in the curriculum. Familiar stories represent children's authentic performance with regular classroom activities (Gonzalez et al., 1997). About six pictures are used in three groups so that young children can focus their attention while identifying the beginning time sequence of events in the story. Six items are suggested to have a sample that represents children's performance.

Instructions (All Levels)

Read a story to the child and say, "I want you to place these pictures to show what happened yesterday, today, and tomorrow."

Yesterday	Today	Tomorrow	Correct	Incorrect

Scoring

Stages indicate children's level of understanding of the concept of time. According to socioconstructivistic theory (Gonzalez et al., 2006; Piaget, 1964, 1967, 1970), three stages can be identified in children's responses: (1) Stage 1—the child can understand only one dimension of the concept of time: today; (2) Stage 2—the child can understand two dimensions of the concept of time: today and yesterday; and (3) Stage 3—the child can understand three dimensions of the concept of time: today, yesterday, and tomorrow.

Paula's Performance

Paula could understand three dimensions of time for both languages of administration. So Paula's performance was at Stage 3 in both languages because she could place pictures using the concepts of present (today), past (yesterday), and future (tomorrow). Paula placed pictures according to the three conventional spatial dimensions of the concept of time at the nonverbal level (she placed pictures of events in the story that happened in the past to the left, pictures of events in the story that happened in the future to the right, and present events in the center). Paula could also explain in English why she had placed some pictures to the left, some to the right, and some in the middle. However, she could not explain in Spanish her nonverbal placement of pictures in three time-based categories.

Concept of Space Developmental Task

Definition (All Levels)

Even though the objects presented to the child use three-dimensional stimuli such as bears, children can understand the task at any of the three levels (Gonzalez et al., 2006; Piaget, 1964, 1967, 1970). The suggested objects are just examples of common manipulative instructional materials used in preschool classrooms. Teachers should select objects that have been used for instruction and incorporate this type of space activity in to their instruction (Gonzalez et al., 1997).

Instructions (All Levels)

1. Show the child a rectangle or square box with a four-cell division (in the form of a cross).

2. Say, "Here we have some objects. I want you to place them as I tell you in this box."
   - Place the bear inside the box.
   - Place the bear outside the box.
   - Place the bear inside the box on the right cell (division/side) of the box.
   - Place the bear inside the box on the left cell (division/side) of the box.
   - Place the bear inside the box on the right and top cell (division/side) of the box.
   - Place the bear inside the box on the left and bottom cell (division/side) of the box.

Scoring

Stages indicate children's level of understanding of the concept of space. According to socioconstructivistic theory (Gonzalez et al., 2006; Piaget, 1964, 1967, 1970), three stages can be identified in children's responses: (1) Stage 1—the child can understand only one bipolar dimension of the concept of space: inside/outside); (2) Stage 2—the child can understand two bipolar dimensions of the concept of space: inside/outside and top/bottom; and (3) Stage 3—the child can understand three bipolar dimensions of the concept of space: inside/outside, top/bottom, and right/left.

Paula's Performance

Paula could understand three dimensions of the concept of space in both languages of administration. So Paula's performance was at Stage 3 because she could place the bears using three bipolar dimensions of the concept of space present in a consistent manner. Paula placed the bears, and she could explain in English why she had placed some bears to the left, some to the right, some in the middle, some outside, some in the top, and some in the bottom of the box. Paula's explanations in Spanish for her placements were less detailed, as she did not have command of all the vocabulary necessary.

Prosocial Behaviors Developmental Task

Definition (All Levels)

Even though the story presented to the child used one-dimensional stimuli such as words, children can understand the task at any of the three levels (Gonzalez et al., 2006; Eisenberg-Berg & Hand, 1979; Kohlberg, 1987; Kohlberg, Levine, & Hewer, 1987). Teachers should select stories that have been used in instruction and match themes and topics included in the curriculum. Familiar stories represent children's authentic performance with regular classroom activities (Gonzalez et al., 1997). Teachers should introduce the concept of main characters in a story, as well as making children familiar with analyzing their own feelings about characters in stories.

Instructions (All Levels)

1. Say, "I am going to tell you a story, and then I will ask you some questions. So please pay attention to my reading and the story pictures I will show you."

2. Ask, "How do you feel about the main character after hearing the story?" (sad, happy, wanted to cry, hate)

3. Ask, "Why do you think the main character did (or behave like) that? Would you do the same? Why?"

4. Scoring:
   - Can child decenter from self-perceptions? ____YES ____NO
     _____Child's response

   - Can child identify own feelings for the main character?
     ____YES ____NO
     _____Child's response

   - Can child understand the perspective and feelings of the main character? ____YES ____NO
     _____Child's response

Scoring

Stages indicate children's level of understanding of the concept of prosocial behaviors. According to socioconstructivistic theory (Gonzalez et al., 2006; Eisenberg-Berg & Hand, 1979; Kohlberg, 1987; Kohlberg et al., 1987), three stages can be identified in children's responses: (1) Stage 1—the child cannot decenter from self-perceptions, cannot identify own feelings for main character, and cannot understand the perspectives and feelings of the main character; (2) Stage 2—the child starts to decenter from self-perceptions, can identify some of her own feelings for main character, and can understand some of the perspectives and feelings of the main character; and (3) Stage 3—the child can decenter from self-perceptions, can identify own feelings for main character, and can understand the perspectives and feelings of the main character.

Paula's Performance

Paula could decenter from self-perceptions and understood the perspective and feelings of the main character. She could also identify her own feelings for the main character. So Paula's performance was at Stage 3 in both languages of administration because she could decenter and show prosocial behaviors, and she could explain verbally her own feelings in relation to main characters in the story. It seems that Paula had equal command of social competence in both languages, Spanish and English, when using language to express emotions. Most likely, it is because she used Spanish at home to communicate in social situations with her parents and siblings.

Responsibility Skills Developmental Task

Definition (All Levels)

Even though the necklace task presented to the child uses three-dimensional stimuli such as beads, children can demonstrate responsibility behaviors at any of the three levels (Gonzalez et al., 2006; Eisenberg-Berg & Hand, 1979; Kohlberg, 1987; Kohlberg et al., 1987). The suggested necklace task is only an example, and teachers should select tasks that have been used in instruction. Familiar tasks represent children's authentic performance with regular classroom activities (Gonzalez et al., 1997).

Instructions (All Levels)

1. Provide the child with a new task with realia and objects to manipulate (e.g., arts and crafts).

2. Say, "We are going to do some arts and crafts. I will give you some materials, and you are to decide how to complete a necklace, the way you want. We also need to follow some class rules: We need to clean up after ourselves, we cannot stand up until we are done, we need to pick up anything we drop to the floor, and we need to wash our hands when we are done."

3. Say, "Please show me your best work and your best behavior."

4. Scoring:
   - Can child follow classroom rules? ____YES (at least two) ____NO (fewer than two)
   - Can child use self-direction to complete tasks? ____YES ____NO
   - Can the child socially adapt to complete a new task? ____YES ____NO

Scoring

Stages indicate children's ability to take responsibility for safety of self and others, bind actions to rules, use self-direction to complete tasks, and adapt to new tasks (Colby & Kohlberg, 1987; Harrison, 1991; Kohlberg et al., 1987). Three stages can be identified in children's responses: (1) Stage 1—the child cannot take responsibility for safety of self and others, cannot complete tasks by himself or herself, and cannot adapt to new tasks; (2) Stage 2—the child is starting to become responsible for safety of self and others, can engage in tasks by himself or herself but not yet complete them, and cannot yet adapt to new tasks; and (3) Stage 3—the child can be trusted to assume responsibility for safety of self and others, can complete tasks by himself or herself, and can adapt to new tasks successfully.

Paula's Performance

Paula showed understanding of the concept of responsibility at the level of Stage 2 in both languages of administration. Paula's performance in the task showed that the she was learning to become responsible for her own safety, could start tasks by herself but not complete them, and was learning to adapt to new tasks. In the necklace activity, Paula started to place some beads on the thread, but after a while, she needed to ask the teacher for advice on how to complete the necklace. She could not decide by herself what colors and shapes of beads to use. She wanted to give the necklace to her mom, for her birthday, but could not make up her mind on what colors would look best. She was good at completing her necklace, and she did remember to wash her hands, but she needed to be reminded, by her teacher, to clean up after herself.

Sense of Self Developmental Task

Definition (All Levels)

Even though the sense-of-self situations presented to the child used one-dimensional stimuli such as words, children can understand the task at any of the three levels. The suggested situations are only examples, and teachers should select situations for prompting children to construct polite requests that have been used for instruction. Familiar situations represent children's authentic performance with regular classroom activities. About four situations total are used so that young children can focus their attention, and teachers can collect a sample that represents children's performance.

Instructions (All Levels)

1. Call the child by name and see if she can make eye contact.

2. Say, "We are going to play some pretend situations, and I will ask you some questions."

3. Say, "Let's pretend that you are at a birthday party in a friend's house and you want to ask the lady of the house for some water. What do you say to her? Remember to use your nice words (simple polite request)."

4. Say, "Let's pretend that you are at a restaurant and you need some more napkins. What do you say to the server? Remember to use your polite words (simple polite request)."

5. Say, "Let's pretend that you are entering a store and a clerk gives you some candy. What do you say to the person who was nice to you? Remember to use your nice words (complex polite response)."

6. Say, "Let's pretend that you step on another's child and without meaning to do so, and you hurt him. What do you say to this child? Remember to use your nice words (complex polite response)."

7. Scoring:
   - Can child respond to name? ____YES ____NO
   - Can child make eye contact? ____YES ____NO
   - Simple polite response: ____YES ____NO
     _____Child's response
   - Complex polite response: ____YES ____NO
     _____Child's response

Scoring

Stages indicate children's level of understanding of the concept of self. Three stages can be identified in children's responses: (1) Stage 1—the child can respond to name and make eye contact but cannot yet make a simple polite request; (2) Stage 2—the child can respond to name, make eye contact, and make a simple polite request; and (3) Stage 3—the child can respond to name, make eye contact, and make simple and complex polite requests.

Paula's Performance

Paula could understand the concept of self at Stage 2 level in both languages of administration. She could respond to her name, make eye contact, and make polite requests only at a simple level. She could understand the need to make a polite remark, but she had difficulty expressing her thoughts through a complex polite request.

DISCUSSION OF PAULA'S OVERALL PERFORMANCE ACROSS DEVELOPMENTAL TASKS

Paula's performance across developmental tasks was as follows: (1) advanced for her age in language and literacy areas, (2) advanced and at Stage 3 for conceptual or cognitive areas, and (3) normal and at Stage 2 for affective or emotional areas. Overall, Paula's performance ranged from advanced to normal for her chronological age. However, Paula's performance for most developmental tasks was higher in English than in Spanish. Several issues could have contributed to Paula's lower achievement in Spanish for most developmental tasks. First, Paula had received more literacy instruction in English at the BPDC, with about 25% of her schooltime conducted in Spanish. Second, English is the dominant language outside of school, so Paula was mostly exposed to environmental print and media in English. Moreover, although Spanish was used at home, most likely Paula's older siblings also had English as a dominant language because of schooling.

Next, a summary of Paula's performance in each developmental task will be provided. This last section will close Chapter 5 with a discussion of some factors that could have contributed to some patterns found in Paula's performance across developmental tasks.

On the letter recognition developmental task, Paula used a strategy to show her teacher that she knew about the letters: She named students in the class whose names begin with those letters. The use of this strategy shows that Paula was familiar with beginning sounds and had developed phonemic awareness skills. In addition, Paula was familiar with demonstrating knowledge learned in the classroom during testing situations.

Paula's performance on the handwriting and eye-hand coordination developmental tasks was higher in English (with 65% of letters copied correctly, 17 out of 26) than in Spanish (with 46% of letters copied correctly, 12 out of 26), with a similar outcome for familiar and unfamiliar words. While copying the letters, Paula also attempted to name the letters and started sounding out some of the letters to decode the meaning of only familiar words.

Paula's performance for the vocabulary definition developmental task at the index, symbolic, and sign levels was at Stage 3 across languages of administration. Paula could define words at the abstract level using categories and subcategories when using two-dimensional (pictures) and three-dimensional (objects) stimuli. She could make relations to her prior sociocultural knowledge and academic knowledge and skills learned at school (e.g., defining words based on attributes of objects and applying reasoning skills for understanding the meaning of verbal concepts).

On the phonemic awareness developmental task, Paula made several remarks during the test. When the hippopotamus was placed on the table, she said, "A hippo hiccups." This could have been a play on words or a reference to a beginning-sound rhyme; either way, she had knowledge that the letter "H" was the beginning sound of "hippo." Paula also noted, "The orange is really orange," a comment that shows metalinguistic awareness of the relation between the label for the object, its color, and the meaning of both labels (i.e., "orange" denoting color, and "orange" denoting the object fruit).

In the concept of classification and concept of time developmental tasks, Paula performed at Stage 3 level in both English and Spanish administrations. However, her verbal explanations were more elaborate in English than in Spanish, performance that is related to her levels of language proficiency. Moreover, it is interesting to see that in the concept of number and concept of space developmental tasks, Paula scored higher in English (at Stage 3) than in Spanish (at Stage 2). This could mean that her mental processes for the concepts of space, counting, and one-to-one correspondence had become more automatic in English, and she had not yet transferred her knowledge to Spanish (McLaughlin, Blanchard, & Osanai, 1995). Paula had received mathematics instruction in English and Spanish at the BPDC. However, Paula's verbal explanations for both concepts of space and time tasks were more elaborate in English than in Spanish, performance that is related to her language dominance and different levels of language proficiency.

Paula's performance in the prosocial behaviors skills developmental task was at the highest Stage 3 level, for both Spanish and English administrations. However, Paula's performance was at the lower Stage 2 level for the concepts of responsibility and sense of self. As reported by her teachers, Paula's classroom behaviors showed interpersonal skills to establish rapport with classmates and respond to their feelings (behaviors that are consistent with a high level of performance in the prosocial behaviors task). Even though Paula understood the need to make a polite remark and she could make simple requests, she still had difficulty expressing her thoughts through a complex polite request. Paula's performance in the responsibility skills developmental task showed that she was learning to become responsible for her own safety, could start tasks by herself but not complete them, and was learning to adapt to new tasks.

Based on Paula's overall performance across developmental tasks, it seems that she had had a good home situation and had received high-quality preschool education (Gonzalez, 2001b). According to Ovando, Combs, and Collier (2006), both home and school nurturing environments contribute to minority children's development and learning processes.

The evaluation situation that Paula experienced was also ideal for several reasons, and according to Natriello (1987), her performance in developmental tasks probably truly reflects her achievement levels in both Spanish and English languages. First, the classroom-based evaluations included several nonverbal developmental tasks (i.e., concepts of classification, number, time, and space), which are important for preschool children (and especially for bilingual youngsters) who are still in the process of language development (Gonzalez & Riojas-Clark, 1999). Second, the high level of familiarity that Paula had with her evaluators (her teachers) positively impacted her task performance. So when teachers conduct classroom-based assessments with familiar instructional activities and stimuli and in natural situations and settings, young children's performance increases on evaluation tasks (Gonzalez, Bauerle, Black, & Felix-Holt, 1999). Finally, when bilingual children are evaluated in English and in their home language, their performance can be better understood in the complexity of conceptual and language transference and interaction of languages (Gonzalez, Bauerle, & Felix-Holt, 1996). Even though Paula's performance was lower in Spanish than in English across developmental tasks, the dual language of administration strategy provided her with an opportunity to express her prior sociocultural knowledge in her home language and minority culture and, in many instances, her metalinguistic awareness in relation to her bilingualism and bicultural identity (Gonzalez & Riojas-Clark).

In sum, this chapter uses Paula's case study to illustrate how to use developmental tasks as classroom-based assessments. The developmental tasks presented in this chapter are authentic, qualitative, alternative classroom-based assessments that link assessment to instruction. These developmental tasks follow the ethnic-educator approach in its philosophical and theoretical bases, as well as extend its derived pedagogical strategies into assessment strategies. These developmental tasks also apply standards for educational testing (AERA, APA, & NCME, 1999; National Educational Goals Panel, 1998) recommended for young, diverse children. Therefore, the developmental tasks presented are valid and reliable because teachers can adapt their methodology to match idiosyncratic, cultural, and linguistic characteristics of young, diverse children. Developmental tasks are methods of assessment, and not tests, because the language of administration and the activities and stimuli used can be adapted to the particular curriculum and instructional contexts and the educational and developmental needs and characteristics of children. Developmental tasks also complement classroom-based observations discussed in Chapter 4, as well as reading assessments discussed in Chapter 6.

6

Storytelling

Chapter 6 presents storytelling developmental tasks as an alternative tool for assessing semantic development (i.e., the intersection of cognition, culture, and language) in young, diverse children. Storytelling developmental tasks are classroom-based assessments that represent the philosophical and pedagogical principles of the ethnic-educator approach. As a developmental method of assessment, storytelling tasks link assessment to instruction and provide early childhood teachers with measurement tools that tap verbal and nonverbal mental processes and behaviors (i.e., semantic development) in young, diverse children. The storytelling developmental tasks presented in this chapter complement the classroom-based observations presented in Chapter 4 and the developmental tasks of academic content presented in Chapter 5. All the alternative methods of assessment presented in Chapters 4, 5, and 6 are classroom-based assessments that can be used by early childhood teachers for instructional purposes with young, diverse children.

Then, Chapter 6 presents storytelling as an alternative assessment of semantic and narrative development for young, diverse children (with the possibility of dual-language administration for bilingual or English-as-a-second-language [ESL] preschoolers). Actual assessment strategies and examples of young, diverse children illustrate the implementation of this alternative assessment for young, diverse children's semantic and narrative development. The examples represent real-life diverse children who attended the Bilingual Preschool Development Center (BPDC). Storytelling developmental tasks were used in the BPDC to extend the ethnic-educator curriculum and link assessment and instruction. The examples selected are of three- to five-year-old native Spanish-speaking children from Hispanic immigrant low-income families living in the United States. Evaluation insights gained from these alternative assessments show sequential and imbalanced first- and second-language semantic and narrative developmental stages and patterns, with storytelling showing cultural aspects of concept formation skills. Evaluation insights have important, research-based educational implications for the assessment and instruction of young, diverse children.

The first section of Chapter 6 presents a theoretical framework supporting the use of storytelling as an alternative method of assessment. This theoretical framework merges socioconstructivistic and sociocultural perspectives and presents research-based knowledge supporting the use of developmental tasks for the alternative assessment of first- and second-language and cognitive development in young, diverse children. Storytelling provides an opportunity to examine the interaction of cognition, culture, and language processes in bilinguals (Cortazzi, 1993) through the evaluation of narrative and linguistic skills. Culture and language cannot be separated from each other because one influences the other (Fantini, 1991).

In this chapter, semantic development is defined as the formation of verbal concepts that are culturally loaded and represent sociocultural conventions or patterns of meaning and use. We define narrative development as the speaker's ability to tell stories that use language and sociocultural conventions to form and follow scripts (i.e., a sequence of events that follow sociocultural conventions in a particular setting, a visit to a restaurant or the doctor's office) and the structure and characteristics of a story (i.e., in reference to content, staging, and cohesion; Peterson & McCabe, 1991). Then, this chapter presents the use of a developmental task, dual-language storytelling, to gain insight into the cognitive and cultural aspects present in semantic and narrative development in bilingual preschoolers. It is our purpose for the reader to gain insight into the use of developmental tasks as an alternative tool for assessing semantic development (i.e., the intersection of cognition, culture, and language) in young, diverse children. Developmental tasks link assessment and instruction and provide teachers with classroom-based assessments that tap verbal and nonverbal mental processes and behaviors in young children.

The second section of Chapter 6 applies research and theoretical knowledge about semantic and narrative development to using developmental tasks in the alternative assessment of young, diverse, bilingual children. The second section examines closely developmental similarities (i.e., stages and patterns), individual differences, and culturally and linguistically loaded factors in the interface between cognition, culture, and language. Moreover, a third section of Chapter 6 applies research-based knowledge to support the validity of storytelling as a developmental task and alternative assessment method for identifying patterns and stages in first- and second-language semantic and narrative development in young, diverse children. Through vivid examples of bilingual Hispanic children, this chapter provides a fascinating insight into the interaction of cognitive, cultural, and linguistic processes when young children form concepts (i.e., semantic development) and tell stories (i.e., narrative development) in their first and second languages (L1, L2).

RESEARCH-BASED KNOWLEDGE SUPPORTING STORYTELLING AS AN ALTERNATIVE ASSESSMENT

The theoretical framework selected merges socioconstructivistic with sociocultural perspectives on language and cognitive development. This theoretical merger proposes that language and thought processes develop in social environments and, thus, become culturally and socially influenced and loaded, but also present developmental similarities and individual differences. These two perspectives form the research-based support for storytelling as an alternative assessment method of cognition and language in young, bilingual children. Thus, bilingual preschoolers' semantic and narrative development goes through a continuous and flexible set of milestones and stages, and presents developmental similarities and individual differences when comparing first- and second-language performances in the same bilingual child and across bilingual children.

This first section provides a review and discussion of core terminology, definitions, and research-based support for the use of storytelling as a developmental and alternative assessment method for young, diverse children. The four points discussed include (1) storytelling as an assessment method of first- and second-language and cognitive development, (2) developmental stages in narrative and semantic development in children, (3) a socioconstructivistic perspective for language development, and (4) a sociocultural perspective for language development.

STORYTELLING AS AN ASSESSMENT METHOD OF FIRST- AND SECOND-LANGUAGE AND COGNITIVE DEVELOPMENT

This chapter presents storytelling as an alternative assessment tool for measuring the interaction of cognition, culture, and language processes in the form of semantic and narrative development in first- and second-language performance. Discourse language allows children to symbolize, fantasize, and imagine in relation to prior or unconscious experiences. When bilingual children are assessed, it is imperative that they be allowed to demonstrate their first- and second-language abilities in their unique way (McLaughlin, Blanchard, & Osanai, 1995). Storytelling allows for the expression of language competence and provides the opportunity for individual interpretation and creativity. Narratives are related to cognitive skills and, in particular, problem-solving processes and developmental characteristics of children's performance, which are key components of alternative assessments (Gonzalez, 1999; Snow & Dickinson, 1990). Narrators need a variety of skills when telling a narrative, including the use of background knowledge, monitoring vocabulary and grammar, keeping the listener in mind, and planning (Snow & Dickinson, 1990). As a result, storytelling incorporates problem solving and complex thinking at its core, which requires cognitive and linguistic interactive processes. Thus, storytelling used as a developmental task allows teachers to measure, in an alternative manner, semantic and narrative developmental processes.

Another advantage of using storytelling as an alternative assessment is that it provides a link with instructional practices (i.e., classroom-based assessments that can measure students' competence; see Gonzalez, 1999; Shepard, Kagan, & Wurtz, 1998). Storytelling has been used as a learning and teaching strategy, for eliciting language samples and as a developmentally appropriate and efficient method of gathering data in the reality of normal classroom interactions (McLaughlin et al., 1995). In this chapter, we recommend a systematic application of storytelling that collects language samples and assures that results are comparable and lead to the identification of patterns and stages in semantic and narrative development.

In addition, language is very much related to cultural environments because mastering the dimensions of communicative competence is influenced by culture. Consequently, assessments of young, diverse children must be appropriate developmentally and culturally while considering linguistic backgrounds for language proficiency (McLaughlin et al., 1995). In relation to developmental, cultural, and linguistic appropriateness, Fantini (1991) stated, "The language we acquire leads us to categorize the world which orients their users to particular ways of knowing and viewing the world" (p. 112). With this statement, Fantini argued that language influences its user's view of the world. Then, bilinguals must make sense of the world from a linguistic standpoint, in two ways through two languages. That is, bilinguals develop representational systems through internalization, transformation, and dual conceptual representation in their L1 and L2 (Gonzalez & Schallert, 1999). This triple-interaction model suggests that children construct first- and second-language concepts at three different levels: (1) cognitive or abstract, (2) symbolic or sociocultural, and (3) linguistic or verbal (Gonzalez, 1999). There are always challenges in life, as there will be in school. In this chapter, we demonstrate the use of storytelling tasks as an alternative assessment method of gathering information and insight into the language and cognitive skills and cultural aspects present in first- and second-language development in Hispanic preschoolers.

DEVELOPMENTAL STAGES OF NARRATIVE AND SEMANTIC DEVELOPMENT IN CHILDREN

Although research studies on storytelling in young, bilingual children are scarce, a few noteworthy studies have been conducted with young, monolingual children. Past studies show that as young as two years old, children can recount past events and describe present situations. Therefore, even at the earliest stages of language development, narrative skills are emerging (Hicks, 1990). Narrative talk during the preschool years shows that the linguistic environment of the child is a strong predictor of literacy development (Dickinson, 2001). Conversation, especially with family members, provides a child with opportunities to improve vocabulary and grammar and to practice narrative structures (Piper, 2003). As children develop their use of language, particularly, their expressive abilities increase.

Furthermore, Wigglesworth (1990) conducted a detailed study on storytelling and used the three-phase developmental model proposed by Karmiloff-Smith (1991) to categorize narrative units. The first procedural stage is recognized by correct syntax, abundant vocabulary, use of pronouns, and a lack of narrative organization. The second metaprocedural stage is characterized by less vocabulary, development of themes, and increased narrative organization. Narratives in the third stage exhibit organization, more details, and superior vocabulary, which were fundamental aspects of classifying and gaining insight into the stories told by the bilingual children in this study. In addition, Wigglesworth maintained that children's narratives are not fully cohesive and organized until approximately age seven. This means that preschool-age children may not have yet developed the ability to tell well-organized stories and, thus, move from one topic to another without connection between topics. Younger children tend to stress actions more than fictional characters and leave out details on the interrelationship between ideas (Hudson & Shapiro, 1991; Wigglesworth, 1990). Consequently, young children's stories resemble more descriptions than stories (Hudson & Shapiro). The importance of these prior studies is that certain characteristics are evident in the development of children's language and ability to tell narratives. However, these studies were conducted with monolingual-English children. Thus, this chapter translates research with monolingual children into culturally and linguistically appropriate practices for young, diverse children and examines similarities and differences in mainstream and young, diverse children's semantic and narrative developmental patterns and stages.

In addition to developmental characteristics, stories can be examined for common narrative structural characteristics (Peterson & McCabe, 1991). Stories can be characterized by content, staging, and cohesion. Content includes structure, mainline events, and contextualizing clauses. Staging refers to how the storyteller controls the perspective of the narrative presentation. Cohesion can be determined by temporal sequences, cause-effect relationships, antithesis, and continuity. Peterson and McCabe (1991) cited Grice's *maxim of orderliness*, which stated that two sequential events are assumed by the listener to have occurred in the order mentioned, as another indication of cohesion. With this in mind, the evaluator would presume that the chain of events in a narrative would be in chronological order.

In a 1983 publication, Peterson and McCabe very specifically organized and described narrative structural components. From their research, they concluded that narratives could be analyzed by high-point, episodes, or syntactic dependency methods. They described high-point narratives as episodes that build up to a high point of suspense and often end with a resolution of this suspense. Episodic analysis was described as narratives comprising a series of events or episodes that involve problem-solving processes. Syntactic dependency is more closely associated with discourse than narratives. This type of analysis is concerned with how coherent a narrative is in regard to its syntactic structures rather than its content (Peterson & McCabe). Structural elements tie into the developmental stages cited by Wigglesworth (1990). The manner in which context, cohesion, and staging are used relates to the organization patterns of the developmental stages. How children tell narratives in terms of structural organization is a factor in the sophistication of their narratives. Thus, in this chapter we demonstrate the use of storytelling as a method of first- and second-language and cognitive development assessment. This chapter focuses on similarities and individual differences in patterns and stages of semantic and narrative development when comparing the performances of young, bilingual children with different degrees of first- and second-language development.

SOCIOCONSTRUCTIVIST PERSPECTIVE FOR LANGUAGE DEVELOPMENT

According to research findings since the 1990s (see Díaz & Klinger, 1991; Gonzalez, 1996, 1999), bilingualism has been shown to have a positive relationship to concept formation, classification, creativity, analogical reasoning, and visual-spatial skills. The level of bilingualism and the fluency in at least one language (i.e., threshold level in relation to additive bilingualism) affects the degree to which these factors influence cognitive development. In verbal, nonverbal, and metalinguistic tasks, bilingual children show advantages over monolingual children and have better control over language processing (Gonzalez, 2006). Vygotsky suggested that exposure to two languages creates an awareness of language and directs intelligent behavior (Bjorklund, 2000; Díaz & Klinger, 1991). For bilinguals, this generates an awareness of metalinguistic, noncommunicative, and cognitive uses and functions of language, such as thinking about the coincidences and differences of word meanings across languages, finding humor in language, and realizing social connotations of meanings. Bilinguals seem to be more aware of how language is used as a cognitive tool to convey concepts and ideas, which is a metalinguistic awareness ability that produces a more efficient use of language as a cognitive tool and thinking process among bilinguals (Díaz & Klinger, 1991). The diversity of language experiences that bilingual children are exposed to creates a more varied effect on cognitive development. Then, because of the exposure to multiple languages, bilinguals have experiences that are more diverse and, therefore, develop higher levels of cognitive capacities, such as the symbolic ability to use language to construct meanings and to communicate in socially and culturally appropriate ways. Thus, this chapter shows that bilingual preschoolers have advantages in their semantic and narrative development, at least in their dominant language, resulting from their ability to think and perform in two languages.

SOCIOCULTURAL PERSPECTIVE FOR LANGUAGE DEVELOPMENT

Cognitive and linguistic developmental processes are affected by the child's culture, family, and social setting, such as school, neighborhood, community, and many other environmental factors. That is, language development is intertwined with social interaction and activities (Rogoff, 1998). Thought processes and language use are indications of sociocultural influences because people in different social situations and cultural environments display differences in their thinking and language. Thinking is not rigid or static but rather flexible and continuous and subject to dynamic changes. Children's acquisition of knowledge and strategies occurs through maturation, formal education processes, life experiences, and interactions with adults and peers, which Vygotsky deemed scaffolding (Bjorklund, 2000; Rogoff, 1998; Vygotsky, 1986). With adult help, children can work and achieve at a higher level than they are able to think and act on their own. Children are constantly absorbing and learning from their formal and informal social interactions with people and sociocultural surroundings in their lives, experiences that directly influence their development.

Then, following a sociocultural developmental perspective, real-life examples of diverse children presented in this chapter show that they do not have a set manner of thinking dependent on their developmental stage, but rather that they can display multiple ways of thinking and acting at any point in development (Siegler, 1996). This model of cognitive development is founded in the notion that there are alternative ways of thinking and that development does not mean substituting one way of thinking for another (Gonzalez, 2001b). That is, there is not one way to think or act that is of significance to bilinguals because they already must make multiple meanings of languages and cultural behaviors. Therefore, this chapter merges a socioconstructivistic with a sociocultural perspective, in which it is expected that language and thought processes develop in social environments and, thus, become culturally and socially influenced and loaded yet also present developmental similarities and individual differences. Thus, language development in bilingual preschoolers may not go through parallel stages and milestones and will present individual differences when we compare first- and second-language performances across bilingual children. A synthesis of relevant points represented in socioconstructivistic and sociocultural perspectives on language and cognitive development applied to the use of storytelling as a developmental and alternative assessment method include the following:

1. Children develop cognitively and linguistically following universals from infancy until early childhood years, with predictable patterns and stages. However, these universal language-developmental stages are influenced by the interaction of cultural and social environments (external factors) and individual differences (internal factors; e.g., neurological maturational factors affecting reaching developmental milestones).

2. Children develop the cognitive, emotional, and social skills to use their particular language as a tool for thinking, learning, communicating, and socializing.

3. Language acquisition is influenced when one becomes bilingual, which is a dynamic and complex process that can add culturally and linguistically loaded patterns to children's cognitive development (including semantic and narrative development). Therefore, we expect similarities (developmental

universals) but also differences (individual differences and culturally and linguistically loaded patterns) when bilingual children's first- and second-language semantic and narrative developmental skills are assessed.

APPLICATION OF RESEARCH-BASED KNOWLEDGE TO ACTUAL ASSESSMENT STRATEGIES

Actual assessment strategies and examples of using storytelling are presented in this second section. Actual implementation of the developmental and alternative assessment method for the case of bilingual (Spanish/English) children's semantic and narrative development is presented through real-life examples. The examples represent real-life diverse children who attended the BPDC. These children were native Spanish-speaking three- to five-year-old preschoolers from Hispanic immigrant low-income families living in the United States.

To gain insight into educationally applied strategies for using storytelling as a developmental and alternative assessment method of semantic and narrative development for diverse children, the two main steps necessary to assess narrative and semantic development in young, diverse children are presented next.

Step 1: Collect linguistic samples for storytelling developmental tasks — stimuli and procedures

Step 2: Analyze linguistic samples with substeps clustered into four areas:

1. Transcript of recorded narratives

2. Coded responses in five nominal categories (i.e., units of speech, concepts, cognitive processes, language functions, and word functions)

3. Recommended strategies for clustering coded responses using patterns
   - Description of using vocabulary and actions
   - Recommendations for the use of grammatical structures
   - Description of developmental characteristics of narrative structures and elements
   - Description of sociocultural components
   - Description of language proficiency

4. Four recommended strategies for interpreting evaluation results
   - Do oral first- and second-language developmental processes show similar or different patterns?
   - What developmental stages of first- and second-language semantic and oral-language development are present in bilingual preschoolers?
   - How do linguistic, cognitive, and semantic abilities reflect in the narratives constructed by bilingual preschoolers?
   - What semantic and narrative developmental patterns in both first- and second-language performances are present in bilingual preschoolers?

Step 1: Collection of Linguistic Samples for Storytelling Developmental Tasks (Stimuli and Procedures)

Stimuli to Collect Linguistic Samples

In our educational practice, when assessing young, diverse children, we have used six different drawings from the Children's Apperception Test (CAT) (Bellak & Bellak, 1991) as stimuli to collect linguistic samples of storytelling. The CAT is designed as an individually administered projective-personality technique appropriate for clinical use with children 3 to 10 years of age. By presenting a series of pictures and asking a child to describe the situations and make up stories about the people or animals in the pictures, an examiner can elicit information about the personality traits, attitudes, and psychodynamic processes (i.e., relationships, sibling rivalry, and aggression) in young children. Even though we used the CAT for its original purpose, as a technique for eliciting stories in young children, we analyzed the collected linguistic samples with the educational purpose of assessing semantic and narrative development in young, diverse children.

We selected three pictures from the CAT for the Spanish assessment (the first picture was of three monkeys in a school setting, the second picture was of a cat standing upright and dressed in an apron, and the third picture was of a kangaroo using crutches and with its tail and foot wrapped in bandages) and three other pictures for the English assessment (the first picture was of a large bear holding a smaller bear in its lap; the second picture was of a rabbit dressed as a doctor examining a smaller rabbit, a stethoscope and medicine bottles be seen in the background; and the third picture was of two mice having a tea party, other toys seen around them).

All the pictures are black-and-white drawings and are shown in the same order to each child. Some degree of control of stimuli needs to be exerted so that each child has the opportunity to respond to the same picture prompts and verbal instructions in the storytelling task, which are presented in a systematic order. When shown the picture, the children were asked by the evaluator to tell a story about the picture they were viewing and to identify characteristics in the pictures. For both language administrations, the evaluator needs to give initial prompts and then ask questions to encourage children to say more about the picture. Across language sessions, the evaluator must make an effort to individualize assessment and clarify verbal instructions as needed. Moreover, the evaluator must allow children to use code switching (i.e., the use of Spanish and English sequentially between complete sentences in each language) and code mixing (i.e., the use of Spanish and English simultaneously in the same sentence). When evaluating bilingual children, it is best to have bilingual examiners who have experience in the minority culture of the children. Instructions for collecting the linguistic samples for the CAT are included.

Spanish Instructions

Este es el dibujo de una historia pero yo olvidé las palabras de la historia. Quiero que me digas una historia sobre este dibujo. Dime todo lo que puedas sobre este dibujo.

Examples of questions that can be used to encourage the children to talk more about the story include the following: ¿Qué más me puedes decir sobre el dibujo? ¿Qué más pasó? ¿Qué otras ideas se te ourren?

English Instructions

This is a picture of a story, but I forgot the words. I want you to tell me a story about this picture. Please tell me all you can about this picture.

Examples of questions that can be used to encourage the children to talk more about the story include the following: What else can you tell me about the story? What else happened? Do you have more ideas of what happened?

Procedures for Collecting Linguistic Samples

Procedures used to collect linguistic samples for storytelling have an analytic approach. Storytelling samples can be collected in the form of children's spontaneous narratives during a period of two to six months. Samples can be collected during individual sessions or during group participation in storytelling activities. In the case of bilingual children, dual-language data collection can take place, with some Spanish and some English storytelling sessions. Language sessions can last for as long as the child speaks about a story in response to verbal and visual stimuli. Therefore, some language sessions can be quite short, approximately two minutes, while others can last longer, approximately 8 to 10 minutes, depending on how much a child wants to say while telling a story. It is better to audiotape sessions by recording and transcribing language samples; we can achieve a greater level of validity and reliability in our evaluation of language processes in young children.

Step 2: Analysis of Linguistic Samples

The goal is to identify developmental patterns and then compare them across first- and second-language semantic and narrative development. However, because the children's verbal and nonverbal responses are open-ended, a wide variety of developmental patterns can be identified. Variety in responses is possible because the storytelling task allows for individualization of assessment.

More specifically, the process of analyzing linguistic samples has several steps. First, after meeting with the children and recording their narratives, the conversations between the evaluator and the children need to be transcribed verbatim from the recordings. Second, the narratives need to be broken into *units of speech*, according to the following operational definitions of coding categories. A unit of speech is determined by the content of the utterance. When a new idea is introduced, a new unit is identified. Third, each unit of speech needs to be coded according to the five *nominal categories*, including concepts, cognitive process, language function, and word function, as explained next.

The five nominal categories developed by Gonzalez (2006) are defined operationally in the following examples

1. *Unit of speech* is defined operationally as a set of verbal and nonverbal responses that are centered on one idea and initiated either by the observed child (production level unit) or by someone else such as the teacher or peer(s) (comprehension level unit) (Gonzalez, 2006).

   Example:

   Child: (looking at the sky) A bird.

   Teacher: Speak louder, so I can hear you.

   Child: A bird.

   Teacher: The cloud looks like a bird?

   Teacher: Do you think it looks like a bird?

   Child: Yes, it does.

   Teacher: Good. Thank you.

2. *Concept* is operationally defined as a category for grouping ideas, (Gonzalez, 2006) and includes *state* (operationally defined as an aspect of someone or something during a particular point in time, such as actions, amount, animate or inanimate objects, direction, and manner) and *event* (operationally defined as something that happens such as property and place).

3. *Cognitive processes* are operationally defined as mental processes that involve thinking, knowing, and understanding (Gonzalez, 2006). Cognitive processes include seven subcategories:

   a. *Problem solving* is operationally defined as using prior learning and/or past experiences to find one or more possible solutions to a perceived problem situation (Gonzalez, 2006). An example is a child who does not know how to complete a task assigned by the teacher, such as painting a worksheet. Instead of asking the teacher, the child decides to solve the problem by looking at what peers are doing to their designs.

   b. *Symbolic play* is operationally defined as the creation of symbols in order to express through a verbal or nonverbal behavior internalized past life experiences (Gonzalez, 2006). For example, a child plays with a block of wood as if it was a car and pretends there is a traffic signal, and says, "Stop now. Okay. Green, go now."

   c. *Creativity* is operationally defined as the ability to generate novel and unique ideas (Gonzalez, 2006). For instance a child says, "This is my store, please enter." When another child pretends to enter the store, the first child says in a strong tone, "Not through there. That is the window! Go through the door, over there. Can you hear the music?"

d. *Analogical reasoning* is operationally defined as the ability to make comparisons based on prior conceptual knowledge applied to understand the meaning of a new learning experience (Gonzalez, 2006). An example of this kind of thinking is the following statement uttered by a child: "My stomach does noises like a piano."

e. *Logical thinking* is operationally defined as the ability to do mental transformations such as reversibility of thinking and forming new concepts to categorize prior and new experiences (Gonzalez, 2006). Children can do mental transformations such as reversibility, concept formation, or categorizations that allow them to think in different ways about their experiences. For example, "I don't want more oranges, and no more apples. I don't want more fruit!"

f. *Flexibility of thinking* is operationally defined as the ability to change easily and adapt to different learning situations (Gonzalez, 2006). For instance, the child can produce several ideas or do several mental transformations to think in different ways about the same experiences in a short time.

g. *Metalinguistic awareness* is operationally defined as the ability to think about language and transcend labels to form meaning. That is, it is the ability to use language as a communication tool and to understand the existence of an audience (Gonzalez, 2006). For example, children speak to adults and other children differently. They say to the teacher, "Ms. Cindy, *please* give me that book," but they say to their classmate, "Give me that book."

4. *Language functions* are operationally defined in relation to five functions: (1) Function 1 is operationally defined as the children's use of language to assert and maintain social needs, (2) Function 2 is operationally defined as children's use of language to project into novel situations, (3) Function 3 is operationally defined as children's use of language for controlling the self and others, (4) Function 4 is operationally defined as children's use of language to inform, and (5) Function 5 is operationally defined as children's use of language to forecast and reason (Gonzalez, 2006).

5. *Word functions* are operationally defined in relation to seven parts of speech, including noun, pronoun, verb, determiner, adjective, adverb, and preposition.

A coding form (in Table 6.1) and a narrative report can be written as an explanation and analysis of the unit categorizations. Based on the data from the coding forms, the evaluators can identify patterns in the narratives in each language separately, and then integrate the developmental patterns and stages found in the two languages of administration and response. Examples of coding categories and patterns in relation to the evaluation of bilingual (Spanish/English) Hispanic preschool children are presented in the next section. These examples will be presented in relation to areas of recommended strategies.

Table 6.1 Protocol for Coding Storytelling Developmental Tasks

Child's Name: _____   Observer's Name: _____

Observation Date: _____   Observation Duration _____

Observed Activities: _____

Unit Marking

0, 1, 2, 3, 4, 5, 6, 7, 8, 9, 10, 11, 12, 13, 14, 15, 16, 17, 18, 19, 20, 21, 22, 23, 24, 25, 26, 27, 28, 29, 30

Cognitive Processes

Cognitive Processes	Unit 1	Unit 2	Unit 3	Unit 4	Unit 5
Interacting with	__ alone __ peer(s) __ teacher(s)	__ alone __ peer(s) __ teacher(s)	__ alone __ peer(s) __ teacher(s)	__ alone __ peer(s) __ teacher(s)	__ alone __ peer(s) __ teacher(s)
Comprehension and production	__ comprehension, initiator: observer __ production	__ comprehension, initiator: child __ production	__ comprehension, initiator: child production	__ comprehension, initiator: observer production	__ comprehension, initiator: child __ production
Concepts involved	**State __ Event** __ actions __ property __ amount __ place __ animate thing __ inanimate thing __ direction __ manner __ others	**State __ Event** __ actions __ property __ amount __ place __ animate thing __ inanimate thing __ direction __ manner __ others	**State __ Event** __ actions __ property __ amount __ place __ animate thing __ inanimate thing __ direction __ manner __ others	**State __ Event** __ actions __ property __ amount __ place __ animate thing __ inanimate thing __ direction __ manner __ others	**State __ Event** __ actions __ property __ amount __ place __ animate thing __ inanimate thing __ direction __ manner __ others

Cognitive Processes	Verbal	Nonverbal	Verbal	Nonverbal	Verbal	Nonverbal	Verbal	Nonverbal	Verbal	Nonverbal
Problem solving										
Symbolic play										
Creativity										
Analogical reasoning										
Logical thinking										
Flexibility										
Metalinguistic awareness										

Language Function (Verbal Responses)

	Unit 1	Unit 2	Unit 3	Unit 4	Unit 5	Unit 6	Unit 7	Unit 8	Unit 9	Unit 10
Function 1										
Function 2										
Function 3										
Function 4										
Function 5										

(Continued)

Table 6.1 (Continued)

Parts of Speech

	Unit 1	Unit 2	Unit 3	Unit 4	Unit 5	Unit 6	Unit 7	Unit 8	Unit 9	Unit 10
Noun(s)										
Verb(s)										
Determiner(s)										
Adjective(s)										
Adverb(s)										
Preposition(s)										

RECOMMENDED STRATEGIES
FOR CLUSTERING CODED RESPONSES

The data gathered provide patterns in the oral-language abilities and developmental stages of the preschoolers. However, in the examples provided more extensive data are available for the Spanish narratives than the English ones, based on the sheer fact that the participating children were native Spanish speakers. After the data were collected and coded, common patterns among the English and Spanish narratives emerged. In this section, the patterns will be discussed, and then they will be related to the recommended interpretation strategies in the next section. These narratives lend insight into the language development of bilingual preschoolers with six patterns found: (1) use of vocabulary and actions for describing pictures, (2) use of grammatical structures, (3) developmental characteristics of normative structures and elements, (4) developmental stages of narratives, (5) cultural components of narratives, and (6) language-developmental levels. These patterns were obtained from actual bilingual (Spanish/English), Hispanic preschoolers using a qualitative framework that identifies theses, themes, and topics (Bodgan & Biklen, 1982). Each pattern is discussed in relation to themes or topics found in each pattern.

First Pattern: Describing Using Vocabulary and Actions

The first notable theme in the storytelling samples of bilingual (Spanish/English) children collected is the use of vocabulary in the narratives. Although the amount of language produced is relatively small in the English narratives, the children were able to name and describe various items in the pictures. The words used by the children are overwhelmingly placed in the nominative word-function category. What is particularly interesting is that the children put together long strings of nominative words while using a few conjunctive or transitional words, as shown in the examples provided.

Umm . . . baby, daddy, umm . . . a bear, tiger, umm . . . elephant, Santa, ice cream. (Daniel, Unit 1)

A person playing with the babies and toys, blocks, and a ball and food and coffee and chairs. (Juanita, Unit 3)

In the first example, Daniel was describing the bear picture in English. Although baby, daddy, and bear are related to the picture being shown, the other words, for example elephant and Santa, in this unit, are seemingly unrelated. It is uncertain whether Daniel really had a handle on the task or the ability to describe the picture or he was just saying all the words he could in his L2.

Unlike Daniel, Juanita described the picture in terms of objects actually visible in the picture. Describing pictures in terms of listing objects was very common among the preschool children in Spanish storytelling as well. In the Spanish examples provided, Julia and Juanita described what is seen in the picture and included their own ideas about the picture as well.

> Un gato . . . no una ama de casa. (A cat . . . no a housewife.) (Julia, Unit 3)

> Es un changuito en la escuela estudiando. (It is a little monkey at school studying.) (Juanita, Unit 1)

A second theme indicated that children preferred to describe animates in their narratives, such as people and animals. It is noticeable that the children identified animals by their common names (bear, cat, or monkey) or in terms of familiar relationships (daddy, baby, or housewife). Describing pictures instead of more original narration is common among all children of this age, including monolingual and bilingual children.

As discussed in the theoretical framework section, preschool children are less likely to tell an actual narrative and more likely to describe pictures and events (Hudson & Shapiro, 1991; Wigglesworth, 1990). Similarly, a third theme indicates that some children's narratives, in these examples, support this claim because they named items on the pictures and described the items in terms of parts of a whole. Body parts were the most frequent parts of a whole named. For example, see Juanita and Lorenzo's quotes; they described the picture of the cat in terms of its body parts.

> Y tiene un vestido y una cola y dos patas y dos manos y una nariz y tiene pelos. (And she has a dress and a tail and two paws and two hands and one nose and she has hair.) (Juanita, Unit 6)

> Brown teeth . . . He had teeth. (Lorenzo, Unit 5)

The examples presented are descriptions of what is seen in the picture, rather than an elaboration about the figure. Naming body parts was a very common pattern found in the Spanish storytelling, and it is interesting that this pattern carries over to the English narratives, albeit less frequently.

A fourth theme indicates that even though most children described the physical aspects of the figures, only few children had a tendency to tell narratives in terms of action. These fewer children described the actions being performed by the figures in the pictures. As a representative of this smaller group, Sara's quote about the picture of the monkeys is presented next. Sara described the picture in terms of what she could see them doing.

> Se está parando este. Y este está sentado. También este. Y está leyendo. Este quiere que se siente. Y no se sienta. (This one is standing. And this one is sitting. Also this one. And this one is reading. This one wants to sit down. And he doesn't sit.) (Sara, Unit 2)

Although it was found that children tend to emphasize actions in their narratives, this is not entirely applicable to their English narratives because they used few predicate-word functions to express action. The majority of the actions were used to describe the tea party scene on the third picture card. For instance, for this picture, some of the children said the following:

They're playing. (Josefina, Unit 4)

A person playing with the babies. (Juanita, Unit 3)

The examples quoted earlier illustrate a common word choice and descriptive action because the children were able to use actions in their descriptions. Other children could be more creative in their descriptions. For instance, as the next quote illustrates, while telling his English narrative about the first picture with the bear, Lorenzo was more imaginative in his description, but repeatedly used a form of the same action verb: to go.

He can go to McDonald's. He got to Chuck E. Cheese. He go to the high school. He go to Chuck E. Cheese. He go to McDonald's. He blind. He go to the doctor. He go to the ballgame. (Lorenzo, Unit 3)

All three examples presented by Josefina, Juanita, and Lorenzo show that some children could use verbs to describe the pictures. However, these three are among the only utterances that were categorized as an action in the concepts category. Thus, these three children focus their narratives on actions instead of just mere descriptions of objects. In general, most children did follow the established theoretical developmental premise that preschoolers tend to describe rather than tell narratives, but some individual differences or specific higher developmental patterns were also found in some bilingual preschoolers.

A fifth theme indicates that although some of the children's descriptions were merely a verbal reflection of what was drawn in the picture, many of the children did invent activities for the depicted characters. In the examples provided next, the children's narratives went beyond what was seen on the card and became very imaginative, creative activities that the figures performed.

Se estaba bañando . . . está cocinando. Se está bañando y se está cambiando. Está comiendo. También, le da de comer a sus niños. Y también baña a sus niños. También busca . . . también busca a sus bebes. Y también, también le da algo de comer a su *kitty*. También, también, juega con su *kitty*. (She is bathing. She is cooking. She is bathing and is changing. She is eating. Also, she feeds her children. And she also bathes her children. Also, also she looks for her babies. And also, also she feeds her kitty. Also, also she plays with her kitty.) (Catalina, Units 6–7)

Y otra vez a casa. Y fueron [fueron] a Boobie [Burger] King y fueron a Chuck E. Cheese y a McDonald's y otra vez a Chuck E. Cheese y a McDonald's y Boobie King. (And again home. And they went to Burger King and they went to Chuck E. Cheese's and to McDonald's and again to Chuck E. Cheese's and to McDonald's and Burger King.) (Lorenzo, Unit 11)

He can go to McDonald's. He got to Chuck E. Cheese. He go to the high school. He go to Chuck E. Cheese (Lorenzo, Unit 2)

In these examples, the children were departing from what is shown in the picture to create something entirely their own. In the last example, Lorenzo described characters going to various American fast-food restaurants. This is not only an embellishment beyond basic description but also an indication of familiar cultural aspects related to his real-life sociocultural experiences. Because some children did not limit themselves to explaining the picture, they allowed for narratives that were more detailed.

Thus, in general, this first pattern, with its five themes, shows that the description of items through nominative words dominates the narratives in both the L1 and L2 in bilingual, Hispanic preschoolers. Identification of items and their parts is characteristic of preoperational perceptual-level children. However, the use of actions, especially in L1, gives a good indication that the children were mature in their narrative abilities. By using actions, some children displayed characteristics of a preoperational functional level. These children were expanding beyond labeling of items to discuss activities and events. In the Spanish narratives, the nominative use is not disproportionate, as is the case for the English narratives. This is not surprising, however, because Spanish was the L1 of the children. The English narratives, on the other hand, relied heavily on nominative words and identification of items. This was expected because English, as the children's L2, was less developed and was still in the midst of being acquired in the bilingual preschool classroom setting.

Second Pattern: Use of Grammatical Structures

The first emerging theme indicated that children used single words or a string of words during the English assessment. Speaking in complete English sentences was rare, with the exception of Lorenzo and Gabriela. As their quotes indicate, they showed a higher level of narrative and language development in English.

He go to the doctor. He go to the McDonald's. He go to the ballgame. (Lorenzo, Unit 3)

The boy is sleeping. Call the doctor. Call the mom. The daddy is sleeping. (Gabriela, Unit 3)

In these previous examples, the children used complete sentences to convey their ideas. The difference between the two children's utterances was that Gabriela's sentences were more grammatically correct. However, both children produced a nominative and predicate part in their sentences. The difference, however, is that Gabriela was able to conjugate her verbs correctly to match her subject, which shows a greater command of the English language. In the Spanish narratives, the children sometimes used single words to describe the pictures, but more often described pictures using complete sentences.

A second theme indicated that few children used both single words and full sentences. For instance, in the next narrative, Jacinta used both single words and full sentences.

Changos. Libros. (Monkeys. Books) (Jacinta, Unit 1, 3)

Va a decir que pide su camisa. Se va a poner su pantalón . . . a su camisa. Se va a poner la falda. (She is going to ask for her short. She is going to put on her pants . . . her shirt. She is going to put on the skirt.) (Jacinta, Unit 7)

A third theme was the use of past tense by some children. Inclusion of the past tense is seen as a narrative grammatical structure that starts to develop in young children and is considered to indicate a more advanced narrative (Hudson & Shapiro, 1991). The past tense in Spanish is noted primarily by using the preterit and imperfect tenses and occasionally the past progressive. For example, Gabriela used the past tense to explain what happened to the kangaroo, and Julia used the past progressive.

Se lastimó. (He injured himself.) (Gabriela, Unit 7)

Estaba corriendo. (He was running.) (Julia, Unit 6)

In the English narratives, use of a past tense was uncommon. Only Lorenzo, on two occasions, used the simple past tense in English.

He got to Chuck E. Cheese. (Lorenzo, Unit 2)

He had teeth. (Lorenzo, Unit 4)

A forth theme indicated that semantic organization of ideas by using complete sentences was a skill that the majority of the children possessed. Eleven children spoke in complete sentences during their Spanish narratives and only two during the English narrative. Moving beyond single-word utterances to organized sentences is a clear indication of semantic development. Presenting information in the present tense develops sooner than the past tense. Therefore, use of the past tense is a more sophisticated semantic ability. Only four children used the past tense in their Spanish narratives, clearly indicating a more advanced semantic development. However, the children's English narratives showed adequate semantic development for age. Thus, the four themes found in the second pattern refer to the use of grammatical structures. These four themes indicated that children used single words or a string of words in their English narratives, with only a few children able to form full sentences. Most children could use the past tense in a variety of complex forms in Spanish, but only a few children could use the simple past tense in English. Most children showed advanced semantic organization abilities in Spanish and a lower level in English, although adequate for age.

Third Pattern: Developmental
Characteristics of Narrative Structures

A first theme indicated that even though some children could tell more-complex narratives, the use of formal narrative structural elements was lacking. These formal structural elements include a typical plot sequence or a classic high-point analysis pattern for narratives, such as a formal beginning, initiating events, a problem, a resolution, and a formal ending (Peterson & McCabe, 1983). But the Hispanic, bilingual children's narratives did not follow this traditional plot sequence model. None of the children's narratives began with an opening statement or phrase. The actions described by children in their narratives were not described as events leading up to a problem and its resolution. The closest any child could come to a classic high-point plot sequence was Josefina's narrative about the kangaroo.

> Se cayó. Fue al doctor. Lo curó. (He fell. He went to the doctor. The doctor healed him.) (Josefina, Units 5–7)

Although the children, in general, did not use the classic pattern for high-point analysis, this does not mean that their narratives were devoid of any narrative structure. Many children displayed the impoverished pattern or miscellaneous pattern for high-point analysis because they did not provide enough information or structure to recognize a high point or other type of pattern. This lack of structure resulted in an impoverished pattern showing a string of words or very little narrative responses and repetition of events (Peterson & McCabe, 1983). Because of these two main characteristics of lack of structure, Kaleo and Lorenzo's narratives, shown next, could be placed into this impoverished pattern because they repeat the same activities repeatedly in their narratives. Kaleo did this repetition of events only in his Spanish narrative, but Lorenzo, on the other hand, showed this repetition of events in both English and Spanish performances.

> Luego lleva una cosa a su casa y va para su casa. Luego . . . luego . . . iba a la casita. Luego va a . . . a la aldea. Luego se bañaba. Luego iba a . . . a . . . ir a la casita. Luego . . . y se bañaba y se va a dormir. Y luego se va . . . se va a comer. (Later he brings something to his house, and he goes home. Later . . . later . . . we went to the little house. Later he goes to . . . to the town. Later he bathes. Later he went to . . . to go to the little house. Later . . . he bathes, and he goes to sleep. And later he goes . . . he goes to eat.) (Kaleo, Unit 23)

> He go to the doctor. He go to the McDonald's. He go to the ballgame. (Lorenzo, Unit 3)

Not only could Kaleo and Lorenzo be using impoverished patterns characterized by repetition of events, a case could be made that they were also displaying a chronological pattern, which involves a succession of actions or an episodic analysis of action sequence, which is a list of actions in seemingly chronological order of what happened first to last according to the speaker (Piper, 2003). These action sequences can also be seen in Catalina and Gabriela's narratives, which follow.

> Está bañando . . . está cocinando. Se está bañando y se está cambiando. Está comiendo. (She is bathing . . . she is cooking. She is bathing, and she is changing. She is eating.) (Catalina, Unit 6)

> Uh umm . . . the doctor wanta go to the house and the doctor (?) the baby . . . the boy is sleeping. Call the doctor. Call the mom. The daddy is sleeping. (Gabriela, Unit 3)

A second theme displayed, which is linked with the narrative structure, is the use of dialogues as narrative elements. In only two narratives, dialogue was present, and this happened only in the Spanish storytelling and was not present at all in the English narratives. Beatriz and Lorenzo were the only ones to add character speech into their narratives.

> Dijo el gato, "¿Qué . . . Por qué estabas cocinando?" Dijo la niña, "Porque me gusta cocinar." Y dijo, "¡Ah! ¿Qué te gusta cocinar? Porque tu eres doctora." (The cat said, "What . . . Why were you cooking?" The girl said, "Because I like to cook" And she or he said, "Ah! What do you like to cook? Because you are a doctor." (Beatriz, Unit 7)

> Fuerlon [fueron] a la escuela y dicen, "¿Qué comieron?" Yo comí una boqueza. Dicen, "Ya me voy otra vez a mi casa." (They went to school and say, "What did they eat?" I ate a sandwich. They say, "I am going home again.") (Lorenzo, Unit 11)

It should be noted that Beatriz used dialogue on more than one occasion during her storytelling, and while doing so, she changed the intonation of her voice. Using dialogue was a rare but interesting occurrence and indicated a more sophisticated level of narrative abilities.

A third theme was the presence of the final narrative element recognized in the narratives as the formalized ending. Two children used common sociocultural convention or phrases to indicate narrative termination; During Unit 2 Pablo said, "Ya se acabó" (It is now finished), six times through his narrative to indicate that he was finished talking about the topic. Ironically, most of the time, he continued to tell more about the characters after stating that the narrative was over. The most formal ending used came from Beatriz. At the end of the narratives (from Unit 8) about the cat and the kangaroo, she said, "Este cuento se ha acabado" (This story has finished). This statement is usually preceded by "colorín, colorado," which is a very commonly used story ending in the Hispanic culture. Even though formal narrative elements were lacking in the Spanish narratives, there were instances of their use sprinkled throughout the children's narratives. Unlike the Spanish narratives, the narratives in English employed no narrative elements. For the most part, the participants did not employ structural narrative elements; however, there were some notable exceptions.

Thus, the third pattern with its three themes shows that the use of formal narrative structures and elements were not prevalent among the Spanish or the English narratives. The vast majority (13 Spanish and 5 English narratives) had little to no structural organization, which is not uncommon for children of this age. More complex structures and elements were used, though rare, during the Spanish narratives. Two children used repetition of events as a form of episodic organization. One child's narrative fits in the classic high-point analysis and uses chronological order of narrative structure. In regard to elements, two children used dialogue, and two used formalized endings. Placement beyond the impoverished pattern and use of narrative elements signals narrative development.

Fourth Pattern: Developmental Stages of Narratives

The main theme emerging from the data follows Karmiloff-Smith's (1991) three-phase developmental model. The procedural first stage is characterized by little detail and lack of organizational structure. Eight children can be placed in this first developmental narrative phase based on their Spanish narratives: Carmen, Gabriela, Isabel, Josefina, Julia, Jacinta, Natalia, and Pablo. Based on their English narratives, three children, Daniel, Josefina, and Juanita, can be placed in this first category as well. Thus, only one child, Josefina, could be placed in the first developmental narrative phase based on her Spanish and English performance. The narratives of these children tended to be more simplistic, as they merely included a description of the picture.

The second or metaprocedural stage is recognized by more development of organization and theme, which was displayed by Alicia, Catalina, and Sara in their Spanish narratives and by Gabriela in her English narrative. Their narratives were more organized and detailed than those in the first stage but lacked the structural elements and complexity of those in the third stage. The third phase is the most advanced stage and incorporates both organizational structures and detailed narratives. Beatriz, Kaleo, and Lorenzo belong to this third stage for Spanish narratives. Interestingly, only Lorenzo can be placed in this third phase for his English narratives. It is important to highlight that the complexity of the story, activities of the characters, and use of structural elements determined the placement of the students in the most advanced developmental phases, and not the length of their narratives.

Thus, the themes found in the fourth pattern indicated that although the children are all approximately the same age and attend the same bilingual preschool, a continuum of developmental stages in their Spanish and English narratives is obvious. The children and their Spanish- and English-language abilities are maturing at different rates, and, thus, their narratives reflect this same range of variation in individuals across their L1 and L2 and between individuals in languages.

Fifth Pattern: Sociocultural Components

In Spanish, adults and children alike use diminutive suffixes to convey smallness, to express affection, to reduce items to a manageable emotional size, and to produce pleasant reactions in others (Gooch, 1967). The first theme showed words, with the diminutive suffix, that were sprinkled throughout the children's narratives. The situations when the preschoolers used the diminutives were in reference to a figure, indication of location, and description. For example, many children referred to the monkeys in the first picture as "changuitos" (small monkeys) and the cat in the second picture as "gatito" (little cat). Others described locations with the diminutive, such as "casita" or small house. In these two situations, the children may be using the diminutive as an indication of size. The pictures are much smaller than the actual object would be. When mentioning an outside character, some children used diminutive endings. In one case, a baby was referred to as "chiquitito" (small one). In another situation, a grandfather was introduced as "abuelito," which is similar to grand pappy. In these circumstances, the children may be using the diminutive as terms of endearment and affection toward another person. Using diminutive suffixes is typical among Hispanics and is quite evident in the narratives told by these Hispanic preschool children.

A second interesting theme found, but infrequently occurring, was the children's use of linguistic gender in their Spanish narratives. In Spanish, every noun regardless of use or meaning is marked by either masculine or feminine linguistic gender. Modifiers, such as articles and adjectives, must agree in number and linguistic gender with the noun that they modify (Gonzalez, Schallert, de Rivera, Flores, & Perrodin, 1999). The second picture used as a stimulus for the Spanish storytelling showed a cat wearing an apron and a beaded necklace and was the catalyst for this issue to come to light in Lorenzo and Alicia's Spanish narratives. The word "gato," Spanish for cat, can be marked by either a masculine or a feminine linguistic gender (as in gato, he cat or gata, she cat). Because the picture depicts a female cat, the children place a feminine definite article, *una*, with the feminine noun *gata* (Lorenzo, Unit 5, and Alicia, Unit 4). In doing so, Lorenzo and Alicia were acting on metalinguistic knowledge because they knew that Spanish needs markers for linguistic gender and that the modifiers must reflect the linguistic gender of the noun. The children were also showing problem-solving behaviors because they could obviously see that the picture was portraying a female cat and were attempting to reflect physical gender of animates through language.

This intriguing cultural aspect was also evident in the English narratives and depicted a third theme in the data. Gabriela and Lorenzo incorporated very American characteristics into their narratives as illustrated in these quotes.

Mama wanta make . . . uh mmm . . . the mama wanta sip it . . . umm . . . the daddy wanta sip it. (Gabriela, Unit 2)

The doctor wanta go to the house. (Gabriela, Unit 3)

Gabriela's examples show a sociolinguistic pattern common in American speech patterns: using *wanta* instead of *want to*. This is a phenomenon typical of native English speakers from the United States. By using wanta, Gabriela was showing that she was a product of the English environment in which she lived. Lorenzo also demonstrated cultural aspects in his story, as portrayed in this quote.

He can go to McDonald's. He got to Chuck E. Cheese. (Lorenzo, Unit 3)

Interestingly, Lorenzo talked about McDonald's and Chuck E. Cheese in his Spanish narratives also. These two fast-food restaurants, especially McDonald's, are the epitome of the American culture. Putting these aspects in their narratives showed that these children were influenced by their American surroundings.

Thus, the fifth patterns showed that living in a sociocultural environment and experiencing certain events influence a person's thinking processes. Therefore, it is not surprising that cultural elements permeated the children's narratives. Culturally relevant grammatical structures (e.g., diminutives and linguistic gender in Spanish) and word pronunciation and phrases (e.g., American pronunciation) were among the most frequent cultural indicators present throughout the children's narratives. Incorporation of cultural events and places was also common to the children's first- and second-language narratives.

Sixth Pattern: Language Proficiency

After considering the various areas of analysis, the issue of language proficiency must be addressed. The first theme refers to language proficiency levels. Because of the fact that only five children were able to give responses in English, it can be surmised that the children who gave no English response were either not available during the English assessment or are a part of the beginning level of the Teachers of English to Speakers of Other Languages (TESOL) standards. A beginner has little to no knowledge of English and uses it infrequently. Even when responses were given in English, they were often single words or strings of words. These types of responses would also be considered as beginner level. Daniel, Josefina, and Juanita were beginners in English proficiency because they struggle responding in English. Gabriela and Lorenzo are more successful in expressing their ideas in English. They use more complex vocabulary and grammar, which would place them at the intermediate proficiency level. In Spanish proficiency, the TESOL standards were also considered. Because Spanish is the L1 of these children, it is not shocking that they are more proficient in Spanish than in English, their L2. According to TESOL standards, all the children would be advanced language speakers in terms of their L1 because they have the ability to relate information easily. It should be recognized that these children have not yet reached Piaget's formal operations stage and do not think abstractly. Their language use is limited by their cognitive processing because they do not yet express abstract concepts, which is a characteristic of the superior proficiency level.

FOUR RECOMMENDED STRATEGIES
FOR INTERPRETING EVALUATION RESULTS

The four recommended strategies for interpreting evaluation results, discussed next, can be used with the five areas of recommended strategies for coding, explained in the next section. That is, the recommended strategies for coding and interpreting linguistic samples of storytelling developmental tasks complement each other and can help evaluators and educators better understand the actual patterns and developmental stages represented in a young, diverse child's collection of samples. In addition, the examples illustrating the recommended interpretation strategies helps evaluators see the verbal behaviors that lead to coding categories.

The four recommended strategies include (1) similar and different patterns on first- and second-language developmental processes; (2) developmental stages of L1 and L2 present in young, bilingual children; (3) linguistic, cognitive, and semantic abilities reflected in the narratives of bilingual preschoolers; and (4) semantic and narrative developmental patterns in first- and second-language performances present in bilingual preschoolers.

Do Oral First- and Second-Language Developmental
Processes Show Similar or Different Patterns?

The evaluation of bilingual (Spanish/English) preschool, Hispanic children provided very good examples of coding categories and patterns across their two languages. Taking into account all the aspects of diverse children's narratives and considering their bilingual backgrounds, we can identify an increasing ability in their first- and second-language development. English and Spanish narrative comparisons provide a fascinating insight into linguistic, cognitive, and narrative development.

Examples are presented as a summary of patterns of similarities and differences shown in Table 6.2. The L1 (Spanish) is the dominant and much more developed language, as it is the children's native and home language in the examples provided. Patterns found in these children indicate that they were able to produce in their Spanish narratives adultlike speech that shows (a) organization of words by category and word and schema relationships, (b) advanced grammatical structure, and (c) recognition of sociocultural and sociolinguistic elements. The children who could provide English narratives were clearly moving from simplistic or babylike talk toward adultlike speech. They were able to identify items in the pictures and, on occasion, describe action. This item and action description is the most prevalent overlap between the English and Spanish narratives and provides developmentally appropriate narratives in both languages. Children of preschool age are expected to emphasize items and actions rather than tell elaborate narratives involving fictional characters and extensive details (Hudson & Shapiro, 1991; Wigglesworth, 1990). Thus, both the first- and second-language narrative samples support the presence of developmentally appropriate semantic and narrative performances in these bilingual children.

Table 6.2   First Area of Recommended Strategies: First- and Second-Language (L1, L2) Similarities and Differences

First Area of Recommended Strategies	Spanish (First-Language, L1) Narratives	English (Second-Language, L2) Narratives	L1 and L2 Narratives
• Do oral L1 and L2 developmental processes show similar or different patterns?	• Adultlike speech • Organization of words into categories and relationships • L1 higher developed than L2	• Moving toward adultlike speech • Words used label items and some actions	• L1 and L2 not at equal levels • Labeling of items and actions

What Developmental Stages of First- and Second-Language Semantic and Oral-Language Development Are Present in Bilingual Preschoolers?

The examples provided by bilingual (Spanish/English) children can be considered typical developmental profiles of rapid sequential bilinguals because they were introduced to English after passing the initial language developmental stages in Spanish. Because the children lived in families where Spanish was spoken at home and attended a bilingual (English/Spanish) preschool classroom, they were exposed to an abundance of language in Spanish and English. As it may be expected, the children's Spanish abilities were stronger than their English abilities, and hence, they seem to be imbalanced or sequential bilinguals with Spanish as an L1 (see Table 6.3). According to the TESOL language-proficiency levels, the children, in Spanish, would be rated superior with Spanish as their first and dominant language. This is obvious because more children were able to complete the Spanish administration and gave more lengthy and detailed responses in Spanish. Even though not all Spanish narratives were equally as detailed and sophisticated, the proficiency level was still at a superior level compared to their English abilities. Because very few children could complete the English administration, it is possible that a large portion of the children were in the nonverbal period of language acquisition as presented by McLaughlin Blanchard, and Osanai (1995). The children who could use formulaic and telegraphic speech patterns can be placed in the third stage of sequential language learning, and a few children were even showing signs of moving into the fourth stage because they could control language production.

How Do Linguistic, Cognitive, and Semantic Abilities Reflect in the Narratives Constructed by Bilingual Preschoolers?

Not surprisingly, the narratives provide a wide range of ability levels in L1 and L2 (see Table 6.4). In Spanish, the children were able to speak in complete

Table 6.3 Second Area of Recommended Strategies: First- and Second-Language (L1, L2) Similarities and Differences

Third Area of Recommended Strategies	Spanish (First-Language, L1) Narratives	English (Second-Language, L2) Narratives	L1 and L2 Narratives
• At what developmental stage were the children in terms of L1 and L2 semantic and oral-language development?	• Most children (10) were at the procedural stage, and a few (3) children were at metaprocedural third stage (Karmiloff-Smith, 1991)	• Nonverbal, third, and fourth stages showing sequential language learning • Beginner and intermediate proficiency levels • All children were at a procedural stage (Karmiloff-Smith, 1991)	• Rapid sequential unbalanced bilinguals • Majority of narratives at first or procedural stage (Karmiloff-Smith, 1991) • L1 narratives at a more advanced developmental stage (Karmiloff-Smith, 1991)

Table 6.4 Third Area of Recommended Strategies: First- and Second-Language (L1, L2) Similarities and Differences

Third Area of Recommended Strategies	Spanish (L1) Narratives	English (L2) Narratives	L1 and L2 Narratives
• How do linguistic, cognitive, and semantic abilities reflect in the narratives constructed by bilingual children?	• Usually complete sentences • Present, past, and progressive verb tenses • Nominative and predicate words used • Diminutive endings • Metalinguistic abilities with linguistic gender	• Usually words, few complete sentences • Present and progressive verb tenses, no third person singular markers • Presence of majority of nominative words • American pronunciation	• Cultural influences • Mixing or changing of sentence subjects

sentences and use a variety of verbs tenses (i.e., present, past, and progressive), whereas in English, very few responses involved complete sentences and only simple verb tenses were used. There was a reliance on present and progressive verbs with omission of the morphological third-person singular marker in English. Just from these two points, it can be understood that the children had greater linguistic and semantic abilities in Spanish. In a few instances, the subject pronoun, either explicitly stated or implied through the Spanish verb, was changed mid-narrative. This may indicate confusion in their thought processes or language production.

In addition, cultural influences were evident in their narratives, which can be attributed to linguistic, cognitive, and semantic understanding and ability. The use of the diminutive in Spanish was the greatest example of cultural influence on speech in this research study. Also in Spanish, linguistic gender agreement with articles and nouns was seen as well. Word choices and American English pronunciation was available in the English narratives. These examples illustrate that the children learned languages as a part of a social and cultural reality that they were able to represent verbally and nonverbally using their symbolic function capacity.

What Semantic and Narrative Developmental Patterns in First and Second Language Are Present in Bilingual Preschoolers?

The trends in narrative patterns were consistent across the two languages (see Table 6.5). In both first- and second-language narratives, there was an emphasis on actions. For that reason, many of the narratives are categorized through chronological high-point analysis, episodic action sequence, and repetition of events. The events may not be in conventional chronological order, but they are in order as far as the speaker is concerned. Regarding the English narratives, they are mostly in the impoverished or miscellaneous categories of high-point analysis because there is a lack of organization and content. Only in a few instances in the Spanish narratives is the classic high-point analysis pattern recognizable. The narrative elements dialogue and formalized endings are only employed in the Spanish narratives. In a few of the Spanish narratives, the children digressed from the narrating about the picture on the card to include personal narratives.

Table 6.5   Fourth Area of Recommended Strategies: First- and Second-Language (L1, L2) Similarities and Differences

Fourth Area of Recommended Strategies	Spanish (First-Language, L1) Narratives	English (Second-Language, L2) Narratives	L1 and L2 Narratives
• What semantic and narrative developmental patterns in both L1 and L2 performances are present across all children?	• Narrative elements: dialogue and formalized endings • Few instances of classic high-point analysis • Personal narratives	• Impoverished or miscellaneous high-point analysis	• Chronological high-point analysis • Episodic action sequence • Repetition of events • Preoperational thinking

Overall, the Spanish narratives were more detailed and sophisticated than the English narratives. This is not unforeseen because the first-language levels are more advanced.

CONCLUSIONS

This chapter presents recommendations of strategies for collecting linguistic samples, coding children's storytelling developmental samples, and interpreting their responses based on patterns and stages of semantic and language development in young bilingual Hispanic children. The patterns and stages presented provide support for a sequential and unbalanced process of first- and second-language acquisition for young, Spanish-dominant children who are exposed to monolingual-Spanish-speaking households, even if they are exposed to a bilingual (English/Spanish) preschool program and live in the United States. The children showed a higher semantic and narrative developmental level in Spanish, showing an advanced stage for their chronological age (i.e., metalinguistic abilities) and also showing transference and progress toward moving into more mature narrative and semantic constructions in their English performance (i.e., from beginning to intermediate levels).

The recommendations and ethnic-educator strategies provided are connected with the advantages of using developmental tasks, such as storytelling, as authentic assessment methods of first- and second-language semantic and narrative development in young Hispanic children. The recommended storytelling developmental task can be used by educators with any group of diverse, preschool children (and older elementary-school children), provided that stimuli and interpretations of children's responses are adjusted to their developmental level and cultural and linguistic backgrounds. Finally, teachers can use storytelling as a classroom-based assessment to link assessment with instruction. Chapter 6 centers on the topic of how teachers can conduct classroom-based assessments of narrative and semantic development and do so in a systematic, valid, and reliable manner that fulfills both instructional and accountability purposes of the standards movement. This objective is achieved by integrating research-based knowledge with best educational practices for young, diverse children.

7

Alternative Reading Instruction

Chapter 7 presents an ethnic-educator approach to alternative reading instruction for young, diverse children. These pedagogical reading strategies represent academic content standards endorsed by Teachers of English to Speakers of Other Languages (TESOL, 2005). The first section of Chapter 7 presents a socioconstructivistic theoretical framework, centered on schema theory and proficient readers' research, supporting reading instruction through reading fluency interventions and the guided-reading approach. The second section of Chapter 7 presents appropriate instructional practices for stimulating literacy development and reading comprehension in young, diverse children, with a special focus on reading fluency interventions and the guided-reading approach developed by Irene Fountas and Gay Su Pinnell (1996). Following the guided-reading approach, teams of teachers form small guided-reading groups so that each child receives direct reading instruction on a daily basis, resulting in reading improvement greater than expected. Discussion of certain guided-reading strategies centers on increasing word-recognition skills through practice and repetition of high-frequency words. Some examples of the application of the guided-reading strategies are provided for the language-arts content area.

The third section of Chapter 7 centers on family involvement to increase reading skills in young, diverse children. Teachers can cooperate with parents to provide regular practice rereading texts at home, resulting in even greater improvements in reading skills in children. Chapter 7 ends with concluding remarks about best reading instruction practices for meeting the educational needs of young, diverse children.

INTRODUCTION

The linguistic and cultural diversity among students in American schools is great. According to the U.S. Bureau of Census, in 1990, more than 6.3 million children between the ages of 5 and 17 spoke a language other than English at home (U.S. Bureau of Census cited in Crawford, 2000). During the late 1990s, one out of three children was from an ethnic or racial minority group, one out of seven children spoke a language other than English at home, and one out of fifteen children was born outside the United States (Miramontes, Nadeau & Commins, 1997). By the year 2000, that had grown to more than 9.7 million (U.S. Bureau of Census, 2000). Given this rapid growth, educating children of racially, culturally, and linguistically diverse backgrounds is a major challenge for school systems across the country. For too many of these diverse children, American education has not been a successful experience.

The problem of low academic achievement and excessive high school dropout rates among diverse students may be, in part, because of three disadvantages that many bilingual Hispanic students endure in school: (1) low levels of English-language proficiency for achieving at grade level in monolingual-English classrooms, (2) being part of a minority and an at-risk population because of high poverty rates, and (3) students' parents and extended family members having little formal education and no experience with the American mainstream school culture (Valdivieso & David, 1988). The reasons for diverse students' poor academic performance are complex, but they stem, in part, from a misalignment between educational practices and diverse students' socioeconomic, cultural, and linguistic backgrounds and educational needs. An important pedagogical goal is to develop instructional strategies to improve reading readiness among young, diverse children, skills that will ultimately impact their overall academic achievement.

The most common learning difficulties and developmental delays among young, diverse children are in the areas of literacy development, reading comprehension, and content retention. With a high influx of English-as-a-second-language (ESL) children, the importance of acquiring literacy skills in the primary grades and identifying effective reading strategies is crucial. In the past, some educators believed that students must be fluent in oral-English-language skills before they could learn how to read. However, contemporary research has shown that young, diverse children are able to learn oral and written language simultaneously (see Alyousef, 2005; Araujo, 2002; Fang, 1999; Hadaway, Vardell, & Young, 2002; Ovando, Combs, & Collier, 2006; Peregoy & Boyle, 2005). In fact, the more young, diverse children read, the more language they will learn. Delaying the instruction of reading deprives diverse students of the rich language and experiences that are found in high-quality text. Reading comprehension is a crucial component of effective instruction, whether instructing native English speakers or ESL children.

THEORETICAL FRAMEWORK SUPPORTING READING INSTRUCTION IN YOUNG, DIVERSE CHILDREN

Most contemporary reading theories place an emphasis on the role and importance of comprehension in becoming a proficient reader. The theoretical framework used in this Chapter is based on *schema theory*. As stated by McGee (1992), a growing body of contemporary empirical research attests to the role of schemata in ESL reading comprehension. According to Grabe (1991), schema-theory research centers on readers developing automatic language skills through vocabulary development, comprehension-strategy training, and making reading-writing relations. The schema theory is chosen as a theoretical framework for this chapter because it provides a socioconstructivistic framework to explain the mental representation of knowledge gained by individuals from their sociocultural experiences since infancy until adulthood.

Constructivist theorists Piaget and Inhelder (1969) explained the construction of knowledge and children's language-learning processes as the interaction between innate symbolic representational functions and environmental stimulation. Vygotsky (1986) expanded on this theory to a socioconstructivist perspective by proposing that the social interactions with adults and peers and the general interactions between individuals and the sociocultural environment primarily impacted children's cognitive and language development. Perhaps one of Vygotsky's (1978) most well-known constructs is the *zone of proximal development*, defined as the distance between what a child currently understands and his or her potential level of development. Krashen (2005) later expanded on Vygotsky's constructs and applied them to ESL learners. Krashen proposed the *input hypothesis*, which states that adults and peers functioning as social scaffolds expand children's current levels of knowledge to higher levels of understanding. Reading-comprehension strategies, applying Vygotsky's concept of proximal development, teach young children, in an explicit manner, how to expand their prior knowledge to new knowledge with higher levels of understanding. Both the constructivistic and socioconstructivistic theories provide a framework for reading-comprehension interventions because they take into account authentic sociocultural stimulation of the home environment and extend it to include pedagogical strategies for enhancing language learning.

From a socioconstructivism perspective, Gonzalez, Yawkey, and Minaya-Rowe (2006) explained three levels of constructing and understanding concepts through language: (1) concrete via recalling and transforming direct experiences with objects through manipulative or motor behaviors (index level), (2) perceptual or figurative via recalling and transforming experiences with graphic representations (symbolic level), and (3) conceptual or constructive via recalling and transforming experiences through nonverbal or verbal behaviors (sign level). In relation to the third conceptual level, Gonzalez, Yawkey, and Minaya-Rowe noted that language eventually becomes a "semantic or abstract verbal tool for conveying meaning" (p. 114). The three levels should be fostered in children by way of meaningful and developmentally appropriate activities that show real-life sociocultural applications.

Reading-comprehension strategies recommended in this chapter center on the third conceptual level of understanding concepts through language (i.e., semantic skills) given the abstract quality of high-frequency words and their functionality. Learning at the abstract level is made easier for young children by the age-appropriate materials that are extensions of classroom-taught standards.

Brown (2000) suggested that the understanding of meaning and the development of semantic abilities, such as reading-comprehension skills, are important ways to stimulate children's language learning. For this reason, in this chapter semantic phrases and sentences are recommended components for developing reading comprehension and language learning in young, diverse children.

According to the schema theory, individuals organize and store knowledge in units or schemata, based on their idiosyncratic experiences of a situation or event. Prior schemata affect the way individuals interpret and store new information. Based on the schema theory perspective, ESL students from different countries have different sociocultural schemata, and most have difficulties in processing knowledge like native English speakers (Kang, 1987). Proficient readers are able to activate prior knowledge stored in memory, which is appropriate to the sociocultural situations to integrate new linguistic data in the comprehension process. Therefore, following the schema theory, a reading curriculum for ESL students should include strategies and activities that activate sociocultural prior knowledge in their first language (L1) and adapt it to the sociocultural situations of their second language (L2).

In addition to the schema theory, the theoretical framework supporting the recommended reading instructional strategies presented in this chapter is also based on proficient readers' research synthesized by Pearson, Dole, Duffy, and Roehler (1992). These researchers investigated what proficient readers do to comprehend text, and they proposed the need for explicit instruction of comprehension strategies before, during, and after reading texts. From this research, Pearson, Dole, Duffy, and Roehler identified seven reading-comprehension strategies that successful readers of all ages should use to construct meaning based on text, including the following:

1. Activate prior knowledge: Readers should use what is known about the organization and content of a text and make mental connections between new information and existing knowledge.

2. Monitor comprehension: Readers need to adjust speed and strategies to increase their understanding of different kinds of text.

3. Repair comprehension: Readers recognize when meaning is lost and use fix-up strategies, such as skipping ahead, to move reading back on track.

4. Determine important ideas: Readers can make predictions and identify important ideas before, during, and after reading a text.

5. Synthesize: Readers summarize information to check their comprehension.

6. Draw inferences: Readers combine prior knowledge with text information to make inferences, predictions, and draw new ideas about a text.

7. Ask questions: Readers mentally ask questions about a text to activate prior knowledge, check their text comprehension, clarify ideas, and focus their attention.

The schema theory research by Pearson, Dole, Duffy, and Roehler (1992) is the guiding framework in Debbie Miller's book (2002) titled *Reading With Meaning*, as well as in *Mosaic of Thought*, a book written by Ellin Keene and Susan Zimmerman (1997). The pedagogical approaches utilized by Miller and Keene and Zimmerman are derived from Pearson, Dole, Duffy, and Roehler's identified reading-comprehension strategies and are adapted to meet young children's developmental needs (e.g., thinking aloud, asking questions, visualizing text, clarifying meaning of text, expressing feelings about texts, summarizing and synthesizing texts, making predictions about texts, and reflecting on texts read). The selected reading-comprehension strategies have two important pedagogical characteristics that meet young, diverse children's educational needs: (1) They are explicitly taught for an extended amount of time, which allows at-risk children to have necessary extra developmental time; and (2) they use children's literature that is meaningful for them because it authentically represents diverse children's prior sociocultural knowledge and experiences.

This chapter adapts research derived from the schema theory for teaching reading to mainstream children to strategies for reading instruction for diverse children, such as ESL learners (August & Hakuta, 1997; Snow, Burns, & Griffin, 1998). Although there is not much heuristic research conducted on theory building to teach reading to diverse children, there are a number of research studies conducted on L1 and L2 acquisition. This later research supports maintenance and continued development of L1 competence for more rapid L2 competence (August & Hakuta, 1997; Cavazos, 1990; Barona & García, 1990; Prado & Tinajero, 2000). This chapter adapts mainstream reading interventions that are supported by schema theory, L1, and L2 research, as promising pedagogical options for meeting the educational needs of young, culturally and linguistically diverse children, such as ESL children. The reading fluency interventions and the guided-reading approach recommended in this chapter can significantly increase reading comprehension and academic achievement in young, diverse children. The focus of reading interventions recommended for young, diverse children is on improving reading fluency because of the key role of recognizing high-frequency words in the development of reading-comprehension abilities.

GUIDED-READING APPROACH FOR DEVELOPING READING-COMPREHENSION SKILLS

To understand how one learns to read we must go back to Laberge's theory, stating that a fluent reader decodes text automatically without conscious direction, leaving attention free to be used for comprehension (Laberge & Samuels, 1974). Beginning readers mostly focus their attention on decoding words (Breznitz, 1987) rather than on comprehending meaning of text (Laberge & Samuels, 1974; Nathan & Stanovich, 1991; Stanovich, 1986). The guided-reading approach proposed by Fountas and Pinnell (1996) applies Laberge's theory in a pedagogical approach to increasing automatic reading skills in young children. Learning how to read is a key ability for academic success of all children. All teachers want their students to become independent, strategic, and competent readers, which is central to the guided-reading approach. Guided reading allows teachers the opportunity to work with dynamic small groups that can be reconfigured throughout the school year to address young children's educational needs, reading levels, strengths, and interests. This flexible pedagogical approach to reading is important to developing comprehension in young, diverse children, such as ESL children, at the early levels of literacy development.

Regardless of skill level, teachers want all their students to develop a lifelong love of reading. Yet for below-grade-level readers, like most diverse and ESL students, this can seem far from their reach. With a guided-reading approach to literacy, teachers can differentiate learning with leveled books; they can integrate word-solving strategies; and they can coach language and concept development to ensure success for young, diverse children. The small-group interaction and opportunity for one-on-one instruction can be a very successful strategy for young, diverse readers, especially for ESL reading instruction. The next section guides early childhood teachers through an explanation of the application of the guided-reading approach for young, diverse children.

APPLICATION OF THE GUIDED-READING APPROACH

Three instructional strategies of the guided-reading approach have been documented as effective for improving children's fluency and reading-comprehension skills: (1) repeated reading, (2) teacher/expert modeling, and (3) student self-monitoring of progress. In addition, guided-reading strategies reinforce problem solving, comprehension, and decoding through the teacher acting as a role model of a good reader. More specifically, during the instructional process, the teacher focuses on various aspects of good reading, such as an analysis of the book title, seeing who the author and illustrator are, picture walking through the text to make predictions about the text, and also framing words to learn important vocabulary prior to reading the passage. This approach teaches students how to be familiar with a text and the reading process, to work closely with the teacher, to ask questions about the text in general and vocabulary in particular, to discuss concepts, and to monitor progress closely.

Guided reading works in stages, as children develop reading strategies, such as predicting, sampling, and then confirming or correcting the student's reading process. The guided-reading approach includes three stages: (1) *the before reading stage,* with the objectives of eliciting prior knowledge, building background knowledge, and introducing the book; (2) *the during reading stage,* with the objectives of picture walking through the book, reinforcing reading strategies, and practicing the reading strategies learned; and (3) *the after reading stage,* with the objectives of reflecting on the reading strategies used, building comprehension by discussing the story, extending the reading by responding to questions through writing and visual learning and reading independently. Depending on the levels and needs of students, the teacher must determine an appropriate order of strategy instruction. Each of the strategies is taught over an extended period, anywhere from three weeks to two months. This framework ensures that young, diverse children have a strong foundation of each reading strategy and provides extra developmental time for making at-risk learners more effective readers.

APPLICATION OF THE SCHEMA THEORY

The application of the schema theory to improving children's reading skills is based on research conducted by Pearson, Dole, Duffy, and Roehler (1992). They identified reading-comprehension strategies for constructing meaning based on text, some of which are discussed in this chapter, including (1) activating schemas and making connections with prior knowledge, (2) creating mental images, (3) asking questions, (4) determining most important ideas or themes, and (5) retelling stories read.

It is always a good idea to begin the school year by introducing the first strategy of reading comprehension—activating prior knowledge or schemas in children. A reader's knowledge of the world provides a basis for understanding, learning, and remembering facts and ideas found in texts (McGee, 1992). Building and activating students' schemas can begin by introducing the concept of *schema* through an instructional activity suitable for the children's age. For instance, a song and related lessons that demonstrate how a reader's schema can change and grow can help young children become more proficient readers. Early childhood teachers can be hesitant to introduce a big word, such as schema, to their young students. However, an instructional activity, such as a song, is a key element to help young children understand an abstract concept. Besides helping children develop the concept of schema, the use of a song as an instructional strategy involves making connections between what children know and what they read. The children are taught to make connections between the text read, their ideas, and real-world experiences.

The second strategy for enhancing children's reading-comprehension skills is visualizing or creating mental images. The children are taught how to "make a movie in their heads," allowing for their own interpretations of the text results in enhanced understanding of text meanings. Teachers encourage children to listen to stories and poems with their eyes closed and compare the images they created inside their heads to the images of the book illustrator or the mental images of fellow classmates. Children are challenged to consider why their mental pictures are similar or different from the book illustrators' images or their classmates' mental images. Through these reflective activities, children are stimulated to understand that mental images are different for each person because the creation of schemas is a subjective process that occurs inside the heads of individuals. Children also learn to understand that book illustrators (who may be the book authors) draw pictures based on their subjective mental images they created for the stories. Children also learn that their schemas are dynamic because mental images grow and change through reading and engaging in discussions with classmates.

The third strategy for enhancing children's reading-comprehension skills is asking questions. Children are introduced to the activity of asking questions by looking at the cover of a book and playing the "I wonder" game. Teachers can model several questions about "I am wondering what the book will be about." Then, the children ask their own questions in three stages: before, during, and after the book is read. Together, the teacher and the students complete an anchor chart with three questions: (1) When do good readers ask questions? (2) Why do good readers ask questions? (3) How can good readers find the answers to their questions? The goal of these three questions is for the children to clarify meaning, speculate about what is to come, and deepen their comprehension of a text.

It is important to note that prior to beginning this third strategy, teachers need to do a lot of work on *how* to ask a question, focusing on language structure, particularly for diverse and ESL students. Teachers need to provide diverse children with practice on the language structure of a question, such as question words (i.e., who, what, when, where, why, and how) and how to form questions (i.e., using proper grammar and syntax rules). A solid grasp of the questioning strategy is crucial when young children begin learning about most important ideas or themes in books, which covers a large amount of content in the curriculum in primary grades. Young children have intrinsic motivation for learning, so questioning strategy seems to come naturally. Children are expected to use their schemas, along with new information found in the text and other books, to answer questions. Teachers can help children answer their posed questions by explaining important information and main ideas or themes in the text.

The questioning strategy is also related to the fourth strategy of determining most important ideas or themes in texts, as both strategies enhance children's understanding of meanings and concepts presented in texts. Mastery of this conceptual skill requires children to have a firm understanding of how all the elements come together in a story. This broad strategy requires teachers to delve into the realm of fiction and nonfiction and to be able to distinguish between the two. Character webs, setting comparisons, and discussions of beginning, middle, and end of stories are all elements of this strategy. Once children are able to verbalize the important people and events in a story, they are ready to move to the ideas and themes found in nonfiction stories.

The fifth strategy for enhancing young children's reading-comprehension skills is retelling or synthesizing what was read. Children can gain a better understanding of the parts of a story and how they fit together to make meaning. Together, the teacher and students can develop a chart of what should be included in a good retelling of a story. Not only is it important for children to know who the characters are, where the setting is, and what the events are, but also to explain this information in their *own words*. Children can use rubrics as checklists for retelling stories. Children can work with peers and their teacher as partners to practice how to tell stories effectively. This strategy, rather than focusing solely on decoding the text, can be a good measure of the children's level of understanding the meaning of texts. Giving students the opportunity to explain the meaning of texts is a good assessment of their reading-comprehension skills, but it is also a measure of verbal elaboration and language flexibility, as children share their ideas with their teacher and peers (Anderson & Roit, 1996).

In summary, there are many benefits for both students and teachers when using guided reading that focuses on the explicit teaching of reading-comprehension strategies. The students benefit because they (1) develop as individual readers while being involved in a collaborative activity; (2) have the opportunity to use higher-level reading-comprehension strategies to read progressively difficult texts at an independent level; (3) interact with readers at different levels (i.e., emergent readers, early readers, and fluent readers) to learn collaboratively from each other's experiences with texts; (4) experience success in reading appropriate texts; (5) learn how to problem-solve with new texts independently; and (6) learn how to think critically with information and the analysis of underlying meanings and concepts presented in texts. Teachers also benefit from using a guided-reading approach because they (1) observe individual students as they problem-solve while working with new texts, (2) assess individual students using running records before or after group reading on a regular basis, and (3) provide students with scaffolding opportunities to build expert reading strategies and a print-rich environment (Fountas & Pinnell, 1996).

Thus, the explicit instruction of effective reading-comprehension strategies is crucial to the development of proficient young readers. Learning reading-comprehension strategies enables young, diverse children to become critical thinkers when working with texts. That is, children can draw from their prior knowledge, think aloud, ask questions, visualize the text, monitor their understanding, and synthesize what they read. Then, the guided-reading approach gives children an active role in the process of learning how to read. This means construction and the use of critical-thinking skills has a central role in the continuous development of young readers' comprehension strategies. Besides the five main reading-comprehension strategies discussed in this section, practice and repetition are an important way in which reading comprehension becomes an automatic process for young, diverse children. In the next section, practice and repetition for improving recognition of high-frequency words are reviewed.

REPETITION AND PRACTICE
MAKE PERFECT

Many American homes consist of afternoon snacks, homework time, and even a little TV or outdoor playtime. This more relaxed after-school time is made possible by mainstream or minority, middle-class parents who are familiar with the mainstream school culture and can help their children with homework. However, in many minority households that are poverty stricken, parents do not have adequate English-language skill and literacy skills in their L1, and they are not familiar enough with the mainstream school culture to be able to help their children with their homework. Some minority children who are fortunate enough to receive community support and have access to transportation are taken to after-school programs where volunteers kindly assist them with their homework. Some minority children might also have the help of their older siblings, who have developed some level of English competence and academic content knowledge. But most minority children have to endure doing their homework on their own, without a computer, Internet, or other resources that have become basic today.

If parents do not possess the English-language skills and prior academic content knowledge to assist diverse children with homework, it is even more important that children develop reading-comprehension skills to help improve their overall academic achievement. Reinforcement and repetition are necessary educational strategies for developing fluent and automatic reading and writing processes in young, diverse children (Flood, Lapp, Tinajero, & Hurley, 1997). They become even more essential as diverse children move up through the grades and reading materials become more difficult (Delgado-Gaitan, 2006). The gap between parents' English-literacy abilities and schools' expectations only grows as children become older. Many researchers have linked school failure to a lack of early literacy skills among young children, regardless of race (Fang, 1999). The lack of early literacy skills becomes a compounded problem when considering language barriers in ESL children.

High-frequency words occur with such regularity in texts that the development of automatic decoding skills in young children is helpful in increasing their overall reading-comprehension skills (Fang, 1999). Fountas and Pinnell (1996) outlined three rationales for the usefulness of memorizing high-frequency words. First, these commonly found words "facilitate fluent reading and allow the reader to pay attention to new words" (Fountas & Pinnell, 1996, p. 171). Second, high-frequency words may be used as a springboard for solving new words and add fluency and speed to the writing process. Last, many high-frequency words have nonphonetic-based spelling patterns (Cunningham, 2005; Fang, 1999). Cunningham pointed out that a child's instinctual reaction when approaching a new word is to use the decoding skills taught in primary grades. The letters are first interpreted with the association of letter-sound phonemes and then retrieved as a phonological representation of the word. The problem with a nonphonetic language, such as English, is that although the initial decoding process is based on prior knowledge of the phonological association, many English words do not fall in the logical phoneme-letter patterns (Vaughn & Linan-Thompson, 2004).

Although classroom teachers use various techniques to introduce and learn high-frequency words, Gonzalez, Yawkey, and Minaya-Rowe (2006) pointed out that most textbooks do not offer meaningful hands-on activities that use differential learning techniques. The basal system for teaching reading, used in most school districts, dictates many of the activities found in the classroom, often supplemented with phonics-based instruction. Although these instructional methods for teaching reading may work for mainstream children, ESL children have culturally and linguistically diverse educational needs that should be considered (Trueba, 1999). Because diverse children do not use high-frequency words in everyday conversation, their comprehension of the meaning of these words is lacking.

Piper (2003) defined five reading processes that children can use to learn high-frequency words, including (1) automatic recognition of letters and words without conscious effort, (2) acquisition of memory strategies, (3) use of prior knowledge, (4) ability to self-monitor reading comprehension, and (5) adaptation of strategies to different reading tasks. These five reading processes clearly show a sequence that begins with simple tasks and builds to more independent learning strategies, all applicable to learning the automatic decoding of high-frequency words. More specifically, Cunningham (2005) outlined the process taken when a child is presented with a new word, beginning with the task of decoding. Although a working knowledge of the decoding process may help with phonetic-based words, a working knowledge of irregularities can also aid in decoding new high-frequency words. Automatic reading-comprehension processes also create a working knowledge of the irregular patterns sometimes found in the English language. As stated by Peregoy and Boyle (2005), "The more words a student recognizes immediately, the more fluent [he or] she will be at processing the language of textbooks and constructing meaning" (p. 386). Thus, the automatic recognition of the meaning that is carried by high-frequency words creates a bridge to vocabulary across academic content areas (Peregoy & Boyle).

Although vocabulary flashcards are used by many teachers for stimulating language development in young children, there are studies indicating that flashcard-based programs can have lasting benefits for increasing children's reading abilities (McGee, 1992). Johnson (1981) indicated that although learning words in isolation could have some negative impact on learning how to read, oral repetition and visual associations in the context of texts can increase students' abilities to correctly identify high-frequency words. Similarly, Wang and Koda (2005) found that even adults acquired sensitivity to word frequency and regularity when taught in context-framed repetition drills.

Although it may be much easier for a child to associate a word with a picture, Armbruster, Anderson, and Meyer (1991) concluded that learning words in isolation negatively impacts reading comprehension. Johnson (1981) noted that even sounding out the word correctly impaired the child's comprehension, as did long pauses taken to recall a high-frequency word. Because of the possible negative connotations of learning words in isolation, Johnson suggested that words be put into a meaningful phrase or sentence. That is, a context provides children with opportunities to create and associate meanings with drills of repeated readings of texts to increase their reading fluency. In a study conducted by Grabe (1991), two groups were studied for syntactical gains; the control group received the information with vocabulary words highlighted but the meaning of the vocabulary not highlighted, and the experimental group received the information with both vocabulary words and meanings highlighted in their computer studies. Grabe found that the experimental group did better on posttests than the control group. Findings suggested that meaning and context increase students' ability to learn high-frequency words and improve their decoding and reading-comprehension skills.

Many states have required school districts to adopt a list of high-frequency words to meet academic standards. For instance, the Hamilton City school district located in southwestern Ohio has chosen the Dolch (1936) list of 220 high-frequency words that students must recognize by sight at the end of first grade. This standard is much higher than the 20 words students are required to know at the end of kindergarten. Typically, in most school districts, the high-frequency word lists continue to grow as students climb through the grade levels, each building on the previous year. Delgado-Gaitan (2006) noted that the growing word lists demand more not only of the students but of the parents as well because children must have a support system at home to become successful at memorizing so many words. Most lists of words are nonphonetic based, making word-attack skills learned useless.

Typically, these word lists are also among the most commonly used words in any text, ensuring that each child will find 50% or more of them in any piece of literature chosen. Although some children struggle with these words, most children eventually pick them up because of extended exposure, practice, and repetition. Teachers work through many repetition exercises during their daily routines and assignments; however, reinforcement at home is essential to ensure acquisition of basic decoding reading skills in young children. Therefore, it is very important for teachers to develop collaborative partnerships with diverse parents to ensure that their children become competent readers.

Though there have been debates regarding which words should be taught and learned because of their high frequency, educators typically use the lists of Dolch (1936). This first list was created based on the frequency with which words occurred in the most common basal texts. Dolch commented that nouns are not included on any list because of their tendency to be subject specific, changing as students moved on to new topics. For this reason, high-frequency words tend to be relatively meaningless words, valued only for their *connectability* (Cunningham, 2005).

Despite the seeming meaninglessness of high-frequency word lists, Johnson (1981) stated,

> Of the approximately 600,000 plus words in English, a relatively small number appear frequently in print. Only 13 words (*a, and, for, he, is, in, it, of, that, the, to, was, you*) account for more than 25% of the words in print and 100 words account for approximately 50%. . . . The Dolch Basic Sight Vocabulary contains 220 words (no nouns). Although this list was generated more than 40 years ago, these words account for more than 50% of the words found in textbooks today." (pp. 49–50)

Thus, young, diverse children can increase their reading-comprehension skills by practicing repetition and recognition of high-frequency words and by learning automatic decoding processes. Teachers and parents need to collaborate in supporting diverse children's learning efforts by reinforcing the memorization of high-frequency word lists in meaningful contexts, such as sentences and phrases, and by doing repetitive readings of texts. Most school districts select high-frequency word lists that represent words commonly found in textbooks across content areas, which increase dramatically with grade levels. Research supports the stimulation of automatic decoding skills in young children to increase their ability to focus on meanings and concepts found in texts and, ultimately, to improve their academic achievement.

ACTIVITIES FOR INCREASING READING ABILITIES

In this section, some instructional methodologies based on contemporary research in word recognition are presented. One of the research-based instructional methodologies recommended by Cunningham (2005) is the use of a word wall in daily classroom activities. Cunningham provided complete, step-by-step, and sequential phonics activities to build the word wall. He suggested that the word wall be chanted, written, copied into personal dictionaries, and referenced in guided reading and writing during daily activities. The presence of a word wall in the classroom increases the time and frequency of children's exposure to high-frequency words, and teachers should implement the use of lists of words into practical daily applications.

Some researchers, however, have recognized that the display of a word wall in the classroom is not enough to acquire high-frequency words (Peregoy & Boyle 2005). Johnson (1981) recommended repeated readings of texts to (1) increase reading fluency and practice with spelling, (2) stimulate conceptual processes, (3) develop automatic decoding, and (4) understand the meanings of words in different contexts. Although repetition and practice are reinforced in most classrooms, they should also be included in activities at home.

Multiple studies explore the use of electronic media to aid in reinforcing reading at home (Johnson, 1981). For instance, García and McLaughlin (1995) and Freeman (1998) found that by using a tape recorder as a model, students increased the words correctly read and decreased the mean error rate. They also proposed that tape-recorded material be modified and used for young children in phonics-based programs designed to teach reading fluency, phrasing, inflection, and other skills needed for reading. More modern technology, such as a CD, can provide an accessible and easily reproducible source of audio material for instructional reading activities at school and home. Next, some additional instructional activities to stimulate reading processes are highlighted in relation to writing activities in the language-arts classroom for young, diverse children.

Additional Suggestions for Applying Reading and Writing Strategies in Language Arts

1. Educators may utilize the language-experience approach (LEA), in which children tell their teacher, or a more capable peer, a story in their own words as the teacher transcribes it. Then, the teacher reads the story back to the children. With guidance, the students eventually begin to read the text on their own. This activity can help connect children's words and personal stories to experiences with print, and it supports the development of phonemic awareness (Diaz-Rico, 2004; Hadaway, Vardell, & Young, 2002).

2. Dialogue journals can be an excellent and flexible follow-up activity to reading a text. Typically, there is no established topic, the teacher is the only reader of the journals, and the grading rubric used by the teacher provides corrections of form but does not evaluate children's writing (Diaz-Rico, 2004). This activity can be adapted for beginning writers by creating *frame sentences* based on the initial text, which students complete by filling in the gaps (Diaz-Rico, 2004).

3. Reading aloud is an excellent practice activity that Hadaway, Vardell, and Young (2002) recommended to stimulate young children to develop "big words and literary sentences" (p. 108). A similar option is to provide children with audio recordings of stories that they can listen to on their own.

4. Children can respond to wordless picture books by predicting with peers what will happen in the story, telling the story as they see it in the illustrations, or writing the events depicted in the pictures (Hadaway et al., 2002).

5. Igoa (1995) encouraged teachers to use artwork. Moreover, Hadaway, Vardell, and Young (2002) suggested that beginning writers respond to stories by drawing and then labeling key points of the illustrations with words and phrases.

6. Engaging in collaborative work, young children can compose the text for a big book. Each child is assigned a page of the book to illustrate, and then each of the pages is bound together to create a big book (Diaz-Rico, 2004).

7. Igoa (1995) described how young children transform stories they write into a simple filmstrip. First, children write their stories, and then they divide the text of the story into sections to accompany each film slide. Then, children record themselves reading the text for each film slide, which becomes the narration for the film. Next, children create the graphics for the story by drawing a series of illustrations on a long strip of paper, which will be fitted to a reel for viewing. Finally, classmates are gathered around to listen to the story, offer constructive feedback, and decide together on sound effects. After practicing the sound effects, the film is viewed again with the audience providing the sound effects.

8. Diaz-Rico (2004) suggested that teachers observe children carefully to discover their interests. Then, teachers can locate texts that support children's interests, with the goal of motivating children by showing them reading is related to their reality and their daily lives.

9. Authenticity in writing may translate as having a real reason and audience for writing (Diaz-Rico, 2004). This may take the form of requesting something, thanking someone for an action or present, writing to a pen pal, writing someone directions to get to a particular place in the community, or other authentic communication purposes.

FAMILY INVOLVEMENT FOR INCREASING READING SKILLS

There have been long-running debates surrounding uncaring parents and uncommunicative schools. The solution lies in each party, parents and teachers, releasing their preconceptions and meeting the other halfway. The typical expectation of mainstream schools is that parents take an active stance in their children's education, ensuring homework is completed, and attending parent-teacher conferences and other school events. Parents, in turn, expect to be informed by the school of their child's academic progress and other activities.

However, it takes a joint effort and the establishment of a partnership between parents and teachers to ensure that communication between home and school is a smooth process. McGee (1992) defined family-school partnerships as "involving school personnel, children, parents, and family members working together to ensure the success of children in school" (p. 2). He also defined four levels of establishing family-school partnerships: individual child, classroom, building, and district. At the individual child level, McGee stated that although parent-teacher conferences and regular communication are necessary, the parent and teacher team should share perspectives and work toward common goals set for the individual child.

McGee (1992) defined both family and teacher as equals, and he broke down the roles of the partners into three aspects: supporting, guiding, and implementing. The implementation role is the strongest of the three, making both teacher and parent responsible for mutually setting goals, establishing an agenda, and implementing goals. McGee stated that many parents do not have the time or energy to take part in building- and classroom-level partnering. But almost all parents, at some point, will be involved with the school regarding their individual child's homework. Supporting this point, many research studies show that at-home activities increase and reinforce previously learned skills (e.g., Diaz-Rico, 2004; Fang, 1999). This point suggests that when students complete their homework, they increase their chances of mastering essential mathematics and literacy skills (Fang, 1999). Teachers typically use or create homework activities that are expected to reinforce the concepts taught in class. Although homework is a widely known convention, its application is often burdensome to diverse families because of language barriers, lack of parents' mainstream academic content knowledge, or survival priorities present at home (Trueba, 1999).

The development of literacy skills in young children is preceded by exposure to books in the early years of their life. Cunningham (2005) stated that children who read more encounter the same words more frequently, increasing their reading fluency rates and comprehension skills. Similarly, Delgado-Gaitan (2006) noted, "home literacy activities provide a framework for observing parents as educators in their natural social milieu" (p. 53). Thus, early literacy exposure at home supports instruction provided at school by teachers (Piper, 2003).

BRIDGING THE GAP BETWEEN
SCHOOL AND HOME CULTURES
THROUGH PARENTAL PARTICIPATION

Research findings support linking new academic materials to students' prior knowledge and real-life sociocultural experiences as an especially effective instructional strategy for young, diverse children (August & Hakuta, 1997). However, a major challenge for educators has been identifying children's prior sociocultural knowledge without relying on myths, preconceptions, and cultural stereotypes. For instance, a common stereotyped perception held by many educators is that Hispanic immigrant parents hold low educational aspirations for their children and are not interested in participating in their children's education. Teachers need to dispel these misconceptions and myths because diverse parents can help identify sociocultural knowledge that their children learn at home. Parents use language and culture as socialization tools for their children, and they act as role models of cultural expectations and behaviors. Lack of resources can also prevent collaboration between educators and diverse parents through school events, such as lack of transportation, lack of access to care for younger children at home, hectic work schedules, and so on.

Early literacy skills begin in the home where a child is raised. Early literacy skills are formed by nightly bedtime stories or songs, daily conversations with parents and siblings, reading labels during a trip to the store, or, perhaps, through the mere glimpse of billboard signs outside the car windows. Regardless of how early literacy skills are developed, they provide the initial springboard for primary education. Many homes of diverse, immigrant families offer rich opportunities to develop bilingual literacy knowledge, yet these children often become monolingual because of limiting English school curriculums. Because of cultural and language differences, there is often miscommunication between educators and parents of diverse children regarding the level of participation or involvement expected (Fang, 1999). It is essential that diverse parents be made equal partners in the children's education as early as possible to maximize the time spent developing literacy skills (Fang, 1999). Although each party acts on behalf of the best interests of the child, goals may be mutually agreed on to bridge the gap between current knowledge and expected learning. This not only involves open communication between home and school but also requires culturally and linguistically appropriate instructions and educational materials sent home by teachers to assist parents with their child's education.

Despite the evidence supporting home literacy practices, the question remains how diverse parents with limited English proficiency and educational background implement homework activities. Several other variables appear to be important for children's academic success, including parents' provisions for academic resources and materials. Fang (1999) pointed out that it becomes the teachers' responsibility to provide adequate materials for learning if the family environment is not already conducive to homework activities. Because most immigrant families are focused on meeting their basic needs, educational materials are seen as a nonpriority, and the academic practice at home provided for children is, therefore, nonexistent. This puts the responsibility on educators to provide adequate educational materials to complete homework activities (e.g., textbooks, access to computers with Internet connection, reference books at nearby public libraries, and access to educational supplies and materials), so that diverse children's learning may continue at home.

Other factors reducing home-literacy practice may include parents' limited English proficiency and illiteracy in their L1 because of limited schooling opportunities in their home country. Stanton-Salazar (2001) commented, "Mexican parents are themselves cognizant of their own limitations, and do express them, often in lamenting fashion" (p. 86). Diaz-Rico (2004) suggested sending homework with instructions in the children's L1, but still some Hispanic immigrant low-income diverse parents may lack sufficient L1 literacy skills. In addition, helping children with homework assumes that diverse parents understand concepts and academic content taught at school. Many teachers misunderstand parents' lack of ability to help with academic homework activities as a lack of concern for their children's learning. Instead, if proper steps were taken to make parents partners in their child's education, the learning would take place twofold, for parents and their children. Wong-Fillmore (1991) suggested that when American teachers expected that Mexican working-class mothers would help their children with their schoolwork, they were making assumptions about academic abilities that the parents did not have. Because of lack of opportunities for their own formal education in their countries of origin, most immigrant parents are unprepared to help their children with schoolwork. Moreover, teachers were also making assumptions about the universality of what, in American schools, counts as academic content knowledge (Wong-Fillmore). If school expectations would be clearly communicated to immigrant parents, the academic success rates of diverse children would improve.

CONCLUSIONS

Early childhood teachers must provide high-quality instruction for young, diverse children. The increase in the diverse population in American schools should be viewed as a time to reform and restructure education to foster equal opportunities for education. It is only by giving diverse children genuine and high-quality educational opportunities to learn that they will increase their reading skills and related academic achievement. A successful reading program should be built on children's prior sociocultural backgrounds and language heritage, resulting in rich knowledge of cultural themes and topics associated with their native language. Schools with diverse populations should have an articulated parent/teacher-partnership program to help educators discover valuable prior sociocultural knowledge. Diverse parents and other family and community members should be supported to build home environments that promote literacy, including a program to encourage reading for pleasure outside of school and after-school programs to provide support with homework through tutoring. School districts need to adopt the state-of-the-art reading strategies by building effective staff-development components that also include diverse parent and teacher partnerships.

8

Conclusions and Recommendations for Educating Diverse Young Children

Chapter 8 presents excerpts of interviews with teachers who were participants in the Bilingual Preschool Development Center (BPDC) and in English-as-a-second-language (ESL) graduate-level courses and with parents of BPDC children. These teachers and parents' interviews are used as illustrations of patterns and transparent conclusions for the book. The teachers and parents' interview excerpts represent the topics covered throughout the chapters of the book. As a main objective, Chapter 8 will represent the teachers and parents' end-of-the-school-year reflections on their teaching and parenting experiences and their feedback about some lessons learned from praxis.

The first section of Chapter 8 presents a reflection of a language-arts teacher of diverse children, who was taking an ESL graduate-level course with the book author as an instructor. This reflection illustrates the importance of providing professional-development opportunities for teachers serving diverse children. Exposing this teacher to the ethnic-educator philosophical principles and socio-constructivistic theoretical perspectives helped her to develop advocacy, commitment, and practical knowledge to better serve her ESL students. The second section of this chapter provides patterns and conclusions through interviews with actual teachers who have implemented the ethnic-educator philosophy and pedagogical model for instructing and assessing young, diverse children. This section shows that teachers can benefit from (1) taking an ethnic-educator approach, (2) learning about diverse early childhood assessment and instructional models and practices, and (3) gaining insight from implementing the ethnic-educator philosophy and praxis in a diverse classroom.

The third section of this chapter presents lively excerpts from interviews with diverse and mainstream parents of young children who participated in the BPDC laboratory preschool, which implemented pedagogical recommendations presented in the book. Parents' interview questions focus on their perceptions about how much learning was observed in children's behaviors at home across cognitive, language, and socioemotional developmental areas during the academic year. Chapter 8 ends with patterns and concluding remarks about best pedagogical recommendations to meet the educational needs of young, diverse children.

INTRODUCTION: THE BPDC AS A LEARNING CONTEXT

The philosophy of the ethnic-educator approach implemented in the BPDC classroom is based on a socioconstructivistic perspective. Participating teachers in the laboratory classrooms were trained to create a context for learning in which young, diverse children could become engaged in interesting activities that encourage and facilitate creativity, discovery, social interactions, and personal interests. Following an ethnic-educator approach, teachers need to function as role models for children to take an active role in their learning. At the same time, teachers facilitate learning at high levels for children to develop critical-thinking skills about real-life situations and for integrating learning across academic content areas. Teachers guide students as they approach problems, encourage students to work in small groups to think about issues and questions, and support students with encouragement and advice as they tackle problems and challenges that are rooted in real-life situations. Teachers also individualize instruction to the interests of their students and provide learning situations that are developmentally adequate and satisfying in terms of the results of their work. Moreover, teachers use peers as tutors and role models for higher levels of learning and development, as children mainly learn from social interactions in small mixed-aged groups. Finally, teachers view parents as social partners to, stimulate in children to grow and developing and to match and integrate cultural and linguistic home backgrounds between family and school contexts.

Thus, in the context of an ethnic-educator classroom, teachers facilitate growth in children's social, emotional, cognitive, language, and literacy skills and learning processes—as do peers, parents, siblings, and other members of the child's community. All classrooms that use instructional strategies compatible with an ethnic-educator and socioconstructivist approach apply the following principles: (1) Learning and developmental processes are viewed as social collaborative activities that occur between children, peers, and their teachers; (2) School learning processes occur in a meaningful context and in relation to children's prior knowledge and real-world learning; and (3) The children's home, cultural, and linguistic experiences should be related to their school experiences.

Consider the reflection of a mainstream language-arts teacher who has accepted the challenge of serving diverse students in an inner-city, northern Ohio school district. This teacher, Cindy, decided to get a master's degree in the Teaching English as a Second Language (TESL) program where the book's author works, and she wrote the reflection while she was taking a graduate-level methods-in-ESL course that the author was teaching. This reflection is chosen as a very good example of how formal exposure to ethnic-educator philosophical principles and socioconstructivistic theoretical perspectives through graduate-level coursework can help teachers develop advocacy, commitment, and practical knowledge to better serve ESL students. Teachers who chose to serve diverse students and their families need to develop personal commitment, advocacy, and social responsibility to care for the educational and social challenges that economically disadvantaged students bring to the classroom.

CINDY'S REFLECTION ON HER TEACHING CAREER

As a professional educator, I have undergone a wonderfully informative journey as a teacher. It began in my undergraduate experience. For the first time, my lifelong dream of being a teacher seemed to come to life in front of me. I loved the different courses, professors, and readings about just *how* to be a teacher. I left college with the enthusiasm and background to begin my career.

Then reality set in. My first teaching job was in an inner-city school in northern Ohio, where the challenges serving poor students were daily, and the experience was beyond any college text. I literally hit the ground running. What helped me to face this challenge was that I was blessed to have a large group of colleagues who provided a collaborative working environment, where I could try new ideas, and we could work together for the betterment of our diverse students. I truly felt that I was making a difference in the lives of my students with my day-by-day work.

From that experience, I knew that I would always be drawn to work with diverse students with some type of educational or social challenges. I just was not sure what those challenges would be. This May, I learned what my new set of challenges would be. This coming fall will be my first experience as an ESL teacher. This new challenge has filled me with excitement and anticipation, as well as a few nerves. A helpful first step in my development as a professional in the ESL area is identifying and articulating my role in the lives of my diverse students, especially the new responsibilities of working with an ESL population. So as part of my formal training in ESL courses, I am engaging in a reflection about my role as an ESL educator.

My Role as an ESL Educator

I believe that my primary responsibility to my students is to be an advocate for them. As an educator, and especially as an important link in their English-language development and cultural adaptation to schooling, I need to be someone who represents their best interest. In doing so, that means that I will create a classroom of diverse and meaningful lessons. I will make every effort to collaborate with their parents and family

(Continued)

(Continued)

members. I will attend relevant staff meetings and assist other classroom teachers in adding insight to the ESL student's development. I will take the time to get to know each student as a person, not just as a learner.

For students who may be new to the area, or country, I believe that it is important to include aspects of their background, homeland, and culture in the classroom. I think that by integrating these personal aspects, I will better engage my diverse students, interest them in learning, and help them feel integrated in the classroom. This will also show my students that I care about them. As my former principal stated regularly, "Students do not care what you know until they know that you care." As an educator in the ESL field, I also consider it a priority to constantly develop as a professional. By meeting with other teachers, attending workshops, reading relevant and new articles and books, and taking courses, I am committed to keep my teaching fresh, current, and up-to-date. I believe that my diverse students deserve the best teacher possible, and it is my responsibility to fulfill that expectation. I think that the professional-development responsibilities of every teacher are amplified for ESL teachers. I also think that this responsibility comes with a distinct privilege: to make a profound difference in the lives of our ESL students.

Strategies for Teaching ESL

As an educator in the ESL field, I believe that is a variety of strategies should be implemented in my classroom. First and foremost, I believe that the lessons that I plan should be meaningful and important. There are many different requirements in place for my students' social development, English-language demands in the curriculum, state testing, district requirements, and I must assure that my lessons are reaching toward these academic goals. I believe that it is important to plan lessons in relation to the interests of my students and relevant to their lives. I also believe that the students' cultural and linguistic backgrounds, knowledge, and skills should be taken into consideration in advance so that appropriate scaffolding can be implemented in teaching and learning. I think that variety is the key—students should not feel like they are participating in the same lesson format over and over again. As an ESL teacher, I am constantly looking for new instructional and learning strategies to try with my students. This may include a different way to present a topic or different instructional strategies, such as creative arts, drama, songs, visualization, peer tutoring, cooperative group work, or the use of technology integration. Teachers need to have a big bag of tricks—and adapting our instruction to the individual educational needs of our diverse students will give each student the opportunity to learn.

Professional Growth and Development

This summer, I have had the privilege to begin my journey as an ESL educator. Along with the skills and beliefs that I already held as an educator dedicated to my diverse students, this summer, my professors have introduced me to many practical ideas and theories that will serve my ESL students well. I have begun to discuss and collaborate with other educators about challenges and struggles as well as successes and joys that come with teaching ESL students. I have been introduced to new research, theorists, and practical strategies associated with ESL instruction and learning processes. I have started to learn about best teaching practices for ESL students as well as develop my own ideas and beliefs about them.

For me, taking graduate-level courses in ESL has been a wonderfully interesting process. In the past, when I used to teach language arts in regular classrooms for mainstream, poor students, I have felt very comfortable with my subject area. The opportunity of teaching English to students who were not native speakers presented a new set of challenges for me. Honestly, it scared me to feel so unprepared for my ESL subject area. How could I teach ESL students when I did not really know how? Luckily, the first two courses in the ESL field opened my eyes to the theories of second-language acquisition and the teaching skills and methods of instruction that go along with it. My most interesting revelation, however, is that the more I learn about ESL instruction, the more I see just how close it is to any other kind of "good" teaching. In taking ESL courses, I have reinforced my belief that good teaching, for any subject area, is "good teaching." This understanding has not only left me more confident about my upcoming new ESL courses in the master's program, but also it has excited me in new ways. I now see my role as an ESL educator to take my enthusiasm and skills that I already have for teaching and combine that with my growing knowledge of ESL theory and practice.

I am so glad that I began on this journey as an ESL educator. Specifically, I feel that the best experience of taking these first three graduate-level ESL courses for me was to engage in online discussions with other educators, the readings that explained practice combined with theory, and the direct exposure to case studies of ESL students and their families. Hearing about the experiences of ESL students with their ESL teachers, in the students' own words, through digital recordings of interviews and digital video clips of classroom interactions, has made a great impact on my view of my role in the classroom.

I end the methods in ESL course with much to look forward to. I look forward to walking into my new classroom this fall with an excitement and a plethora of ideas to share. I look forward to September, when my next ESL course in the series begins. I look forward to continuing to develop as an ESL educator and as an advocate for my students.

As Cindy's reflection illustrates, ESL teachers are faced with many challenges, such as teaching content and the English language simultaneously to students. But ESL teachers are also faced with the privilege of serving as role models, cultural bridges, and facilitators for diverse children and their families. As Cindy's reflection shows, ESL teachers need to make a special commitment to becoming advocates and invest the care and time in ESL professional development. Next, interview excerpts of teachers working in the BPDC show how experience in a bilingual classroom can be the most useful opportunity for professional development.

INTERVIEWS WITH TEACHERS
PARTICIPATING IN THE BPDC PROJECT

An Interview With Connie: A BPDC Teacher Aide

[Interviewer (I); Connie (C)]

I: What is your language and cultural background?

C: I am a monolingual-English speaker, with some knowledge of a little
Spanish. I am an assistant teacher, supporting the bilingual teachers at a
BPDC bilingual classroom. I am a first-year bachelor student in an early
childhood-teacher education program. I just completed my second year in
a bilingual classroom, so by now, I have learned some Spanish phrases and
commands to use in the classroom with the children. I always had an interest in working with diverse children, and I find the bilingual classroom a
very interesting learning environment that the children and I enjoy a lot.

I: What are your views about how children develop?

C: I believe in exposing young children to a lot of interaction in small groups
and in using modeling and social interaction to learn a language from teachers
and peers. I like group interaction to teach because through listening to
adults and peers, children can learn a lot of language. I think that exposure
to language is very important for social development and learning literacy
skills. I also think that children develop at different paces depending on their
home background and degree of exposure to academic materials before they
enter preschool. They primarily learn through play at home and daily life situations in the family settings, as well as in the community and social situations, like going shopping at the supermarket, going to a restaurant, and
visiting their local library. I also believe that children need one-to-one interaction with teachers and that we need to adapt instruction to individual differences and follow the children's interests.

I: What have you learned from your experience teaching in the BPDC?

C: I have learned how to apply my teaching skills when working with bilingual children. Especially the children whose first language, and only one,
was Spanish have made a lot of progress learning English and also improving their Spanish up to age level. The monolingual-English-speaking
children have also picked up quite a bit of Spanish, like their colors, songs,
the alphabet, and many phrases and words. By the middle of the school
year, monolingual-English children started to communicate with the
Spanish-speaking children in Spanish, at least with simple sentences and
phrases. The same happened with the Spanish-speaking children. All of a

sudden, the Hispanic children were interested in talking to their main-stream peers in English.

I: What developmental patterns have you observed in the children through-out the school year?

C: Children have learned a lot of social skills. The first few months of school, children got acclimated to our classroom routine and got adapted to new teachers and classmates. When children came back from Christmas break, they started to show a lot of progress in their language and social develop-ment. The Spanish-speaking children started to use English in the classroom with teachers and peers. They could understand instructions and commands in English. Before the Christmas break, Hispanic children did not speak English at all. It was like an eye-opening experience for me! Of course, there were individual differences, for example, age and personality made a differ-ence in how much language they had learned. The more shy children did not like to speak a lot, and we had to prompt them to talk more in the classroom, whereas the more sociable children were more talkative and used more lan-guage on a spontaneous level.

Also, in general, all children showed more interest and enthusiasm in learn-ing after the Christmas break. Of course, again, there were individual differences. I believe that academic achievement depends on individual dif-ferences because some children are more interested in books and curious about asking questions and knowing about how things work and are named. Overall, the children learned a lot of academic content, and I also learned a lot from their behaviors. I learned a lot of Spanish as well, and it was quite interesting to learn new strategies for teaching children from different cultures and languages. I also learned that children adapt easily to speech in different languages and to children and teachers from different cultures. Teaching in the bilingual classroom was indeed quite an interesting learn-ing experience for me!

An Interview With Blanca: A BPDC Teacher and TESL Master Student

[Interviewer (I); Blanca (B)]

I: What is your language and cultural background?

B: My first language is Spanish because I am from Colombia. I also studied Italian for five years and English as a foreign language (EFL) since I was in primary school until I finished college in Colombia.

I: How long have you been living in the United States?

B: I have been living in the United States for two years. But I visited the United States several times before as a tourist. I also studied English for so long back in my home country that I thought that my adaptation to live here would be easier. However, my cultural adaptation has been very difficult, a very hard process. As a result, my views of the world, and how people are supposed to behave, have changed a lot in the past two years.

I: What is your experience teaching ESL?

B: I have taught EFL at an international school back home, which was serving Americans living in Colombia. This particular international school served high-socioeconomic-status (SES) students and helped them learn Spanish as they maintained their academic English. In the United States, it is very different; at the BPDC, I am teaching ESL to minority, low-SES, Hispanic children, who need to learn English as a survival tool for cultural adaptation.

I: What are your views about how children develop?

B: I believe that children need to learn their first and second language at the same time using a natural approach. I also believe that the acquisition of a first language is very important for learning a second language, and also for learning content areas. Language is the medium for learning, and there are internal and external factors affecting language learning. Teachers need to provide a balance between lack of resources at home and adequate school resources for poor minority students. Some minority children need extra developmental time for learning, and all of a sudden, they express all they had been assimilating for a long time. These children are probably shy, and language helps them to become more sociable and less conscious of their language differences. Some minority children, when provided with extra stimulation and developmental time, become less encapsulated, and all of a sudden, their development blossoms!

I: What are some of the instructional strategies that you prefer to use with ESL children?

B: I am a socioconstructivist. I believe that there is an important role of learning from interactions with others. But I also like to structure my classroom because that is how I was taught during my undergraduate years. Now, I have managed to become semistructured in my teaching approach. But I still use some structured instructional activities. For instance, I need to have group time and talk with children about content, and other days, I do free activities. I also believe in adapting instruction to individual differences. I believe that we, as teachers, are facilitators and guides for our students. Every child is unique and has strengths and weaknesses. For example, one student only wanted to work in small groups, so I would give her choices, but all options were good matches for her learning style and preferences. In all learning situations, we were achieving instructional objectives but adapting lessons to how she learned. We had the luxury of individualizing instruction and working on one-to-one situations because we had a low ratio between children and teachers at the BPDC.

I: How has your personal background affected your teaching preferences?

B: My personal background has definitely influenced my teaching. I have changed a lot my teaching style in comparison to how I used to teach in Colombia because in the United States I am also a language-minority individual. My new identity also affects how I communicate with minority parents, as I identify with them, and I want my Hispanic students to succeed in academia. Here I am more attached to the Hispanic children because they belong to my same minority group. We all belong to the same group of Hispanic immigrants, and we are experiencing the same process of identification with the United States-Hispanic group. So I am definitely going to be an advocate for dual-language immersion in bilingual programs for Hispanic children. Children in the BPDC classrooms also develop a special bond with me because they realize I speak two languages, Spanish and English, and they want to become bilingual like me.

I: What are the most important lessons that you have learned through your BPDC teaching experience?

B: I have seen, through real-life children, how important it is to maintain their first language to accelerate the process of ESL and also for development and learning across content areas in general. Teachers need to be facilitators and allow a collective-teaching process to take place in their classroom. Teachers need to incorporate real-life tasks, like writing children's names for mailing letters to their grandparents, for a real-life purpose. The BPDC classroom offers children a nurturing environment, where teaching and learning become a dual process because children are learning from their teacher, and teachers are learning from the children.

I: Did you observe any developmental milestones in the BPDC children throughout the school year?

B: Children learned English and Spanish through imitation from peer models and from teachers. Children were constantly trying to imitate words they had heard and started talking in their second language by the middle of the school year. Children were also telling their parents about the new words they had learned in their second language. It was incredible to watch some children blossom learning their second language in a few months. Some shy children who would never talk even in their first language at the beginning of the school year started to overcome their shyness and talk constantly in their first and second language in the classroom. Most of them go through an *incubation* or *encapsulated* period; I think it is a developmental period in which children gather information and gain experience in their second language in a silent manner. Other students gained confidence and motivation in learning a second language by identifying with their bilingual teachers as role models. These students needed a "push" and a model that would validate their bilingual and bicultural identity to start speaking in both their first and second language. For instance, some minority children learned to like American food and snacks at school, but at the same time, they continued to like their food, language, habits, and traditions at home. That is, children added the second language and American culture and did not lose any of their valuable first language and home culture. Another pattern I observed was that most children became more developmentally mature as the school year went by. Children learned how to fulfill their teachers' expectations and showed much more social and emotional maturity. For instance, some children who were very shy at the beginning of the school year started to communicate more easily with peers and teachers as the year went by. Children also developed school readiness in a short period of time because they arrived to us as "little babies" with underdeveloped first language and no second language at all, and they ended the school year with preliteracy skills and conceptual thinking abilities in both languages. I am a witness that real learning took place for children in the BPDC classrooms, and they developed first- and second-language maturity as a tool for learning all content areas to appropriate grade levels. I believe that all children developed cultural adaptation and, hopefully, can do better at school.

The BPDC teaching has been the best experience during my master TESL program. Teaching at the BPDC has helped me learn how to teach according to the children's developmental levels, to go with their own learning pace, and to use first and second languages as instructional tools and as a support system to partner with minority parents. Teaching at the BPDC has made me a better person. My teaching has made me improve as a person because I learned to identify with the minority Hispanic children and their parents I was serving. It has taught me that teachers always need to expect a little more from their students. It has been a great experience!

We will continue our conversation with BPDC diverse and mainstream parents about the children's language development and learning throughout the school year. Then, in the final section, patterns and concluding remarks from both teachers and parents will be presented.

INTERVIEWS WITH DIVERSE AND MAINSTREAM PARENTS PARTICIPATING IN THE BPDC PROJECT

Interviews With Hispanic Parents

About half of the children and their families served at the BPDC were from a Hispanic background. All these families immigrated from Mexico, Puerto Rico, or other Latin American countries during the past two to eight years. Some children were born in their home countries and others in the United States. Most parents and children spoke Spanish at home, with some older children introducing English as a preferred language to communicate with siblings at home. Most stay-at-home mothers hardly spoke English; however, mothers who worked outside the house had some command of English. Most fathers spoke English at an intermediate level because they needed it to communicate at work. Most fathers worked in construction or in landscape jobs. Most families immigrated to the United States looking for better jobs, economic situations, and educational opportunities for their children. Overall, the Hispanic-immigrant families were doing their best to culturally adapt to living in the United States and welcomed the opportunity to provide a bilingual education for their preschool children.

All the interviews took place by the end of the school year. The book author interviewed all parents either face-to-face or via a phone call to the household. The interviews with the Hispanic parents were recorded and then transcribed, and the interviews were conducted in Spanish and translated into English by the author.

An Interview With the Father of a
Three-Year-Old Puerto-Rican Boy

Ignacio was four years and one month when the book author interviewed his father. He had attended the preschool since the start of the preschool year, and the interview took place at the end of the school year.

[Interviewer (I); Father (F)]

I: What languages do you speak at home?

F: We speak Spanish at home all the time because both my wife and I are from Puerto Rico. Ignacio did not speak English at all when he started coming to the preschool at the beginning of the school year. He was barely three years old when he started coming to the preschool. My wife and I thought that he needed to interact with children his age so that he could learn some English. Perhaps, he did speak a few words in English that he had learned on his own from watching children's television programs. Now, Ignacio can say complete phrases in English because he has learned some English at school. He likes to mix phrases in Spanish and English when he speaks at home with us. I can speak English, but my command of Spanish is much better, as it is my native language. My wife can only speak Spanish. She is learning some English now, but still her pronunciation is problematic, and she can only speak a few phrases in English. When we respond in Spanish, Ignacio responds back in Spanish. Ignacio does not have any friends in the neighborhood who speak English because we live in an apartment and people move all the time.

I: Does Ignacio have any brothers or sisters?

F: He has a baby sister. Teresa is only nine months old now, and so she does not speak yet. Ignacio is still kind of an only child at home because his sister is still too young and does not interact with him yet. They were both born in Cincinnati.

I: How long has your family been living in the United States?

F: I came first to Cincinnati to study my master's in engineering. I had finished my bachelor degree in Puerto Rico and learned some English back home. However, when I came here I realized I needed to continue learning more English, so my adaptation was not easy. Then, after one year, I went back to Puerto Rico and married my fiancée. We moved back together to Cincinnati, and Ignacio was born a year after.

I: How has the adaptation process to living in the United States been for you and your family?

F: At the beginning, it was difficult, especially with my studies at the university because I did not speak English fluently. I also felt out of place because I was the only Hispanic student in my program of studies. I like the services better here than in Puerto Rico, especially the health services and the high-quality doctors you can find here. But I find it difficult to adapt to the social group; it is a completely different culture. The problem for my family is that we have not been able to develop friendships with American families, and we do not have family here. When we go back to Puerto Rico for a visit, we have so many family members with whom to share and enjoy family celebrations and social gatherings. Now, with the preschool, it is better because we have been able to meet some people, the teachers, and other families, and Ignacio has found many children with whom to play and learn English from. My wife and I also chose the bilingual preschool program for Ignacio because he could speak Spanish. So we thought it would be easier for him to understand the teachers and start learning English.

I: Have you noticed any progress in Ignacio's language and social development since the beginning of the school year?

F: Ignacio has made lots of progress. Now he can count from 1 to 11 in English and Spanish, and he also likes to sing many songs he has learned at school, including the alphabet song. He also likes to draw and speaks much more than before. He speaks a lot now and has started to mix both languages, with some phrases in Spanish and some phrases in English. He has also learned how to play with other children.

Interview With the Mother of a Three-Year-Old Hispanic Girl

Silvia was 3 years and 11 months by the end of school year when the book author interviewed her mother. The interview took place in Spanish, and it has been translated into English by the book author. Silvia had been coming to the BPDC since the beginning of the school year.

[Interviewer (I); Mother (M)]

I: What languages do you speak at home?

M: We only speak Spanish at home. Silvia still prefers to speak Spanish at home, but she has started to speak English at home with more frequency since she started attending the preschool. She is our only child, and so there are no other children who she socializes with when she is at home. I only speak a little English, but her father can communicate in English. So Silvia prefers to speak English with her dad, even though he responds in Spanish to her questions. She insists on speaking in English to me, even though I only speak a few words of English. She has also started to mix both languages since she is attending the preschool. She says phrases in which she uses words of both languages. For instance, she says, "Esto es mi (this is my) foot," and "This is my silla (chair)." We insist that she only speaks Spanish at home, but she continues with mixing both languages or talking to us in English. She also prefers to speak English when we go out. For instance, when we go shopping, Silvia likes to speak in English with the store clerks. She also prefers to watch television in English. Now that she has become more interested in playing with children, she also has started to play with English-speaking children in our neighborhood.

The other day we had a very interesting experience with our communication at home. I am now taking some English classes, and so my teacher had asked me to use some simple phrases at home so that I could speak in English to Silvia. I said to her, "Go to bed," and she was very surprised to hear me talking in English for the first time. Her face illuminated with happiness, and she liked it a lot that her mom could speak in English to her.

But I can only say a few phrases, and I cannot yet read to her in English because my pronunciation is bad. So I only read stories to her in Spanish.

I: How long have you been living in the United States?

M: My husband came first from Guatemala, and he has been here for seven years. I came from Mexico about six years ago, and we met here in Cincinnati through my cousin. I came because I wanted to become independent from my family of origin back home. I also wanted to change my lifestyle.

I: How has the adaptation process to living in the United States been for you and your family?

M: The difficulty has been not being able to communicate in English at my jobs and also during my pregnancy for my visits with the doctors. Now, I also experience communication problems when I have to take Silvia to the dentist and to the pediatrician. But overall, we have a better life than back in our home countries because we can have jobs and be economically independent from our families of origin. I also like that at the preschool I can communicate with teachers and other parents who also speak Spanish. I feel that the bilingual preschool classroom setting is better for Silvia because I do not speak English well, and I do not want Silvia to forget how to speak Spanish.

I: How has the preschool changed Silvia's behaviors?

M: Silvia has always been an independent child at home, but she did not know how to play with other children. She had, especially, a problem of sharing her toys with other children because she was a very egotistic and shy child. Now, Silvia has become even more independent than before attending the preschool, and she also has become much better at keeping her toys organized and neat at home. She also has made tremendous progress in her language skills in both Spanish and English. Now, she also tries to share her things with adults and other children at home. Her play has also become much more creative. She enjoys looking at books much more, likes to be read to, and enjoys listening to music and songs. Most definitely, I can say that Silvia has made a lot of progress since the middle of the school year in many behaviors. At the beginning of the school year, Silvia did not want to go to school, but then she would return home happy saying that she liked her school day. But my most difficult battle was that she did not want to go to bed early enough to be able to get up early the next school day. She would wake up in a bad mood. But what was funny is that after a few weeks, she would also wake up early on her own on Saturdays saying that she wanted to go to school.

Interview With the Mother of a Four-Year-Old Hispanic Boy

Felipe was four years and three months by the end of school year when the book author interviewed his mother. The interview took place in Spanish, and it was translated into English by the book author. Felipe had been coming to the BPDC since the beginning of the school year.

[Interviewer (I); Mother (M)]

I: What languages do you speak at home?

M: We speak only Spanish at home. Felipe is the third born in our family; he has two older siblings, a girl who is 11 years old and a boy who is six years old, and a younger sister who is two years old. Even though my older sons go to school and have learned how to speak English, still, they prefer to speak Spanish at home with Felipe. Part of the reason for my children's preference to speak Spanish at home is that I only speak Spanish. My husband speaks a little English, and so he also speaks in Spanish at home with our children. My older daughter likes to read storybooks in English to her younger siblings. So when Felipe started attending the preschool, he only spoke a few words of English. He has improved a lot in how he speaks Spanish and has learned many more words and phrases in English.

I: How has your adaptation process to living in the United States been?

M: My husband and I only spoke Spanish when we came to the United States, so the most important problem has been to learn English and be able to communicate with people. My husband and I are from Mexico, and I came to the United States over eight years ago, and my husband came 13 years ago. We have been living in Cincinnati for over one year now, and before we lived in Columbus, Ohio, for six years. My husband immigrated first to the United States; he came to work as a cook, at a restaurant in North Carolina. Then I came, and we started looking for a better job for him. I do not work because I dedicate all my time to take care of the children and the house.

Other than the language difficulties, I do not see many differences between living in the United States and Mexico. We had access to good schools for the children also in Mexico, the same as here. The only difference is that I have difficulties communicating with the teachers in the United States. So I have to communicate through my older daughter; she translates for me at parent-teacher conferences.

The main reason motivating us to come to the United States was that my husband could get a better job with a higher salary. We also like that our children have the opportunity to learn how to speak English at school, even though we still want to keep their Spanish alive, and so we continue to speak only Spanish at home.

I: Have you noticed any changes in Felipe's behaviors since he started attending preschool?

M: Felipe is now able to play by himself. He can play more games now, and he sings and talks a lot more while he plays. He has become more active and engages in many spontaneous activities at home more often now than before attending preschool. Felipe has also become more sociable, and he enjoys playing with his siblings a lot more. He has learned to count to 10 in English, but he still uses his fingers to count. He has learned the colors and attempts to do some scribbles. He does not know the alphabet yet, but he has developed an interest in doing scribbles and drawings. He also has learned pieces of the alphabet song in English that he sings at home.

An Interview With the Mother of a Three-Year-Old Hispanic Girl

Rosa had been coming to the BPDC since the middle of the school year, and the interview took place when Rosa was three years and eight months by the end of her second school year. The interview was conducted in Spanish, and it was translated into English by the author of the book.

[Interviewer (I); Mother (M)]

I: What language do you speak at home?

M: We speak Spanish at home, but lately my older son (he is 10 now) prefers to speak English at home. But I only speak Spanish, so still Spanish is mostly spoken at home. Rosa has started to mix Spanish and English lately, but still most of the time she prefers to speak Spanish at home.

I: How long have you and your family been living in the United States?

M: My husband came from Mexico to Cincinnati about four years ago. He was looking for a job that would pay him better than back home so that he could earn a living for his family. He was studying architecture back home; he was already in the middle of his studies, but it was very difficult because we did not have enough money to pay for our living expenses. As he was doing pretty well here and had found a job in a restaurant, I came from Mexico with our two children about two years ago. None of us spoke any English when we came, so it was very difficult at the beginning. But by now, I have learned at least some English, just some words and useful phrases, and at least, I can get along during our daily life. My husband is learning some English, as he is taking a course in the community college. I work in a factory. I am learning some English at home when I hear my 10-year-old son speaking in English to Rose.

He is doing well at school, and now, he can read and write in English. All of us, including my husband and Rose, are learning some English from my older son.

I: How has the preschool experience changed Rose's behavior at home?

M: Rose's Spanish has improved. She speaks now in full sentences and likes to talk with people when we go out. She speaks some English now, like words and some phrases that she uses often with her brother. She did not speak any English when she started going to the preschool about six months ago.

Interviews With Mainstream Parents

About one-fourth of the children and their families served at the BPDC were from a mainstream background. Parents and children spoke only English at home; however, attending the preschool had prompted children to introduce Spanish at home when speaking to parents and siblings. Children used simple phrases and complete sentences to communicate in Spanish at home, and if parents and children did not understand, children translated from Spanish into English attempting to teach their relatives some Spanish.

An Interview With the Grandmother
of a Five-Year-Old Mainstream Boy

Joshua had been coming to the BPDC since the beginning of the school year, and he was five years and six months at the time of the interview.

[Interviewer (I); Grandmother (G)]

I: With whom does Joshua live?

G: Joshua lives with my husband and me. We are his grandparents. Joshua also has a one-year-old brother. We are the legal guardians for both boys. He also spends some weekends with his mother, who also lives in Cincinnati. Both boys were born here.

I: Why did you choose to place Joshua in the bilingual classroom?

G: I thought that Joshua could learn some Spanish and that would be good for his development. It has been a good decision. Joshua is now talking in Spanish using some words and phrases at home and translates back to English for me. He likes to watch television programs in which children also talk some Spanish, like "Dora the Explorer." He repeats the Spanish words that he hears on television. He also has improved his English a lot. Now, he speaks English more clearly and can use complete sentences. He is now more interested in playing with other children and likes the outdoors.

Overall, the bilingual classroom has been a good experience for Joshua. He likes it a lot and has improved his language and learned a lot of new things at school, like colors and numbers and songs. He also has learned to like books, and he asks me to take him to the public library; it has become his favorite outing. I have received good reports from the teachers saying that Joshua has made lots of progress in his social and academic behaviors since he started school.

An Interview With the Mother of a Four-Year-Old Mainstream African American Girl

Bridget had been coming to the BPDC since she was three years old. The interview took place by the end of her second school year when Bridget was four years and 11 months old.

[Interviewer (I); Mother (M)]

I: What language do you speak at home?

M: My husband and I only speak English at home, and so does Bridget's older sister; she is nine years old. We are a mixed marriage; my husband is black, and I am mainstream. However, we were both born and raised in Ohio, so we share similar middle-class backgrounds. I decided to place Bridget in the bilingual preschool because I believe speaking another language is an advantage. I learned some Spanish in high school, and I liked it.

I: Have you noticed any progress in Bridget's development since she started preschool?

M: I have seen a lot of progress in this past two years in Bridget's behaviors at home. She can comprehend much more Spanish than last year. She has been using more Spanish at home this year, even though she started saying some Spanish words at home since last year. She can say all the letters of the alphabet, many colors, and words in Spanish now. She is also mixing Spanish and English more this year than before. She says phrases like, "May I have some agua (water)?" Bridget tries to talk to her older sister and me in Spanish. I have tried to respond to her using some Spanish words and even to read to her some story-books in Spanish. But she is not interested in listening to me talking in Spanish; I guess because I cannot pronounce Spanish words well.

We have no exposure to the Hispanic community at home. However, Bridget has made good friends with a Hispanic girl at the preschool, whose name is Carolina; she also happens to be black, like Bridget's father. This little girl came with her family from the Dominican Republic, and so she is a Spanish-dominant speaker. They help each other at school, as they translate for each other, explaining what the teacher or peers said in their first language. For instance, Bridget would translate into Spanish what the teacher said in English so that Carolina can understand. This friendship has helped both of them learn their second language (Spanish for Bridget and English for Carolina) faster. It is very interesting to see how they are helping each other become bilingual at a faster rate together. They complement each other very well and enjoy helping each other.

I have also noticed progress in her English-reading skills. Bridget can read some words in English now. She has improved her phonic skills in English and can sound out letters. She is also using more complex words in English when she talks. However, she is not much interested in talking; she is rather shy, and so when she does talk she is brief and goes to the point.

So Bridget has learned a lot in the bilingual preschool, and that is why I decided to send her for a second year. She is learning a lot from her bilingual teachers. I like that the bilingual preschool has a low ratio between teachers and children. Bridget is a social person, and so she enjoys a lot the teachers' attention that she gets at the bilingual preschool. Bridget likes to answer teachers' questions and to interact with her peers. Bridget is definitely enjoying her experience at the bilingual preschool. And as a mother, I am very satisfied as well to see so much progress in Bridget's learning!

Interviews With the Parents of Mainstream Hispanic Children

About one-fourth of the children and their families attending the BPDC were from a mixed mainstream and Hispanic background, such as the mixed marriage between a mainstream mother, born and raised in Ohio, and an immigrant father who was born and raised in Mexico. Most mothers spoke some Spanish or were making the effort to learn it because their husbands and their children used Spanish and English to communicate at home. All children were born in the United States. Some mothers were homemakers, and others worked outside the home. Most fathers worked in construction companies or in landscape businesses.

An Interview With the Mother
of a Four-Year-Old Mainstream Hispanic Boy

Jack had been coming to the BPDC since the middle of the school year. The interview took place by the end of his second school year when Jack was four years and seven months old.

[Interviewer (I); Mother (M)]

I: What language do you speak at home?

M: We speak Spanish and English at home. Jack prefers to speak English at home more often. But since attending the preschool, Jack has become more interested in talking in Spanish with his father. My husband is from Mexico, and he speaks both Spanish and English at home. He is a construction worker here, and he used to work in construction in Mexico. I only speak English, but I am taking some Spanish lessons at church so I can also talk in Spanish with my family. I especially need to learn Spanish to speak with our Mexican relatives, who only speak Spanish. I am a stay-at-home-mother. My husband and I are both high school graduates.

I: What progress have you observed in Jack's behaviors since he started attending preschool?

M: Jack is now more talkative than before; he also has become more sociable and interested in playing with other children. He also likes more to be read to and enjoys doing puzzles and listening to music at home. Jack has more initiative now in helping at home, like setting the table and picking up his toys. He has also improved a lot in respecting the toys of his siblings and taking care of his baby sister.

An Interview With the Mother
of a Five-Year-Old Mainstream Hispanic Girl

Florence had been coming to the BPDC since the beginning of the school year, and the interview took place by the end of her second school year when Florence was five years and three months old.

[Interviewer (I); Mother (M)]

I: What language do you speak at home?

M: We speak English and Spanish at home. Florence prefers to speak in English at home. Her father is from Mexico, so he prefers to speak in Spanish at home. But he speaks English well, which has helped him to find a better job at a store. I am the general manager for a restaurant. We are both high school graduates. I was born and raised in Ohio, but through interacting with my husband and his Spanish-speaking friends, I have learned to communicate in Spanish. My Spanish may not be perfect, but I can establish a conversation with native Spanish speakers. My oldest child also prefers to speak in Spanish at home. We have three children, a seven-year-old son, then Florence, who is five years old, and a one-year-old baby girl.

I: How has the experience of attending preschool changed Florence's behaviors at home?

M: Florence now has become more confident to speak Spanish at home. She is a shy child, so she did not like to speak in Spanish before because she was afraid of making mistakes. Now she is starting to talk in Spanish to her father and siblings at home. She also has started to mix both languages. For instance, she would respond to an English question in Spanish. In general, she has become more confident in her use of Spanish and has also improved her English skills. She can also entertain herself at home and become more independent about taking care of herself. I am happy with all the progress I have seen in Florence's development.

An Interview With the Mother of a Four-Year-Old Mainstream Hispanic Girl

Patricia had been coming to the BPDC since the beginning of the school year, and the interview took place by the end of her second school year when Patricia was four years and four months old.

[Interviewer (I); Mother (M)]

I: What language do you speak at home?

M: We speak both English and Spanish at home. Patricia's father speaks Spanish as a first language. He is from Mexico and came to the United States eight years ago. He works with a landscaping company. I am a homemaker. Both of us studied only until middle school grades. We have been married for eight years now. I am from Ohio. I can understand Spanish, but still speaking Spanish is somewhat difficult for me. So I mostly speak in English at home. I am learning, though, a lot of Spanish now, both from my husband and my children. Patricia mixes Spanish and English when she speaks.

I: How has the experience of attending preschool changed Patricia's behaviors at home?

M: She has become more talkative and likes to play with children more than before. Patricia has also developed more independence from me, like she can now ask for something she needs to an adult without my help. Before she wanted me to ask questions or for things she wanted, like when she attended a birthday party she did not want to stay by herself. Now, I can leave her at a birthday party and then come back to pick her up, and she can deal with taking care of her needs. Patricia also enjoys going places and meeting people more now than before. She has become more outgoing and knows and can say what she wants and needs. I guess she was shy and had less language before. She also likes to help around the house, like setting the table and bringing things we need. She is more interested in pleasing adults and taking care of the needs of others. Overall, she has become more mature and confident.

OVERALL CONCLUSIONS

As can be observed in the interviews of parents and teachers, some patterns emerged in the changes of children's behaviors resulting from attending bilingual preschool classrooms. The first pattern refers to language development during the academic year. Most children had increased their language development in both Spanish and English significantly from the beginning to the end of the school year. This progress in bilingual language development happened for the three groups of children attending the BPDC, including (1) Hispanic, monolingual-Spanish children, (2) mainstream, monolingual-English children, and (3) mainstream, Hispanic, English- and Spanish-speaking children. However, the group of children who made the most progress was the Hispanic, monolingual children because they entered the preschool with lower levels of Spanish proficiency and speaking no English. By the end of the school year, the Hispanic children were speaking Spanish clearly and in full sentences, having made progress at age level, and speaking English at an intermediate level with phrases and ability to use social language with teachers and peers.

The second group of mainstream, monolingual-English children had learned some Spanish phrases and words, enough to communicate in Spanish with teachers and peers and to be able to understand classroom instructions and general commands. The third group of mainstream Hispanic children had become more confident using their Spanish for social interaction with teachers and peers and had increased their command of more complex English-language patterns and vocabulary. By the middle of the school year, all children were communicating with each other using both languages. It was quite interesting to see that English-dominant children made an effort to use the dominant language of their Spanish-speaking peers to interact with them and vice versa. In contrast, at the beginning of the school year, only monolingual groups of children emerged, with children more interested in communicating with the teacher who had their same dominant language. The *language-segregated* groups tend to dissolve by the middle of the school year.

Finally, all children had started to mix both languages when interacting at school and home. Children both mixed languages in the same sentence (i.e., *code mixing*) and used *code switching* after completing sentences in one language. Both social communication strategies, code mixing and code switching, are normal patterns of language development in bilingual children. These social communication strategies indicate that bilingual children are transcending the use of language as a code to focus on symbols or meanings and the formation of concepts. Therefore, these social-communication strategies indicate the advantages of bilingualism for cognitive development, that is, the attainment of higher levels of semantic development. Children also liked to translate phrases in their more dominant language for friends and teachers at school, as well as for parents and siblings at home. The mainstream children were also attempting to teach Spanish at home to their parents and siblings.

The second pattern refers to teachers and parents reporting progress for most children in social development gained since attending preschool. For instance, changes in behaviors at home and school referred to increased interest in playing with other children outside the household, ability to respect others' feelings and property, ability to share toys, ability participate in group games and follow rules, interest in participating in larger groups, interest in helping peers and siblings (such as helping as translators for parents, peers, and teachers), more assertiveness in talking to adults and peers using their second language, and an overall enthusiasm and motivation for interacting with people. Most parents and teachers reported that children had become more assertive about expressing their feelings, needs, and wants and about initiating social interactions with adults and peers. This increased assertiveness was related to learned socialization skills that had made children more extroverted and sociable. The bilingual preschool teachers were hopeful that evidence of children's progress in socioemotional development would translate in gained cultural adaptation to schooling that would match mainstream teachers' cultural expectation of socioemotional maturity. This gain would certainly help preschool children in their transition to public schools.

Minority parents reported difficulties with socially adapting to their new lives in the United States because of the lack of English-language proficiency, the social isolation, and the lack of social interaction with other mainstream families. However, the children's participation in formal schooling had helped minority families develop social networks with their community. Minority parents reported that their children were helping their siblings and parents learn English at home and gain sociocultural adaptation to the mainstream school culture through developing friendships and social contact with teachers and other families. Minority children showed increased interest in teaching English to their parents and siblings and liked to see their parents use both Spanish and English at home to assert their new bilingual identity modeled at the preschool. Minority children showed increased used of both languages at home, with a preference for code switching and code mixing. In fact, the more language skills children developed in both languages, the more they enjoyed and preferred to use code switching and code mixing with parents and siblings at home.

Still, minority parents reported difficulties with social adaptation to their new life in America because of distance from their relatives still living in their home countries. All minority parents reported a major motivation for immigration to the United States was to improve the economic situation of the family and provide better educational opportunities for their children. All minority parents considered that learning English was necessary to attain a better education for their children, better jobs, and a better income for the family. However, all parents also wanted their children to maintain their Spanish language and Hispanic culture because it was part of their home life and cultural heritage.

Mixed Hispanic and American families also had issues with the use of two languages at home by children because parents may only be proficient in one of the two languages. All mixed marriage situations comprised an American mother and a Mexican father (family situations that were represented by about one-fourth of the children in bilingual classrooms). These dual-language home settings resulted in fruitful situations for children becoming more secure about using Spanish at home. In turn, the children's use of two languages at home resulted in mothers who were more motivated to improve their Spanish skills. Finally, all family members were becoming proud of being bilingual and self-assured about their minority identity.

The third group of mainstream children showed an increased interest in using Spanish at home and in modeling for parents and siblings the use of Spanish words and phrases. Children also liked to watch television programs in Spanish and to imitate words learned in their play. Most mainstream children also had made good progress in their English-language skills, with most parents reporting an increase in clarity and the use of complete sentences at home.

The third pattern in parents and teachers' interview responses referred to progress in learning academic content since starting attending the bilingual preschool. Most children had learned how to count, the alphabet, colors, and songs in both Spanish and English, abilities that were used spontaneously in their play. For instance, children liked to sing and talk more in their games, resulting in their play becoming more creative with the introduction of dialogue between dolls and complex language. Teachers reported their observations that most children developed in spurts and milestones, including a silence period, in which children internalized language patterns, and then an emerging speech period, in which second language emerged in chunks or memorized phrases that were applied correctly to social situations. Teachers reported that most children had gained prereading skills, such as interest in books and listening to stories, ability to do phonics or identify letters and familiar words, and ability to sound out letters and write their names. Bilingual preschool teachers were confident that evidence of gained academic achievement and prereading skills in most children was connected to gains in verbal and nonverbal conceptual ability and critical-thinking skills. Teachers attributed the children's academic achievement and cognitive progress to increased first- and second-language ability and to using both languages as tools for thinking and methods of instruction.

The fourth pattern refers to satisfaction in lessons learned from the experience of teaching in the BPDC reported by teachers and satisfaction with the progress made by the children in their learning and development reported by the parents. Teachers felt that the actual observation of children's progress in response to the dual-language, ethnic-educator curriculum had been an eye-opening experience for them. Teachers observed the positive impact of individualizing instruction to the children's interests, strengths, weaknesses, and developmental needs. Teachers in the BPDC acknowledged the value of real-life contact with diverse students for them to realize the positive impact of bilingual education for young, diverse children's development and learning processes. The use of ethnic-educator pedagogical strategies contributed to teachers' professional development and their realization that the development of commitment and a caring attitude proves to be a good teaching strategy. Teachers reported learning as much from observing the children's development as the actual children learned from their teaching. The learning of both the children and the teachers attests to the value of social interaction in real-life experiences.

Best wishes for teaching successes with young, diverse children!

Appendix

Alignment of Philosophical and Pedagogical Principles and Pedagogical Strategies Endorsed by the Ethnic–Educator Approach for Young, Diverse Children

Philosophical Principles	*Pedagogical Principles*	*Pedagogical Strategies*
Principle 1 *Developmental and Humanistic View of Learning*	*Socioemotional Nature of Teaching and Learning Processes*	
• **Holistic developmental perspective** for learning across cognitive, linguistic, and socioemotional developmental and academic areas (language arts, mathematics, science, and social studies)	• **Developmental and humanistic** view of learning processes and academic achievement • View of **teaching and learning processes as a social and affective experience**	• **Holistic** and **thematic curriculum** that aligns content across developmental areas with **children's interests,** idiosyncratic differences, and sociocultural backgrounds • Need for teachers to develop **personal rapport** and knowledge of young, diverse children's sociocultural backgrounds
Principle 2 *Holistic View of Learning and the Curriculum*	*Internal and External Factors Affect Resilience and At-Risk Conditions*	
• **Socioconstructivistic** perspective with the interaction of internal (maturational, psychological, and biological) and external (cultural, social, schooling, and family settings) factors in development and learning	• Teachers need to help young, diverse children develop **conceptual frameworks** *across* knowledge and problem domains, that can be connected to real-world experiences	• **Individualizing the curriculum** • Development of **critical-thinking skills** (metalearning, metacognitive, cognitive, and metalinguistic strategies) • **Connection** of concepts learned and content areas taught to prior sociocultural knowledge and real-world experiences

(Continued)

(Continued)

Philosophical Principles	Pedagogical Principles	Pedagogical Strategies
Principle 3 *Pluralistic and* *Transcultural Perspectives*	*Culture and Language* *Represented in Assessment* *and Instruction*	
• **Pluralistic pedagogical approach** because it celebrates cultural and linguistic diversity as an asset enriching the learning potential of young, diverse children in multicultural and multilingual minds and spirits	• **Language is a conceptual tool** for learning and representing sociocultural and emotional processes • **Language as a cultural process** to socialize children to be literate • Teachers develop **alternative pedagogical approaches that link assessment to instruction**	• **Use language as a method of instruction** for additive bilingualism and biculturalism • Use **cultural styles of learning and thinking** of diverse cultures and languages • Use **alternative assessments** that measure **potential for learning** and represent **cultural and linguistic diversity**
Principle 4 *Teachers as Advocates and* *Cultural Mediators*	*Teachers as Advocates and* *Cultural Mediators*	
• **Advocacy position** that calls teachers to develop cultural awareness and *personal connections* between their family history and their students' sociohistorical backgrounds	• Teachers need to **develop nurturing learning communities** • Teachers need to act as **mentors for developing rapport** with young, diverse children and *partnerships* with their parents	• Role of teachers as **sociocultural mediators or bridges, advocates, mentors, and role models** for young children and their families • Teachers need **to integrate diverse cultures and languages into the curriculum**

References

Adler, P. S. (1975). The transitional experience: An alternative view of cultural shock. *Journal of Humanistic Psychology, 15*, 12–23.

Alyousef, S. (2005). Teaching reading comprehension to ESL/EFL learners. *The Reading Matrix, 5*(2), 126–137.

American Educational Research Association (AERA), American Psychological Association (APA), & National Council on Measurement in Education (NCME). (1999). *Standards for educational and psychological testing.* Washington, DC: AERA.

Anderson, V., & Roit, M. (1996). Linking reading comprehension instruction to language development for language-minority students. *The Elementary School Journal, 96*(3), 295–309.

Araujo, L. (2002). The literacy development of kindergarten English-language learners. *Journal of Research in Childhood Education, 16*(2), 232–247.

Armbruster, B., Anderson, T. H., & Meyer, J. L. (1991). Improving content-area reading using instructional graphics. *Reading Research Quarterly 26*, 393–416.

August, D., & Hakuta, K. (1997). *Improving schools for language minority children: A research agenda.* Washington, DC: National Academy Press.

Baker, C. (1992). Attitudes and language. In L. M. Malave & G. Duquette (Eds.), *Language, culture, and cognition* (pp. 22–47). Clevedon, UK: Multilingual Matters.

Banks, J. A., & McGee Banks, C. A. (1993). *Multicultural education: Issues and perspectives* (2nd ed.). Needham Heights, MA: Allyn & Bacon.

Barona, A., & García, E. (1990). *Children at risk: Poverty, minority status and other issues in educational equity.* Washington, DC: National Association of School Psychologists.

Bellak, L., & Bellak, S. (1991). *Children's apperception tests* (8th ed.). Larchmont, NY: C.P.S.

Bjorklund, D. (2000). *Children's thinking: Developmental function and individual differences* (3rd ed.). Belmont, CA: Wadsworth.

Bogdan, R. C., & Biklen, S. K. (1982). *Qualitative research for education: An introduction to theory and methods.* Boston: Allyn & Bacon.

Breznitz, Z. (1987). Increasing first graders' reading accuracy and comprehension by accelerating their reading rates. *Journal of Educational Psychology, 79*(3), 236–242.

Brown, D. H. (2000). *Principles of language learning and teaching* (4th ed.). San Francisco: Longman.

Carnegie Task Force on Learning in the Primary Grades. (1996). *Years of promise: A comprehensive learning strategy for American children.* New York: Carnegie Corporation of New York.

Cavazos, E. (1990, November). *An executive initiative for Hispanic education.* Testimony presented before the U.S. House of Representatives, Committee on Education and Labor, Washington, D.C.

Chrispeels, J., & Rivero, E. (2001). Engaging Latino families for student success: How parent education can reshape parents' sense of place in the education of their children. *Peabody Journal of Education, 76*(2), 119–169.

Colby, A., & Kohlberg, L. (1987). *The measurement of moral judgment.* New York: Cambridge University Press.

Collier, V. (1994). *Promoting academic success.* Alexandria, VA: TESOL.

Collier, V. (1995). *Promoting academic success for ESL students: Understanding second language acquisition for school.* Alexandria, VA: TESOL.

Collier, V. P., & Thomas, W. P. (2001, February). *Reforming school for English language learners: Achievement gap closure.* Feature speech delivered at the annual meeting of the National Association for Bilingual Education, Phoenix, AZ.

Collier, V. P., & Thomas, W. P. (2004). The astounding effectiveness of dual language education for all. *NABE Journal of Research and Practice, 3*(1), 1–20.

Cortazzi, M. (1993). *Narrative analysis.* London, UK: Falmer Press.

Crawford, J. (2000). *At war with diversity: U.S. language policy in an age of anxiety.* Tonawanda, NY: Multilingual Matters.

Cummins, J. (1989). *Empowering language minority students.* Sacramento, CA: California Association for Bilingual Education.

Cummins, J. (1991). Interdependence of L1 and L2 proficiency in bilingual children. In E. Bialystock (Ed.), *Language processing in bilingual children* (pp. 70–89). Cambridge, UK: Cambridge University Press.

Cunningham, A. (2005). *Spotlight on comprehension: Building a literacy of thoughtfulness.* Portsmouth, NH: Heinemann.

Delgado-Gaitan, C. (2006). *Building culturally responsive classrooms: A guide for K–6 teachers.* Thousand Oaks, CA: Corwin.

Díaz, M., & Klinger, C. (1991). Towards an explanatory model of the interaction between bilingualism and cognitive development. In E. Bialystock (Ed.), *Language processing in bilingual children* (pp. 167–192). Cambridge, UK: Cambridge University Press.

Diaz-Rico, L. T. (2004). *Teaching English language learners: Strategies and methods.* Boston: Allyn & Bacon.

Dickinson, D. K. (Ed.). (2001). *Beginning literacy with language: Young children learning at home and school.* Baltimore: Brookes.

Dolch, E. U. (1936). *A basic sight vocabulary.* Boston: Pearson.

Eisenberg-Berg, P., & Hand, L. (1979). The relationship of preschoolers' reasoning about moral conflicts to pro-social behavior. *Child Development, 50,* 356–363.

Fang, Z. (1999). The development of literate potential in literature-based and skills-based classrooms. *Journal of Early Reading and Writing, 4*(1), 1–25.

Fantini, A. (1991). Bilingualism: Exploring language and culture. In L. Malave & G. Duquette (Eds.), *Language, culture, and cognition* (Vol. 69, pp. 110–110). Bristol, UK: Multilingual Matters.

Feldman, R. S. (1999). *Child development: A topical approach.* Upper Saddle River, NJ: Prentice Hall.

Flood, J., Lapp, D., Tinajero, J., & Hurley, S. (1997). Literacy instruction for students acquiring English: Moving beyond the immersion debate. *The Reading Teacher, 50*(4), 356–358.

Fountas, I., & Pinnell, G. (1996). *Guided reading: Good first teaching for all children.* Portsmouth, NH: Heinemann.

Freeman, R. D. (1998). *Bilingual education and social change.* Clevedon, UK: Multilingual Matters.

García, E. E., Jensen, B. T., & Cuéllar, D. (2006). Early academic achievement of Hispanics in the United States: Implications for teacher preparation. *The New Educator, 2,* 123–147.

García, E. E., & McLaughlin, B. (1995). *Meeting the challenge of linguistic and cultural diversity in early childhood education.* New York: Teachers College Press.

García, G. G., & Beltrán, D. (2003). Revisioning the blueprint: Building for the academic success of English learners. In *English learners: Reaching the highest level of English literacy* (pp. 197–226). Newark, DE: International Reading Association.

Gauiento, W., & Morley, J. (2001). Text and task authenticity in the EFL classroom. *ELT Journal, 55*(4), 347–353.

Gonzalez, V. (1996). Do you believe in intelligence? Sociocultural dimensions of intelligence assessment in majority and minority students. *Educational Horizons, 75*(1), 45–52.

Gonzalez, V. (1999). The impact of paradigmatic shifts on second language research. In V. Gonzalez (Ed.), *Language and cognitive development in second language learning: Educational implications for children and adults* (pp. 298–302). Needham Heights, MA: Allyn & Bacon.

Gonzalez, V. (2001a). Immigration: Education's story past, present, and future. *College Board Review, 193,* 24–31.

Gonzalez, V. (2001b). The role of socioeconomic and socio-cultural factors in language-minority children's development: An ecological research view. *The Bilingual Research Journal, 25*(1, 2), 1–30.

Gonzalez, V. (2006). Profiles of cognitive developmental performance in gifted children: Effect of bilingualism, monolingualism, and SES factors. *Journal of Hispanic Higher Education, 5*(2), 142–170. Thousand Oaks, CA: Sage.

Gonzalez, V. (Ed.). (2007). *Minority and majority children's development and achievement: An alternative research and educational view.* Bethesda, MA: University Press of America.

Gonzalez. V., Bauerle, P., Black, W., & Felix-Holt, M. (1999). Influence of evaluators' beliefs and personal backgrounds on their diagnostic and placement decisions. In V. Gonzalez. (Ed.), *Language and cognitive development in second language learning: Educational implications for children and adults* (pp. 269–297). Needham Heights, MA: Allyn & Bacon.

Gonzalez, V., Bauerle, P., & Felix-Holt, M. (1996). Theoretical and practical implications of assessing cognitive and language development in bilingual children with qualitative methods. *Bilingual Research Journal, 20*(1), 93–131.

Gonzalez, V., Brusca-Vega, R., & Yawkey, T. D. (1997). *Assessment and instruction of culturally and linguistically diverse students with or at-risk of learning problems: From research to practice.* Needham Heights, MA: Allyn & Bacon.

Gonzalez, V., & Riojas-Clark, E. (1999). Folkloric and historical views of giftedness in language-minority children. In V. Gonzalez. (Ed.), *Language and cognitive development in second language learning: Educational implications for children and adults* (pp. 1–18). Needham Heights, MA: Allyn & Bacon.

Gonzalez, V., & Schallert, D. (1999). An integrative analysis of the cognitive development of bilingual and bicultural children and adults. In V. Gonzalez (Ed.), *Language and cognitive development in second language learning: Educational implications for children and adults* (pp. 19–55). Needham Heights, MA: Allyn & Bacon.

Gonzalez, V., Schallert, D. L., DeRivera, S., Flores, M., & Perrodin, L. M. (1999). Influence of linguistic and cultural variables on conceptual learning in second-language situations. In V. Gonzalez (Ed.). *Language and cognitive development in second-language learning: Educational implications for children and adults* (pp. 19–55). Needham Heights, MA: Allyn & Bacon.

Gonzalez, V., & Yawkey, T. (1993). The assessment of culturally and linguistically diverse students: Celebrating change. *Educational Horizons, 72*(1), 41–49.

Gonzalez, V., Yawkey, T. D., & Minaya-Rowe, L. (2006). *English-as-a-second-language (ESL) teaching and learning: Classroom applications for preK–12th grade students' academic achievement and development.* Needham Heights, MA: Allyn & Bacon.

Gooch, A. (1967). *Diminutive, augmentative, and pejorative suffixes in modern Spanish: A guide to their use and meaning.* Oxford, UK: Pergamon Press.

Grabe, W. (1991). Current developments in second language reading research. *TESOL Quarterly, 25*(3), 375–406.

Green, M., & Piel, J. A. (2002). *Theories of human development: A comparative approach.* Needham Heights, MA: Allyn & Bacon.

Hadaway, N., Vardell, S., & Young, T. (2002). *Literature-based instruction with English language learners.* Needham Heights, MA: Allyn & Bacon.

Hall, G. C., & Barongan, C. (2002). *Multicultural psychology.* Needham Heights, MA: Allyn & Bacon.

Harrison, P. L. (1991). Assessment of adaptive behavior. In B. A. Bracken (Ed.), *The psychological assessment of preschool children* (pp. 317–340). Boston: Allyn & Bacon.

Heath, S. B. (1983). *Ways with words: Language, life, and work in communities and classrooms.* Cambridge, UK: Cambridge University Press.

Hernandez, D. J. (2006). *Young Hispanic children in the U.S.: A demographic portrait based on Census 2000.* New York: SUNY.

Hernandez, D. J., Denton, N. A., & Macartney, S. E. (2007). Young Hispanic children in the 21st century. *Journal of Latinos and Education, 6*(3), 209–228.

Hicks, D. (1990). Narrative skills and genre knowledge: Ways of telling in the primary school grades. *Applied Psycholinguistics, 11*(1), 83–104.

Hudson, J., & Shapiro, L. (1991). From knowing to telling: The development of children's scripts, stories, and personal narratives. In A. McCabe & C. Peterson (Eds.), *Developing narrative structure* (pp. 29–53). Hillsdale, NJ: Lawrence Erlbaum Associates.

Igoa, C. (1995). *The inner world of the immigrant child.* Hillsdale, NJ: Lawrence Erlbaum Associates.

Johnson, P. (1981). Effects on reading comprehension of language complexity and cultural background of a text. *TESOL Quarterly, 15,* 169–181.

Kang, Y. (1987). Content and formal schemata in ESL Reading. *TESOL Quarterly, 21*(3), 461–481.

Karmiloff-Smith, A. (1991). Beyond modularity: Innate constraints and developmental change. In S. Carey & R. Gelmen (Eds.), *The epigenesis of mind: Essays on biology and cognition* (pp. 171–197). Hillsdale, NJ: Lawrence Erlbaum Associates.

Keene, E., & Zimmerman, S. (1997). *Mosaic of thought: Teaching comprehension in a reader's workshop.* Portsmouth, NH: Heinemann.

Kohlberg, L. (1987). *Child psychology and childhood education: A cognitive developmental view.* New York: Longman.

Kohlberg, L., Levine, C., & Hewer, A. (1987). *Moral stages: A current formulation and a response to critics.* Basel, Switzerland: Karger.

Krashen, S. (2005). Let's tell the public the truth about bilingual education. In V. Gonzalez & J. Tinajero (Eds.), *NABE Review of Research and Practice, 3,* 165–173.

Laberge, D., & Samuels, S. J. (1974). Toward a theory of automatic information processing in reading. *Cognitive Psychology, 6,* 293–323.

Mandler, J. M. (1989). Categorization in infancy and early childhood. In M. A. Luszcz & T. Nettelbeck (Eds.), *Psychological development: Perspectives across the lifespan* (pp. 127–139). Amsterdam: Elsevier Science.

Markman, E. M. (1984). The acquisition of hierarchical organization of categories by children. In C. Sophian (Ed.), *Origin in cognitive skills: The 18th Annual Carnegie Symposium on Cognition* (pp. 376–406). Hillsdale, NJ: Lawrence Erlbaum Associates.

McGee, L. (1992). Focus on research: Exploring the literature-based reading revolution. *Language Arts, 69*(7), 529–537).

McLaughlin, B., Blanchard, A. G., & Osanai, Y. (1995). *Assessing language development in bilingual preschool children.* Washington, DC: National Clearinghouse for Bilingual Education.

Miller, D. (2002). *Reading with meaning. Teaching comprehension in the primary grades.* Portland, ME: Stenhouse.

Miramontes, O., Nadeau, A., & Commins, N. (1997). *Restructuring schools for linguistic diversity.* New York: Teachers College Press.

Nathan, R. G., & Stanovich, K. E. (1991). The causes and consequences of differences in reading fluency. *Theory Into Practice, 30*(3), 176–184.

National Education Goals Panel. (1998). *Principles and recommendations for early childhood assessments.* Washington, DC: U.S. Government Printing Office.

National Research Council. (1999a). *How people learn.* Washington, DC: National Academy Press.

National Research Council. (1999b). *Improving student learning.* Washington, DC: National Academy Press.

Natriello, G. (1987). The impact of evaluation processes on students. *Educational Psychologist, 22,* 155–175.

Nieto, S. (2004). *Affirming diversity: The sociopolitical context of multicultural education* (4th ed.). Boston: Pearson.

Ovando, C. J., Combs, M. C., & Collier, V. P. (2006). *Bilingual & ESL classrooms: Teaching in multicultural contexts* (4th ed.). Boston: McGraw-Hill.

Pearson, D., Dole, J. A., Duffy, G. G., & Roehler, L. R. (1992). *Developing expertise in reading comprehension: What should be taught and how should it be taught? What research has to say to the teacher of reading.* Newark, DE: International Reading Association.

Pease-Alvarez, L., García, E. E., & Espinosa, P. (1991). Effective instruction for language-minority students: An early childhood case study. *Early Childhood Research Quarterly, 6*(3), 347–361.

Peregoy, S. F., & Boyle, O. F. (2005). *Reading, writing, and learning in ESL: A resource book for K–12 teachers* (4th ed.). Boston: Pearson.

Peterson, C., & McCabe, A. (1983). *Developmental psycholinguistics: Three ways of looking at a child's narrative.* New York: Plenum Press.

Peterson, C., & McCabe, A. (1991). Linking children's connective use and narrative macrostructure. In A. McCabe & C. Peterson (Eds.), *Developing narrative structure.* (pp. 29–53). Hillsdale, NJ: Lawrence Erlbaum Associates.

Piaget, J. (1964). *The early growth of logic in the child, classification, and seriation.* New York: Columbia University Press.

Piaget, J. (1967). *Mental imagery in the child, a study of the development of imaginal representation.* New York: Oxford University Press.

Piaget, J. (1970). Piaget's theory. In P. Mussen (Ed.), *Carmichael's manual of child's psychology* (Vol. 1, pp. 703–732). New York: Wiley.

Piaget, J., & Inhelder. (1969). Diagnosis of mental operations and theory of the intelligence. *American Journal of Mental Deficiency, 51,* 401–406.

Piper, T. (2003). *Language and learning: The home and school years* (3rd ed.). Upper Saddle River, NJ: Pearson.

Prado, E. B., & Tinajero, J. V. (2000). *Literacy instruction through Spanish: Linguistic, cultural, and pedagogical considerations.* In J. V. Tinajero & R. A. De Villar (Eds.), *The power of two languages: Effective dual-language use across the curriculum* (pp. 42–53). New York: McGraw-Hill.

Rogoff, B. (1998). Cognition as a collaborative process. In D. Kuhn & R. S. Siegler (Eds.), *Cognition, language, and perceptual development* (pp. 679–744). New York: Wiley.

Rueda, R., August, D., & Goldenberg, C. (2006). The sociocultural context in which children acquire literacy. In D. August & T. Shanahan (Eds.), *Report of the national literacy panel on language minority youth and children.* Mahwah, NJ: Lawrence Erlbaum Associates.

Saville-Troike, M. (1987). Bilingual discourse: The negotiation of meaning without a common code. *Linguistics, 25*(1), 81–106.

Shepard, L., Kagan, S., & Wurtz, E. (1998). *Principles and recommendations for early childhood assessments.* New York: Early Childhood Assessments Resource Group.

Shore, C. M. (2004). *Many faces of childhood: The diversity in development.* Needham Heights, MA: Allyn & Bacon.

Siegler, R. S. (1996). Strategic development: Trudging up the staircase or swimming with the tide? In R. S. Siegler (Ed.), *Emerging minds: The process of change in children's thinking* (pp. 84–113). New York: Oxford University Press.

Snow, C., & Dickinson, D. (1990). Social sources of narrative skills at home and at school. *First Language, 10*(29), 87–103.

Snow, C. E., Burns, M. S., & Griffin, P. (1998). *Preventing reading difficulties in young children.* Washington, DC: National Academy Press.

Stanovich, K. E. (1986). Matthew effects in reading: Some consequences of individual differences in the acquisition of literacy. *Reading Research Quarterly, 11,* 360–406.

Stanton-Salazar, R. D. (2001). *Mexican-Americans: A second generation at risk.* Berkeley: University of California Press.

Tabors, P., & Snow, C. (2001). Young bilingual children and early literacy development. In S. Neuman & D. Dickinson (Eds.), *Handbook of early literacy research* (pp. 159–178). New York: Guilford.

Teaching English to Speakers of Other Languages (TESOL). (2005). *PreK–12 English language proficiency standards in the core content areas.* Washington, DC: Author.

Tharp, R. G. (1997). *From at-risk to excellence: Research theory and principles for practice.* Santa Cruz, CA: Center for Research on Education Diversity & Excellence.

Tharp, R. G. (1999). *Proofs and evidence: Effectiveness of the five standards for effective teaching.* Santa Cruz, CA: Center for Research on Education Diversity & Excellence.

Tharp, R. G., Estrada, P., Dalton, S. S., & Yamauchi, L. A. (2000). *Teaching transformed: Achieving excellence, fairness, inclusion, and harmony.* Boulder, CO: Westview.

Tharp, R. G., & Gallimore, R. (1998). *Routing minds to life: Teaching, learning, and schooling in social context.* New York: Cambridge University Press.

Thomas, W. P., & Collier, V. P. (2003). The multiple benefits of dual language. *Educational Leadership, 6*(2), 61–64.

Trawick-Smith, J. (2006). *Early childhood development: A multicultural perspective* (4th ed.). Upper Saddle River, NJ: Pearson.

Trueba, E. T. (1999). *Latinos unidos: From cultural diversity to the politics of solidarity.* Lanham, MD: Rowman & Littlefield.

Trueba, H., & Delgado-Gaitan C. (Eds.). (1988). *School and society: Learning content through culture.* New York: Praeger.

U.S. Bureau of the Census. (2000). American community survey change profile, 2000–2002, California. Retrieved June 10, 2004, from www.census.gov/acs/www/Products/Profiles/Chg/2002/0102/CA.htm

Valdivieso, R., & David, C. (1988). *U.S. Hispanics: Challenging issues for the 1990s.* Washington, DC: Population Trends & Public Policy.

Valencia, S. (1994). *Authentic reading assessment: Practices and possibilities.* New York: International Reading Association.

Vaughn, S., & Linan-Thompson, S. (2004). *Research-based methods of reading instruction: Grades K–3.* Alexandria, VA: Association for Supervision and Curriculum Development.

Vygotsky, L. S. (1978). *Mind in society: The development of higher psychological processes.* Cambridge, MA: Harvard University Press.

Vygotsky, L. S. (1986). *Thought and language.* Cambridge: MIT Press.

Wang, M., & Koda, K. (2005). Commonalities and differences in word identification skills among English second language learners. *Language Learning, 55*(1), 73–100.

Waxman, H. C., & Padrón, Y. N. (2002). Research-based teaching practices that improve the education of English language learners. In L. Minaya-Rowe (Ed.), *Teacher training and effective pedagogy in the context of student diversity* (pp. 3–38). Greenwich, CT: Information Age.

Waxman, S. R. (1990). Linking language and conceptual development: Linguistic cues and the construction of conceptual hierarchies. *The Genetic Epistemologist, 17,* 13–20.

Wigglesworth, G. (1990). Children's narrative acquisition: A study of some aspects of reference and anaphora. *First Language, 10*(29), 105–125.

Witt, J. C., Elliot, S. N., Kramer, J. J., & Gresham, F. M. (1994). *Assessment of children: Fundamental methods and practices.* Dubuque, IA: Brown & Benchmark.

Wodrich, D. L., & Kush, S. A. (1990). *Children's psychological testing: A guide for non-psychologists.* Baltimore: Brookes.

Wong-Fillmore, L. (1991). Second language learning in children: A model of language learning in social context. In E. Bialystok (Ed.), *Language processing in bilingual children* (pp. 49–69). New York: Cambridge University Press.

Index

Note: Page references followed by *f* indicate figures; those followed by *t* indicate tables.

CORWIN

A SAGE Company

The Corwin logo—a raven striding across an open book—represents the union of courage and learning. Corwin is committed to improving education for all learners by publishing books and other professional development resources for those serving the field of PreK–12 education. By providing practical, hands-on materials, Corwin continues to carry out the promise of its motto: **"Helping Educators Do Their Work Better."**